Childhood and Adolescence

COUNSELING THEORY AND TECHNIQUE

•

Edited by

William M. Walsh

Northeastern Illinois University

•

McCutchan Publishing Corporation

2526 Martin Luther King Jr. Way
Berkeley, California 94704

Library of Congress Catalog Card Number 84–61506
ISBN 0–8211–2262–2

Cover design by Terry Down, Berkeley, California
Typesetting composition by Vera-Reyes, Inc., Manila

As always and in everything,
this is dedicated to my
loving family:
Kathleen
Karen
Kristen

Many thanks are given to Ann Marie De Paepe, Roasanne Hanik, and Marilyn Scallon for their dedication in typing this manuscript.

Contents

Contributors

William Appel, College of New Rochelle, New York

Don T. Basse, Director, Special Services, Claremore Junior College, Claremore, Oklahoma

Marilyn Bates, Professor, California State University, Fullerton

Ernst G. Beier, Professor, University of Utah, Salt Lake City

Sherry B. Borgers, Professor, University of Kansas, Lawrence

Leif J. Braaten, Professor, Cornell University, Ithaca, New York

Charles A. Bugg, Elementary School Counselor, American School, Dormstadt, Germany

John H. Childers, Professor, University of Arkansas, Fayetteville

John J. Cody, Professor, Southern Illinois University, Carbondale

Don Dinkmeyer, Communication and Motivation Training Institute, Coral Springs, Florida

Rudolf Dreikurs (deceased), formerly Director of the Alfred Adler Institute, Chicago

Albert Ellis, Executive Director, Institute for Rational Living, New York

Wayne E. Foley, Psychologist, Seattle, Washington

Morley D. Glicken, Professor, Arizona State University, Tempe

Richard R. Gronert, Counselor, Janesville, Wisconsin

Richard M. Hawes, Institute for Reality Therapy, Los Angeles, California

Clarence D. Johnson, Professor, California State University, Fullerton

William Knaus, Consultant, Fort Lee, New Jersey

Arnold A. Lazarus, Professor, Rutgers University, New Brunswick, New Jersey

Stephen Marcus, Psychologist, Newport Beach, California

G. Roy Mayer, Professor, California State University, Los Angeles
Joseph Melnick, Psychologist, Portland, Maine
George W. Murphy, Counselor, Baltimore County, Maryland
Michael S. Nystul, Professor, Portland State University, Oregon
Cecile H. Patterson, Professor, University of Illinois, Urbana
Gerald J. Pine, Professor, University of New Hampshire, Durham
Zander Ponzo, Professor, University of Vermont, Burlington
David W. Roush, Director, Calhoun County Juvenile Home, Michigan
Carl E. Thoresen, Professor, Stanford University, California
Clemmont E. Vontress, Professor, George Washington University, Washington, D.C.
Edwin E. Wagner, Professor, University of Akron, Ohio
Jean C. Waterland, Professor, University of Wisconsin, Milwaukee
Eileen L. Widerman, Social Worker, Philadelphia, Pennsylvania
James L. Widerman, Counselor, Philadelphia, Pennsylvania
John W. Wilson, Counselor, Seattle, Washington

Introduction

There is only one child
And his name is all children.

— *Carl Sandburg*

The counseling of children and adolescents is a relatively recent area of interest for professionals; the major growth in the field has taken place in the past twenty years. The early work of Sigmund Freud, at the beginning of this century, generated initial interest in the early childhood and adolescent years. However, this interest tended to focus on only two areas: the influence of early childhood experiences on later adolescent and adult behavior, and the development of effective therapeutic procedures for treating the severely disturbed client. The developmental needs of the majority of clients in this age group were largely overlooked.

During the past several years, professionals in psychology, counseling, social work, and the allied behavioral sciences have become increasingly aware of the void that exists in the treatment of adolescents and young children. These professionals have begun to respond to the demand for effective delivery systems and treatment processes by designing training and treatment programs to deal with this particular population. However, academicians and practitioners have found that there is a real paucity of published material in this area. There is considerable research in the fields of psychiatry and clinical psychology that concerns itself primarily with aberrant or deviant behavior patterns, but these behavior patterns constitute only a small percentage of the presenting problems of preadolescent and adolescent children. Most of the children in this age group who seek counseling or therapy have less severe developmental and adjustment problems. In short, the counseling needs of children, particularly the preadolescent, have been largely overlooked or ignored.

A brief synopsis of the development of counseling and psychotherapy with children and adolescents may help to clarify the present position of the profession. Counseling as a helping process is not new or modern. It can be traced to the very roots of civilization. Many of the famous people of ancient and modern history performed the helping function of counseling. Other helpers, indeed the vast majority, were unknown, simple people: teachers, friends, relatives, and associates.

Only recently has the concept of interpersonal helping relationships been formalized into an academic discipline or science. The philosophers of the seventeenth and eighteenth century may be considered forerunners of today's psychological theorists. Men like Descartes, Locke, Hobbes, Hume, and Rousseau paved the way for modern theories of behavior. Wilhelm Wundt is generally considered the father of modern psychology. He opened the first psychological measurement laboratory in 1879 in Leipzig, Germany. In following years, the work of William James, Sigmund Freud, Alfred Binet, John Dewey, Carl Jung, Ivan Pavlov, John Watson, and Alfred Adler furthered the development of child counseling and therapy. In the United States, individuals like G. Stanley Hall emphasized the importance of working with children. Jesse Davis and Frank Parsons worked with youngsters at the inception of the vocational guidance movement. Clifford Beers generated interest in the mental health movement. The early twentieth century also witnessed the emergence of the child guidance movement.

After the early years of the discipline, despite world wars and a great depression, interest in child counseling continued to grow. More professionals began specializing in work with children and adolescents, and they primarily used classically oriented treatment models. Although interest in counseling adolescents accelerated prior to World War II with the work of E. G. Williamson and Carl Rogers, little formal emphasis was given to the field of child counseling and psychotherapy until mid-century. In 1958, the National Defense

Education Act provided considerable impetus for school counseling: the number of specialists grew, more counselors were employed in the elementary and secondary schools, and community mental health clinics expanded their personnel and services to provide treatment for adolescents and younger children with less severe adjustment problems.

Today, the growth and expansion of the 1950s and 1960s is continuing. Professional associations have separate divisions for secondary school counselors, adolescent therapists, and child specialists; professional journals aimed specifically at the treatment of adolescents and preadolescents have appeared; and the focus on new and different treatment models and therapeutic approaches has intensified. This book of readings is a response to this continued interest of professionals and the lay population.

The preceding paragraphs, written a decade ago, still hold true today in the mid 1980s. Theoretically and practically, little has changed in the way that professionals treat young people. The search for new treatment methods has become less intense, and the field has become more stable and somewhat institutionalized. Although the older theories are still alive and heavily used, little new has been added to our understanding of the behavior of children. The exception to this is Gestalt therapy. In the last decade, new Gestalt training institutes have been established in major cities throughout the United States, and a quarterly journal has been published since 1978. Gestalt therapists are treating youngsters and are refining theory to explain the behavior of children and adolescents. Consequently, a new section on Gestalt counseling has been added to this book. The purpose of this new edition remains essentially the same: it still surveys the major nonclassical models of counseling and provides a wide variety of techniques for use with children and adolescents. However, the content has been changed to reflect new and enriched thinking in each model.

Classical therapeutic approaches will not be covered in this text. These approaches consist of the analytic models, Freudian and neo-Freudian, that predominate in the fields of psychiatry and clinical psychology. They are employed effectively with patients displaying abnormal or severely deviant behavior patterns in outpatient and in-patient settings. They are generally of longer duration and focus on major personality reconstruction. However, as previously noted, clients displaying severely aberrant behavior are in the minority of the child client population. Most preadolescent and adolescent clients experience adjustment problems that may be more efficiently treated using short-term, nonanalytic counseling techniques. This assumption continues to be a major premise of this book of readings; the text surveys the new, nonclassical models of counseling and therapy with children and provides a wider variety of techniques to help children with adjustment problems.

The various sections present a broad spectrum of therapeutic behaviors and techniques. Each approach is applicable to a variety of therapeutic settings in the school, the home, and the community. Several of the counseling processes emphasize cognitive assessment and directive behavior on the part of the counselor. Rational-emotive therapy, reality therapy, behavioral counseling, and Adlerian counseling are examples of more active, cognitive counseling. Other sections emphasize less directive, more affective client-counselor involvement. Gestalt therapy, client-centered counseling, and existential therapy are representative of this orientation. Play therapy and eclectic counseling generally represent an integration of the different models. The reader should be able to identify with one or several of the approaches and incorporate these methods in his or her counseling practice. There is something for almost everyone: counselor educators, child therapists, counselors-in-training, classroom teachers, administrators, school psychologists, school counselors, special-education therapists, family counselors, or other professionals in allied fields who are concerned with the emotional development of children.

The terms *counseling* and *therapy* are used interchangeably in this text. The word *counseling* may be substituted for *therapy* or *therapist* for *counselor* at any point in the readings. No attempt has been made to distinguish the two terms by way of specific problem orientation, duration of client involvement, or specific techniques. The processes involved in both counseling and therapy are similar, if not identical, and are treated in this manner throughout the entire text.

The readings are organized into sections, and each section treats a relatively distinct counseling model. The sections in this revised book, however, are presented in a different order from the previous edition. Conversations with colleagues and students convinced me that presenting the theories along the directive–nondirective or cognitive–affective continuum would be more appropriate for classroom use. Since most theory courses, they argued, begin by examining the cognitive, directive models and proceed along a continuum to the affective, nondirective theories, why not structure the book in the same fashion? Therefore, the sections have been rearranged to follow how the subjects are commonly presented in theory courses. Additionally, the sections on play therapy and eclecticism have been placed last because they are basically distillations of the preceding major models. These changes in format should produce a more usable academic tool.

Although the sections have all been revised or modified, the format of each remains the same. The introductory article for each section still presents the major theoretical propositions of that model. Several readings follow that deal specifically with the practical application of that model in school or nonschool settings. All of the counseling models are nonclassical; that is, they are not analytically oriented. Each model, however, is a viable, professionally acceptable, and effective process of therapy. The final section contains supplementary readings for each therapeutic model.

SECTION I

Rational-Emotive Therapy

The main goal of the counseling process . . . is to teach the children the main principles of rational-emotive psychology — which is based on the assumptions that people usually become disturbed through acquiring irrational thoughts, beliefs, and philosophies; and that it is these philosophies, and not the events that happen to the individual, which truly upset him and which had better be radically changed if he is to live happily and efficiently.

— *Albert Ellis*

Rational-emotive therapy is the result of the therapeutic work of Albert Ellis. Initially a practicing psychoanalyst, he became dissatisfied with the effectiveness and utility of this classical approach. What gradually emerged from this dissatisfaction he termed *rational-emotive therapy* or simply RET. It is a directive model, a cognitive model, and to some extent a teaching model of therapy. The basic underlying assumption is that "unreason," faulty thinking, can be cured by reason. Rational thought is the key to mental health. It is the individual's faulty reasoning process that causes disturbance and maladjustment.

Ellis postulates an A-B-C theory of personality. The "A" factor is an event that is external to the individual and affects him or her in some way. The "B" factor is related to how the individual perceives the event (A). In other words, "B" is what the individual thinks about

1

the event. "C" refers to the behavior of the individual that results from event (A) and thoughts (B). The therapeutic process of RET is primarily focused on the faulty reasoning that frequently takes place at point "B" and that causes emotional disturbance. The therapist will quickly point out the key thought factor and attempt to replace it with a more rational thought. The replacement of irrational thoughts with rational thoughts will produce more satisfactory adjustment for the individual and a healthier outlook on life.

The therapist using RET functions in a directive manner. It is his or her position to point out faulty thinking and to show the individual how to think and behave more rationally. In this sense, the therapist is a teacher; he instructs the client on how to develop a healthier, more adjusted way of behaving. Although originally developed for adults, it is Ellis's contention that young children can be reasoned with in the same manner as adolescents or adults.

The readings in this section will focus on the application of RET to the preadolescent and adolescent population. The opening article, by Albert Ellis, describes in detail the development of rational-emotive therapy and its major theoretical assumptions.

In the second reading, William Knaus explains how RET can be readily adapted to school counseling situations, and he outlines its application process for counselors and teachers. The counselor in this model could function as a therapist or as a consultant to teachers and other professional staff. The other three articles in this section apply the principles of RET to specific school situations. Edwin Wagner deals with RET from a school psychologist's perspective. His identification of common irrational ideas of disturbed children, as well as his description of concrete counseling techniques to use with the immature client, may be particularly enlightening for counselors. Morley Glicken relates RET particularly to the underachieving student, and in the final selection, David Roush focuses on juvenile offenders and troubled youth. He presents a method of understanding their behavior and offers several intervention techniques for teaching rational thought.

1

Rational Psychotherapy

Albert Ellis

The central theme of this paper is that psychotherapists can help their clients to live the most self-fulfilling, creative, and emotionally satisfying lives by teaching these clients to organize and discipline their thinking. Does this mean that *all* human emotion and creativity can or should be controlled by reason and intellect? Not exactly.

The human being may be said to possess four basic processes—perception, movement, thinking, and emotion—all of which are integrally interrelated. Thus, thinking, aside from consisting of bioelectric changes in the brain cells, and in addition to comprising remembering, learning, problem solving, and similar psychological processes, also is, and to some extent has to be, sensory, motor, and emotional behavior (Cobb, 1950; Ellis, 1956). Instead, then, of saying, "Jones thinks about this puzzle," we should more accurately say, "Jones perceives-moves-feels-*thinks* about this puzzle." Because, however, Jones's activity in relation to the puzzle may be focused *largely* upon solving it, and only *incidentally* on seeing, manipulating, and emoting about it, we may perhaps justifiably emphasize only his thinking.

Emotion, like thinking and the sensorimotor processes, we may define as an exceptionally complex state of human reaction which is

Reprinted from *Journal of General Psychology*, 1958, *59*, 35–49. A publication of the Helen Dwight Reid Educational Foundation. Reprinted by permission.

integrally related to all the other perception and response processes. It is not *one* thing, but a combination and holistic integration of several seemingly diverse, yet actually closely related, phenomena (Cobb, 1950).

Normally, emotion arises from direct stimulation of the cells in the hypothalamus and autonomic nervous system (e.g., by electrical or chemical stimulation) or from indirect excitation via sensorimotor, cognitive, and other conative processes. It may theoretically be controlled, therefore, in four major ways. If one is highly excitable and wishes to calm down, one may (a) take electroshock or drug treatments; (b) use soothing baths or relaxation techniques; (c) seek someone one loves and quiet down for his sake; or (d) reason oneself into a state of calmness by showing oneself how silly it is for one to remain excited.

Although biophysical, sensorimotor, and emotive techniques are all legitimate methods of controlling emotional disturbances, they will not be considered in this paper, and only the rational technique will be emphasized. Rational psychotherapy is based on the assumption that thought and emotion are not two entirely different processes, but that they significantly overlap in many respects and that therefore disordered emotions can often (though not always) be ameliorated by changing one's thinking.

A large part of what we call emotion, in other words, is nothing more or less than a certain kind—a biased, prejudiced, or strongly evaluative kind—of thinking. What we usually label as thinking is a relatively calm and dispassionate appraisal (or organized perception) of a given situation, an objective comparison of many of the elements in this situation, and a coming to some conclusion as a result of this comparing or discriminating process (Ellis, 1956). Thus, a thinking person may observe a piece of bread, see that one part of it is moldy, remember that eating this kind of mold previously made him ill, and therefore cut off the moldy part and eat the nonmoldy section of the bread.

An emoting individual, on the other hand, will tend to observe the same piece of bread, and remember so violently or prejudicedly his previous experience with the moldly part, that he will quickly throw away the whole piece of bread and therefore go hungry. Because the thinking person is relatively calm, he uses the maximum information available to him—namely, that moldy bread is bad but nonmoldy bread is good. Because the emotional person is relatively excited, he may use only part of the available information—namely, that moldy bread is bad.

It is hypothesized, then, that thinking and emoting are closely interrelated and at times differ mainly in that thinking is a more tranquil, less somatically involved (or, at least, perceived), and less activity-directed mode of discrimination than is emotion. It is also hypothesized that among adult humans raised in a social culture thinking and emoting are so closely interrelated that they usually accompany each other, act in a circular cause-and-effect relationship, and in certain (though hardly all) respects are essentially the *same thing*, so that one's thinking *becomes* one's emotion and emoting *becomes* one's thought. It is finally hypothesized that since man is a uniquely sign-, symbol-, and language-creating animal, both thinking and emoting tend to take the form of self-talk or internalized sentences; and that, for all practical purposes, the sentences that human beings keep telling themselves *are* or *become* their thoughts and emotions.

This is not to say that emotion can under *no* circumstances exist without thought. It probably can; but it then tends to exist momentarily, and not to be sustained. An individual, for instance, steps on your toe, and you spontaneously, immediately become angry. Or you hear a piece of music and you instantly begin to feel warm and excited. Or you learn that a close friend has died and you quickly begin to feel sad. Under these circumstances, you may feel emotional without doing any concomitant thinking. Perhaps, however, you do, with split-second rapidity, start thinking "This person who stepped on my toe is a blackguard!" or "This music is wonderful!" or "Oh, how awful it is that my friend died!"

In any event, assuming that you don't, at the very beginning, have any conscious or unconscious thought accompanying your emotion, it appears to be difficult to *sustain* an emotional outburst without bolstering it by repeated ideas. For unless you keep telling yourself something on the order of "This person who stepped on my toe is a blackguard!" or "How could he do a horrible thing like that to me!" the pain of having your toe stepped on will soon die, and your immediate reaction will die with the pain. Of course, you can keep getting your toe stepped on, and the continuing pain may sustain your anger. But assuming that your physical sensation stops, your emotional feeling, in order to last, normally has to be bolstered by some kind of thinking.

We say "normally" because it is theoretically possible for your emotional circuits, once they have been made to reverberate by some physical or psychological stimulus, to keep reverberating under their own power. It is also theoretically possible for drugs or electrical impulses to keep acting directly on your hypothalamus and autonomic nervous system and thereby to keep you emotionally aroused. Usually, however, these steps of continued direct stimulation of the emotion-producing centers do not seem to be important and are limited largely to pathological conditions.

It would appear, then, that positive human emotions, such as feelings of love or elation, are often associated with or result from thoughts, or internalized sentences, stated in some form or variation of the phrase "This is good!" and that negative human emotions, such as feelings of anger or depression, are frequently associated with or result from thoughts or sentences which are stated in some form or variation of the phrase "This is bad!" Without an adult human being's employing, on some conscious or unconscious level, such thoughts and sentences, much of his emoting would simply not exist.

If the hypothesis that sustained human emotion often results from or is directly associated with human thinking and self-verbalization is true, then important corollaries about the origin and perpetuation of states of emotional disturbance, or neurosis, may be drawn. For neurosis would appear to be disordered, over- or under-intensified, uncontrollable emotion; and this would seem to be the result of (and, in a sense, the very same thing as) illogical, unrealistic, irrational, inflexible, and childish thinking.

That neurotic or emotionally disturbed behavior is illogical and irrational would seem to be almost definitional. For if we define it otherwise, and label as neurotic *all* incompetent and ineffectual behavior, we will be including actions of *truly* stupid and incompetent individuals—for example, those who are mentally deficient or brain injured. The concept of neurosis only becomes meaningful, therefore, when we assume that the disturbed individual is *not* deficient or impaired but that he is theoretically capable of behaving in a more mature, more controlled, more flexible manner than he actually behaves. If, however, a neurotic is essentially an individual who acts significantly below his own potential level of behaving, or who defeats his own ends though he is theoretically capable of achieving them, it would appear that he behaves in an illogical, irrational, unrealistic way. Neurosis, in other words, consists of stupid behavior by a nonstupid person.

Assuming that emotionally disturbed individuals act in irrational, illogical ways, the questions which are therapeutically relevant are: (a) How do they originally get to be illogical? (b) How do they keep perpetuating their irrational thinking? (c) How can they be helped to be less illogical, less neurotic?

Unfortunately, most of the good thinking that has been done in regard to therapy during the past sixty years, especially by Sigmund Freud and his chief followers (Fenichel, 1945; Freud, 1938, 1924–1950), has concerned itself with the first of these questions rather than the second and the third. The assumption has often been made that if psychotherapists discover and effectively communicate to their clients the main reasons why these clients originally became disturbed, they will thereby also discover how their neuroses are being perpetuated and how they can be helped to overcome them. This is a dubious assumption.

Knowing exactly how an individual originally learned to behave illogically by no means necessarily informs us precisely how he *maintains* his illogical behavior or what he should do to change it. This is particularly true because people are often, perhaps usually, afflicted with *secondary* as well as *primary* neuroses, and the two may significantly differ. Thus, an individual may originally become disturbed because he discovers that he has strong death wishes against his father and (quite illogically) thinks he should be blamed and punished for having these wishes. Consequently, he may develop some neurotic symptom, such as a phobia against dogs because, let us say, dogs remind him of his father, who is an ardent hunter.

Later on, this individual may grow to love or be indifferent to his father; or his father may die and be no more of a problem to him. His fear of dogs, however, may remain: not because, as some theorists would insist, they still remind him of his old death wishes against his father, but because he now hates himself so violently for *having* the original neurotic symptom—for behaving, to his mind, so stupidly and illogically in relation to dogs—that every time he thinks of dogs his self-hatred and fear of failure so severely upset him that he cannot reason clearly and cannot combat his illogical fear.

In terms of self-verbalization, this neurotic individual is first saying to himself: "I hate my father—and this is awful!" But he ends up by saying: "I have an irrational fear of dogs—and this is awful!" Even though both sets of self-verbalizations are neuroticizing, and his secondary neurosis may be as bad as or worse than his primary one, the two can hardly be said to be the same. Consequently, exploring and explaining to this individual—or helping him gain insight into—the origins of his primary neurosis will not necessarily help him to understand and overcome his perpetuating or secondary neurotic reactions.

If the hypotheses so far stated have some validity, the psychotherapist's main goals should be those of demonstrating to clients that their self-verbalizations have been and still are the prime source of their emotional disturbances. Clients must be shown that their internalized sentences are illogical and unrealistic at certain critical points and that they now have the ability to control their emotions by telling themselves more rational and less self-defeating sentences.

More precisely: the effective therapist should continually keep unmasking his client's past and, especially, his present illogical thinking or self-defeating verbalizations by (a) bringing them to his attention or consciousness; (b) showing the client how they are causing and maintaining his disturbance and unhappiness; (c) demonstrating exactly what the illogical links in his internalized sentences are; and (d) teaching him how to rethink and reverbalize these (and other similar) sentences in a more logical, self-helping way. Moreover, before the end of the therapeutic relationship, the therapist should not only deal concretely with the client's specific illogical thinking, but should demonstrate to this client what, *in general,* are the main irrational ideas that human beings are prone to follow and what more rational philosophies of living may usually be substituted for them. Otherwise, the client who is released from one specific set of illogical notions may well wind up by falling victim to another set.

It is hypothesized, in other words, that human beings are the kind of animals who, when raised in any society similar to our own, tend to fall victim to several major fallacious ideas; to keep reindoctrinating themselves over and over again with these ideas in an unthinking, autosuggestive manner; and consequently to keep actualizing them in overt behavior. Most of these irrational ideas are, as the Freudians have very adequately pointed out, instilled by the individual's parents during his childhood, and are tenaciously clung to because of his attachment to these parents and because the ideas were ingrained, or imprinted, or conditioned before later and more rational modes of thinking were given a chance to gain a foothold. Most of them, however, as the Freudians have not always been careful to note, are also instilled by the individual's general culture, and particularly by the media of mass communication in this culture.

What are some of the major illogical ideas or philosophies which, when originally held and later perpetuated by men and women in our civilization, inevitably lead to self-defeat and neurosis? Limitations of space preclude our examining all these major ideas, including their more significant corollaries; therefore, only a few of them will be listed. The illogicality of some of these ideas will also, for the present, have to be taken somewhat on faith, since there again is no space to outline the many reasons *why* they are irrational. Anyway, here, where angels fear to tread, goes the psychological theoretician!

1. The idea that it is a dire necessity for an adult to be loved or approved by everyone for everything he does—instead of his concentrating on his own self-respect, on winning approval for necessary purposes (such as job advancement), and on loving rather than being loved.

2. The idea that certain acts are wrong, or wicked, or villainous, and that people who perform such acts should be severely punished—instead of the idea that certain acts are inappropriate or antisocial, and that people who perform such acts are invariably stupid, ignorant, or emotionally disturbed.

3. The idea that it is terrible, horrible, and catastrophic when things are not the way one would like them to be—instead of the idea that it is too bad when things are not the way one would like them to be, and one should certainly try to change or control conditions so that they become more satisfactory, but that if changing or controlling uncomfortable situations is impossible, one had better become resigned to their existence and stop telling oneself how awful they are.

4. The idea that much human unhappiness is externally caused and is forced on one by outside people and events—instead of the idea that virtually all human unhappiness is caused or sustained by the view one takes of things rather than the things themselves.

5. The idea that if something is or may be dangerous or fearsome one should be terribly concerned about it—instead of the idea that if something is or may be dangerous or fearsome one should frankly face it and try to render it nondangerous and, when that is impossible, think of other things and stop telling oneself what a terrible situation one is or may be in.

6. The idea that it is easier to avoid than to face life difficulties and self-responsibilities—instead of the idea that the so-called easy way is invariably the much harder way in the long run and that the only way to solve difficult problems is to face them squarely.

7. The idea that one needs something other or stronger or greater than oneself on which to rely—instead of the idea that it is usually far better to stand on one's own feet and gain faith in oneself and one's ability to meet difficult circumstances of living.

8. The idea that one should be thoroughly competent, adequate, intelligent, and achieving in all possible respects—instead of the idea that one should *do* rather than always try to do *well* and that one should accept oneself as a quite imperfect creature, who has general human limitations and specific fallibilities.

9. The idea that because something once strongly affected one's life, it should indefinitely affect it—instead of the idea that one should learn from one's past experiences but not be overly attached to or prejudiced by them.

10. The idea that it is vitally important to our existence what other people do, and that we should make great efforts to change them in the direction we would like them to be—instead of the idea that other people's deficiencies are largely *their* problems and that putting pressure on them to change is usually least likely to help them do so.

11. The idea that human happiness can be achieved by inertia and inaction—instead of the idea that humans tend to be happiest when they are actively and vitally absorbed in creative pursuits, or when they are devoting themselves to people or projects outside themselves.

12. The idea that one has virtually no control over one's emotions and that one cannot help feeling certain things—instead of the idea that one has enormous control over one's emotions if one chooses to work at controlling them and to practice saying the right kinds of sentences to oneself.

It is the central theme of this paper that it is the foregoing kinds of illogical ideas, and many corollaries which we have no space to delineate, which are the basic causes of most emotional disturbances or neuroses. For once one believes the kind of nonsense included in these notions, one will inevitably tend to become inhibited, hostile, defensive, guilty, anxious, ineffective, inert, uncontrolled, or unhappy. If, on the other hand, one could become thoroughly released from all these fundamental kinds of illogical thinking, it would be exceptionally difficult for one to become too emotionally upset, or at least to sustain one's disturbance for very long.

Does this mean that all the other so-called basic causes of neurosis, such as the Oedipus complex or severe maternal rejection in childhood, are invalid, and that the Freudian and other psychodynamic thinkers of the last sixty years have been barking up the wrong tree? Not at all. It only means, if the main hypotheses of this paper are correct, that these psychodynamic thinkers have been emphasizing secondary causes or results of emotional disturbances rather than truly prime causes.

Let us take, for example, an individual who acquires, when he is young, a full-blown Oedipus complex: that is to say, he lusts after his mother, hates his father, is guilty about his sex desires for his mother, and is afraid that his father is going to castrate him. This person, when he is a child, will presumably be disturbed. But, if he is raised so that he acquires none of the basic illogical ideas we have been discussing, it will be virtually impossible for him to *remain* disturbed.

For, as an adult, this individual will not be too concerned if his parents or others do not approve all his actions, since he will be more interested in his *own* self-respect than in *their* approval. He will not believe that his lust for his mother is wicked or villainous, but will accept it as a normal part of being a limited human whose sex desires may easily be indiscriminate. He will realize that the actual danger of his father castrating him is exceptionally slight. He will not feel that because he was once afraid of his Oedipal feelings he should forever remain so. If he still feels it would be improper for him to have sex relations with his mother, instead of castigating himself for even thinking of having such relations he will merely resolve not to carry his desires into practice and will stick determinedly to his resolve. If, by any chance, he weakens and actually has incestuous relations, he will again refuse to castigate himself mercilessly for being weak but will keep showing himself how self-defeating his behavior is and will actively work and practice at changing it.

Under these circumstances, if this individual has a truly logical and rational approach to life in general, and to the problem of Oedipal feelings in particular, how can he possibly *remain* disturbed about his Oedipal attachment?

Take, by way of further illustration, the case of an individual who, as a child, is continually criticized by his parents, who consequently feels himself loathesome and inadequate, who refuses to take chances at failing at difficult tasks, who avoids such tasks, and who therefore

comes to hate himself more. Such a person will be, of course, seriously neurotic. But how would it be possible for him to *sustain* his
neurosis if he began to think in a truly logical manner about himself
and his behavior?

For, if this individual does use a consistent rational approach to his
own behavior, he will stop caring particularly what others think of
him and will start primarily caring what he thinks of himself. Consequently, he will stop avoiding difficult tasks, and instead of punishing
himself for being incompetent when he makes a mistake, he will say to
himself something like: "Now this is not the right way to do things; let
me stop and figure out a better way." Or: "There's no doubt that I
made a mistake this time; now let me see how I can benefit from
making it."

This individual, furthermore, will, if he is thinking straight, not
blame his defeats on external events but will realize that he himself is
causing them by his illogical or impractical behavior. He will not
believe that it is easier to avoid facing difficult things but will realize
that the so-called easy way is always, actually, the harder and more
idiotic one. He will not think that he needs something greater or
stronger than himself to help him but will independently buckle down
to difficult tasks himself. He will not feel that because he once defeated
himself by avoiding doing things the hard way that he must always do
so.

How, with this kind of logical thinking, could an originally disturbed person possibly maintain and continually revivify his neurosis? He just couldn't. Similarly, the spoiled brat, the worry-wart,
the ego-maniac, the autistic stay-at-home—all of these disturbed individuals would have the devil of a time indefinitely prolonging their
neuroses if they did not continue to believe utter nonsense: namely,
the kinds of basic irrational postulates previously listed.

Neurosis, then, usually seems to originate in and be perpetuated by
some fundamentally unsound, irrational ideas. The individual comes
to believe in some unrealistic, impossible, often perfectionistic goals
—especially the goals that he should always be approved by everyone,
should do everything perfectly well, and should never be frustrated
in any of his desires—and then, in spite of considerable contradictory
evidence, refuses to give up his original illogical beliefs.

Some of the neurotic's philosophies, such as the idea that he
should be loved and approved by everyone, are not entirely inappropriate to his childhood state; but all of them are quite inappropriate

to average adulthood. Most of his irrational ideas are specifically taught him by his parents and his culture; and most of them also seem to be held by the great majority of adults in our society—who theoretically should have been but actually never were weaned from them as they chronologically matured. It must consequently be admitted that the neurotic individual we are considering is often statistically normal; or that ours is a generally neuroticizing culture, in which most people are more or less emotionally disturbed because they are raised to believe, and then to internalize and to keep reinfecting themselves with, arrant nonsense which must inevitably lead them to become ineffective, self-defeating, and unhappy. Nonetheless: it is not absolutely *necessary* that human beings believe the irrational notions which, in point of fact, most of them seem to believe today; and the task of psychotherapy is to get them to disbelieve their illogical ideas, to change their self-sabotaging attitudes.

This, precisely, is the task which the rational psychotherapist sets himself. Like other therapists, he frequently resorts to the usual techniques of therapy which the present author has outlined elsewhere (Ellis, 1955a, 1955b), including the techniques of relationship, expressive-emotive, supportive, and insight-interpretive therapy. But he views these techniques, as they are commonly employed, as kinds of preliminary strategies whose main functions are to gain rapport with the client, to let him express himself fully, to show him that he is a worthwhile human being who has the ability to change, and to demonstrate how he originally became disturbed.

The rational therapist, in other words, believes that most of the usual therapeutic techniques wittingly or unwittingly show the client *that* he is illogical and how he *originally* became so. They often fail to show him, however, how he is presently *maintaining* his illogical thinking, and precisely what he must do to change it by building general rational philosophies of living and by applying these to practical problems of everyday life. Where most therapists directly or indirectly show the client that he is behaving illogically, the rational therapist goes beyond this point to make a forthright, unequivocal *attack* on the client's general and specific irrational ideas and to try to *induce* him to adopt more rational ones in their place.

Rational psychotherapy makes a concerted attack on the disturbed individual's irrational positions in two main ways: (a) the therapist serves as a frank counter-propagandist who directly contradicts and denies the self-defeating propaganda and superstitions which the

client has originally learned and which he is now self-propagandis-
tically perpetuating; (b) the therapist encourages, persuades, cajoles,
and at times commands the client to partake of some kind of activity
which itself will act as a forceful counter-propagandist agency against
the nonsense he believes. Both these main therapeutic activities are
consciously performed with one main goal in mind: namely, that of
finally getting the client to internalize a rational philosophy of living
just as he originally learned and internalized the illogical propaganda
and superstitions of his parents and his culture.

The rational therapist, then, assumes that the client somehow im-
bibed illogical ideas or irrational modes of thinking and that, without
so doing, he could hardly be as disturbed as he is. It is the therapist's
function not merely to show the client that he has these ideas or
thinking processes but to persuade him to change and substitute for
them more rational ideas and thought processes. If, because the
client is exceptionally disturbed when he first comes to therapy, he
must first be approached in a rather cautious, supportive, permissive,
and warm manner and must sometimes be allowed to ventilate his
feeling in free association, abreaction, role playing, and other expressive techniques, that may be all to the good. But the therapist does
not delude himself that these relationship-building and expressive-
emotive techniques in most instances really get to the core of the
client's illogical thinking and induce him to think in a more rational
manner.

Occasionally, this is true: since the client may come to see,
through relationship and emotive-expressive methods, that he *is* acting illogically, and he may therefore resolve to change and actually
do so. More often than not, however, his illogical thinking will be so
ingrained from constant self-repetitions, and will be so inculcated in
motor pathways (or habit patterns) by the time he comes for therapy, that simply showing him, even by direct interpretation, *that* he
is illogical will not greatly help. He will often say to the therapist:
"All right, now I understand that I have castration fears and that
they are illogical. But I *still* feel afraid of my father."

The therapist, therefore, must keep pounding away, time and
again, at the illogical ideas which underlie the client's fears. He must
show the client that he is afraid, really, not of his father, but of being
blamed, of being disapproved, of being unloved, of being imperfect,
of being a failure. And such fears are thoroughly irrational because
(a) being disapproved is not half so terrible as one *thinks* it is; be-

cause (b) no one can be thoroughly blameless or perfect; because (c) people who worry about being blamed or disapproved essentially are putting themselves at the mercy of the opinion of *others,* over whom they have no real control; because (d) being blamed or disapproved has nothing essentially to do with one's *own* opinion of oneself; etc.

If the therapist, moreover, merely tackles the individual's castration fears, and shows how ridiculous *they* are, what is to prevent this individual's showing up, a year or two later, with some *other* illogical fear—such as the fear that he is sexually impotent? But if the therapist tackles the client's *basic* irrational thinking, which underlies *all* kinds of fear he may have, it is going to be most difficult for this client to turn up with a new neurotic symptom some months or years hence. For once an individual truly surrenders ideas of perfectionism, of the horror of failing at something, of the dire need to be approved by others, of the notion that the world owes him a living, and so on, what else is there for him to be fearful of or disturbed about?

To give some idea of precisely how the rational therapist works, a case summary will now be presented. A client came in one day and said he was depressed but did not know why. A little questioning showed that he had been putting off the inventory-keeping he was required to do as part of his job as an apprentice glass-staining artist. The therapist immediately began showing him that his depression was related to his resenting having to keep inventory and that this resentment was illogical for several reasons:

(a) The client very much wanted to learn the art of glass-staining and could only learn it by having the kind of job he had. His sole logical choice, therefore, was between graciously accepting this job, in spite of the inventory-keeping, or giving up trying to be a glass-stainer. By resenting the clerical work and avoiding it, he was choosing neither of these two logical alternatives, and was only getting himself into difficulty.

(b) By blaming the inventory-keeping, and his boss for making him perform it, the client was being irrational since, assuming that the boss was wrong about making him do this clerical work, the boss would have to be wrong out of some combination of stupidity, ignorance, or emotional disturbance; and it is silly and pointless blaming people for being stupid, ignorant, or disturbed. Besides, maybe the boss was quite right, from his own standpoint, about making the client keep the inventory.

(c) Whether the boss was right or wrong, resenting him for his stand was hardly going to make him change it; and the resentment felt by the client was hardly going to do him, the client, any good or make him feel better. The saner attitude for him to take, then, was that it was too bad that inventory-keeping was part of his job, but that's the way it was, and there was no point in resenting the way things were when they could not, for the moment, be changed.

(d) Assuming that the inventory-keeping was irksome, there was no sense in making it still *more* annoying by the client's continually telling himself how awful it was. Nor was there any point in shirking this clerical work, since he eventually would have to do it anyway and he might as well get this unpleasant task out of the way quickly. Even more important: by shirking a task that he knew that, eventually, he just had to do, he would lose respect for himself, and his loss of self-respect would be far worse than the slight, rather childish satisfaction he might receive from trying to sabotage his boss's desires.

While showing this client how illogical was his thinking and consequent behavior, the therapist specifically made him aware that he must be telling himself sentences like these: "My boss makes me do inventory-keeping. I do not like to do this. . . . There is no reason why I have to do it. . . . He is therefore a blackguard for making me do it. . . . So I'll fool him and avoid doing it. . . . And then I'll be happier." But these sentences were so palpably foolish that the client could not really believe them, and began to finish them off with sentences like: "I'm not really fooling my boss, because he sees what I'm doing. . . . So I'm not solving my problem this way. . . . So I really should stop this nonsense and get the inventory-keeping done. . . . But I'll be damned if I'll do it for him! . . . However, if I don't do it, I'll be fired. . . . But I still don't want to do it for him! . . . I guess I've got to, though. . . . Oh, why must I always be persecuted like this? . . . And why must I keep getting myself into such a mess? . . . I guess I'm just no good. . . . And people are against me. . . . Oh, what's the use?"

Whereupon, employing these illogical kinds of sentences, the client was becoming depressed, avoiding doing the inventory-keeping, and then becoming more resentful and depressed. Instead, the therapist pointed out, he could tell himself quite different sentences, on this order: "Keeping inventory is a bore. . . . But it is presently an essential part of my job. . . . And I also may learn something useful by it. . . . Therefore, I had better go about this task as best I may and thereby get what *I* want out of this job."

The therapist also emphasized that whenever the client found himself intensely angry, guilty, or depressed, there was little doubt that he was then thinking illogically, and that he should immediately question himself as to what was the irrational element in his thinking, and set about replacing it with a more logical element or chain of sentences.

The therapist then used the client's current dilemma—that of avoiding inventory-keeping—as an illustration of his general neurosis, which in his case largely took the form of severe alcoholic tendencies. He was shown that his alcoholic trends, too, were a resultant of his trying to do things the easy way and of poor thinking preluding his avoidance of self-responsibilities. He was impressed with the fact that, as long as he kept thinking illogically about relatively small things, such as the inventory-keeping, he would also tend to think equally illogically about more important aspects, such as the alcoholism.

Several previous incidents of illogical thinking leading to emotional upheaval in the client's life were then reviewed, and some general principles of irrational thought discussed. Thus, the general principle of blamelessness was raised and the client was shown precisely why it is illogical to blame anyone for anything. The general principle of inevitability was brought up and he was shown that when a frustrating or unpleasant event is inevitable, it is only logical to accept it uncomplainingly instead of dwelling on its unpleasant aspects. The general principle of self-respect was discussed, with the therapist demonstrating that liking oneself is far more important than resentfully trying to harm others.

In this matter, by attempting to show or teach the client some of the general rules of logical living, the therapist tried to go beyond his immediate problem and to help provide him with a generalized mode of thinking or problem solving that would enable him to deal effectively with almost any future similar situation that might arise.

The rational therapist, then, is a frank propagandist who believes wholeheartedly in a most rigorous application of the rules of logic, of straight thinking, and of scientific method to everyday life, and who ruthlessly uncovers every vestige of irrational thinking in the client's experience and energetically urges him into more rational channels.

In so doing, the rational therapist does not ignore or eradicate the client's emotions; on the contrary, he considers them most seriously and helps change them, when they are disordered and self-defeating, through the same means by which they commonly arise in the first place—that is, by thinking and acting. Through exerting consistent interpretive and philosophic pressure on the client to change his thinking or his self-verbalizations and to change his experiences or his actions, the rational therapist gives a specific impetus to the client's movement toward mental health without which it is not impossible, but quite unlikely, that he will move very far.

Can therapy be effectively done, then, with *all* clients mainly through logical analysis and reconstruction? Alas, no. For one thing, many clients are not bright enough to follow a rigorously rational analysis. For another thing, some individuals are so emotionally aberrated by the time they come for help that they are, at least temporarily, in no position to comprehend and follow logical procedures. Still other clients are too old and inflexible; too young and impressionable; too philosophically prejudiced against logic and reason; too organically or biophysically deficient; or too something else to accept, at least at the start of therapy, rational analysis.

In consequence, the therapist who *only* employs logical reconstruction in his therapeutic armamentarium is not likely to get too far with many of those who seek his help. It is vitally important, therefore, that any therapist who has a basically rational approach to the problem of helping his clients overcome their neuroses also be quite eclectic in his use of supplementary, less direct, and somewhat less rational techniques.

Admitting, then, that rational psychotherapy is not effective with all types of clients, and that it is most helpful when used in conjunction with, or subsequent to, other widely employed therapeutic techniques, I would like to conclude with two challenging hypotheses: (a) that psychotherapy which includes a high dosage of rational analysis and reconstruction, as briefly outlined in this paper, will prove to be more effective with more types of clients than any of the nonrational or semirational therapies now being widely employed; and (b) that a considerable amount of—or, at least, proportion of—rational psychotherapy will prove to be virtually the only type of treatment that helps to undermine the basic neuroses (as distinguished from the superficial neurotic symptoms) of many clients, and particularly of many with whom other types of therapy have already been shown to be ineffective.

References

Cobb, S. *Emotions and clinical medicine.* New York: Norton, 1950.

Ellis, A. New approaches to psychotherapy techniques. *Journal of Clinical Psychology Monogram Supplement,* No. 11. Brandon, Vermont: Journal of Clinical Psychology, 1955(*a*).

————. Psychotherapy techniques for use with psychotics. *American Journal of Psychotherapy,* 1955(*b*), *9,* 452–476.

————. An operational reformulation of some of the basic principles of psychoanalysis. *Psychoanalytic Review,* 1956, *43,* 163–180.

Fenichel, O. *The psychoanalytic theory of neurosis.* New York: Norton, 1945.

Freud, S. *Basic writings.* New York: Modern Library, 1938.

————. *Collected papers.* London: Hogarth Press, 1924–1950.

2

Rational Emotive Education

William Knaus

The cumulative effects of technological, economic, political, and moral change have made the task of teaching increasingly complex. Both the school and the educator are forced to modify traditional roles and methods in order to maintain contact with today's students. It is essential that educators mobilize to meet new challenges through the development and implementation of strategies aimed at harmonizing traditional and humanistic principles in education. Our goals now include teaching youngsters not only basic skills but also how to learn and how to cope more effectively in a progressively more sophisticated and demanding environment.

Teaching children how to cope with the stresses of modern living is a valuable educational objective. Unfortunately, due to severe personnel shortages in the mental health field, the gap between available service and need is great. Consequently, many psychologists and educators have sought to develop mental health programs that help prevent emotional/behavioral disturbance and that can be utilized in the school setting. The goal is to foster psychological growth by

Reprinted from *Theory Into Practice*, 1977, *16* (4), 251–255. Reprinted with permission of the publisher, the College of Education, Ohio State University.

teaching skills that enable youngsters to more effectively and objectively deal with personal problems.

Many teachers, however, find themselves trapped into a non–self-selected role of model and teacher of mental health. They experience frustration as they see their already difficult job of teaching compounded. This is due in part to the lack of adequate training and preparation in mental health programs. As a consequence, many teachers feel handicapped, uncomfortable, or overly pressured in trying to develop a sound mental health regimen for their students in an already crowded and demanding curriculum. With this in mind, I developed and piloted (in varied settings) an effective and applicable humanistic approach for helping youngsters cope with the stresses of living and have presented it in a guide entitled *Rational Emotive Education: A Manual for Elementary School Teachers.*[1] In this article, I would like to share some key ideas and concepts and some cogent experiences I have had in piloting this system, which I call Rational Emotive Education (REE). In doing so, my purpose is to focus on several principal ideas and concepts fundamental to this positive mental health system. I will first briefly discuss the program's theoretical-philosophical underpinnings and then describe the REE program, providing explanatory examples. I will try to illustrate how this program can be interwoven into the curriculum as an aid to the teacher interested in integrating traditional and humanistic priorities. Such a teacher, I believe, will find REE a very helpful adjunct. As a result of reading this presentation, teachers will feel stimulated to learn more and, with minimal frustration and fear about instituting such a positive mental health program, will take the first step toward its implementation.

Foundation Ideas

Rational emotive education was developed from the tenets of Rational Emotive Psychotherapy (RET), a highly cognitive and behaviorally oriented psychotherapeutic approach that seeks to teach

---

1. This same program has been used effectively with junior high school, high school, and college students with minor modifications. The manual may be obtained from the Institute For Rational Living, 45 E. 65th Street, New York, New York 10021.

self-acceptance, self-determination, and responsibility. RET represents the pioneering efforts of Dr. Albert Ellis, and is based upon the premise that emotions and behavioral reactions are largely a consequence of how an individual interprets or defines a current situation. The RET approach purges any need for extensive psychological expeditions into an individual's past life experiences and focuses instead on aiding the individual to identify and work out the contradictory current misconceptions and self-created emotional pain. To this end, the efforts of the RET therapist are targeted toward both identifying and expunging faulty thinking (misconceptions, irrationalities) and helping the person strengthen objective thinking capabilities. In essence, the objective of the RET approach is to teach individuals to think straight and to act on the basis of an objective outlook.

The Rational Emotive Education Model

Following these principal tenets of the RET system, REE represents a translation of these and other sound mental health concepts into a teaching design of positive mental health concepts and problem-solving activities that can be understood and applied by both teachers and students. Through a systematic employment of activities, youngsters are provided with opportunities to derive from experience a knowledge of basic and potent human problem-solving strategies. Thus they learn how to approach and cope with their problems through experiential learning.

The REE approach emphasizes experiential learning. While RET concepts are employed, the means of disseminating them are engineered to adapt them to the needs of youngsters in classroom settings. To accomplish this objective, REE emphasizes critical thinking techniques via a flexibly structured thematic sequence of emotive education lessons.

Each REE lesson, as described in my manual, provides both the rationale for the teacher and a series of problem-solving exercises that may be used verbatim or adapted by the teacher to present these concepts concretely and powerfully. The concepts and knowledge that form the program help children to gain an awareness and perceptivity into what feelings are and how to express them; to question ideas underlying inferiority feelings; to discriminate between assumptions and facts; to find, judge, and counteract faulty assumptions that lead to emotional pain; to develop skills for obtaining perspective; to learn better ways to relate to others; to understand and counter specific misconceptions such as prejudices and stereotypes; and to appreciate individual differences.

For purposes of illustration and clarification, I will share some of my own experiences in the use of REE. I will focus particularly on one problem-solving activity as a vehicle for the presentation of several related mental health concepts. I will describe the procedure I used with a sixth-grade class and show how a teacher can helpfully expand a mental health concept depending upon the interest of the class. Next, I will describe how the regular curriculum and REE can be mutually supportive.

The normal sequence of REE activities begins with examining what are feelings and is followed by a guessing game designed to illustrate different ways in which feelings can be expressed. This sequence is normally followed by exploratory activities where youngsters attempt to determine how people come to feel the way they do and where the feelings come from. In the following example, I began a lesson aimed at presenting the concept of individual differences in the expression of feelings. A pantomime game called the "Expression Guessing Game" was used as the vehicle for presentation. This game is designed to continue approximately twenty minutes, which is an ideal length for most REE lessons (to maintain high student interest, lessons are typically presented three times per week for twenty minutes per session). To begin, I explained to the class that we were going to have another in a series of "feeling lessons" and selected a group of three volunteers to pantomime a feeling. After secretly informing the volunteers that they were to portray the feeling "sad," each person in her or his own style, I explained to the class members that their objective was to guess what feeling was being enacted for them. The pantomimers went into action and each guess was written on the board as the class tried to determine what common feeling was being expressed. Then new pantomimers presented other feelings. Using the same process and format, I continued the expression guessing game until the class began to recognize what the lesson was illustrating: some feelings are more difficult to guess than others; sometimes the same feeling can be expressed in different ways; and if you want to be sure how a person feels, you can ask. As an offshoot, the expression guessing game also proved helpful in stimulating awareness of a related concept—guessing can lead to inaccurate assumptions. Furthermore, the group saw that different people looking at the same event and coming to different conclusions about that event could get into conflict.

The implications of youngsters knowing and employing these concepts in the classroom are obvious. Not only does the teacher prosper through reduced discipline problems, but the children themselves can readily feel success in gaining the use of a highly helpful tool to spare themselves much needless emotional pain. The class, in the above illustration, seeing the implications of this tool, adopted a policy of trying to see each other's viewpoints as a way of reducing needless interpersonal friction.

As a result of the expression guessing game experience, some class members began to talk about what can happen if everybody comes to false conclusions at the same time. Then conversation centered upon the issue of prejudice and group pressures to make "everyone think alike." The group seemed fascinated with knowing more about how this happens, so I invited them to participate in an experiment on this topic at our next REE meeting. This experiment represented a departure from the planned sequence of REE lessons, but it was appropriate, as this departure would afford an opportunity to take advantage of the class's motivation to teach an important self-help concept—how to think for yourself. For this lesson, I allowed more than the customary twenty minutes.

The stimulus for the lesson on how to think for yourself arose spontaneously. Believing it wise for an alert teacher to take advantage of serendipitous happenings, I modified my lesson plan to make use of this situation. What follows is the procedure I followed that led up to the lessons on "thinking for yourself."

It seems that a janitor had painted the classroom and written and hung up a "Do not lean your chairs against the wall" sign on a sheet of paper on which I had written notes. I began the lesson using this stimulus. First, I strongly expressed views on the insensitivity of an outsider (the identity of this person was unknown to the class) who had ruthlessly marred and nearly destroyed valuable notes. I continued speaking passionately concerning how the class should band together to defend themselves against those who would endanger their property.

The class by this time knew they were participating in an experiment. However, they continued to become so absorbed in the process that they appeared to forget they were only participating in a game. Indeed, when committees were set up to decide how to attack and destroy the property of members of the other classes before the other classes could mount an assault, the experiment began to take on a frightening realism. When I halted the experiment, the class excitedly examined what had transpired. They talked freely about personal feelings and motivations. They considered how and why the group gathered momentum. They discussed my inciting remarks and emotional provocations and collectively began to comprehend the dynamics of the experiment.

Further in the discussion, we considered ways they could think for themselves so as to avoid being swept away by a group movement. This focus led to the lesson on how to think for yourself or "how to be your own person and not someone else's pawn."

In the learning-to-be-your-own-person lesson, the class role-played asking clarifying questions of group leaders and role-played other methods to ascertain the facts in group discussions. Consistent with an RET approach, the class also examined how their thinking influenced their feelings, and thus the stage was set for an in-depth analysis of this issue in the next lesson—Where do feelings come from?

Students participating in well-managed REE programs will often spontaneously find applications for the taught concepts. However, to reinforce concepts, the REE instructor often contrives activities the student can experiment with outside of the class and then bring to class the results of these experiments. For example, if the class lesson concerns learning the difference between opinion and fact, the assignment could be for each class member to listen to the seven o'clock news on Channel 6 and make a list of opinions expressed and a list of facts expressed. In the next lesson, the class would compare their notes and collectively try to discriminate between facts and opinions by examining the evidence.

REE lessons need not be independent of the regular curriculum as the above examples may suggest. Indeed, important concepts can be integrated into the curriculum and serve to support the validity of the curriculum.

Language arts, current events, science, mathematics, and social studies may all serve as vehicles for teaching mental health concepts. For example, a social studies unit in Greek mythology can be a particularly helpful adjunctive mental health unit. As the class studies the gods of ancient Greece, it can seek to discover how the ancients came to believe in the gods of Mt. Olympus and how such beliefs influenced their behavior. This knowledge of the capability of ancient peoples to create myths can be used to generate discussion on how people currently invent myths and how these modern-day myths influence behavior and engender and promote prejudice. Finally, the class can try to find ways of identifying self-defeating myths to which they ascribe, and alternatives to these myths can be examined.

The above example of integrating REE concepts into the regular curriculum illustrates how simple a process such integration is. Thus, once the teacher has mastered the basic REE tenets, it is easy to generate self-help concepts from regular classroom activities. Furthermore, the REE model can easily be a pivotal system that coordinates the three priorities (basic skills, learning to learn, and coping) without requiring much additional teaching preparation. Indeed, an alert educator will find many opportunities during the day to integrate the priorities, creating learning possibilities in all three areas.

Research strongly supports the efficiency of the REE model in aiding youngsters to build self-confidence, increase tolerance for frustration, and reduce anxiety while maintaining a social viewpoint and thinking in an ethical manner. Like all other systems, the REE system is not a perfect system for solving all emotional-behavioral problems, however, and needs the continuing efforts and attention of a dedicated cadre of educators to further development and refinement. If educators work "smart" they can contribute to the sort of mental health model that has the potential to put most psychotherapists out of business by reducing the need for their services. This, I believe, is a most worthy endeavor because it means that much neurotic misery may be prevented while much constructive human potential is freed to develop.

Lest I leave you thinking I am merely another wild-eyed dreamer, let me hasten to point out I am enough of a realist to know that we will probably fail in this brave venture if we set our criteria of success at a 90 percent reduction in emotional-behavioral problems at the first attempt to institute the program. However, if each classroom teacher can each year help reduce classroom problems by 25 percent by teaching children REE emotional-behavioral problem-solving strategies, I would say that is a really excellent batting average! Let's try for that.

3

Rational Counseling with School Children

Edwin E. Wagner

Rational Counseling is a newly developed approach to counseling with school-aged children which can be easily and effectively applied by the school psychologist and school counselor. It has been developed and adapted in collaboration with a number of school psychologists and is now being successfully utilized within school systems, particularly by Summit County school psychologists. Its efficacy is based not on high-sounding and involved theory but on practical, day-to-day use with children in the primary and secondary grades with a variety of psychological problems. After about two years of experience with Rational Counseling, we are able to state without equivocation that, while it is no panacea, it does work.

Rational Counseling is based on the theory and practice of a psychotherapeutic technique called Rational Therapy which was originated and promulgated by a New York psychologist, Dr. Albert Ellis. Ellis, an erstwhile psychoanalyst, became dissatisfied with the inordinate time demands and uncertain outcomes associated with the use of analytically oriented therapies. Over a period of time he developed Rational Therapy, or as it is sometimes called, Rational-Emotive Therapy, and has used it successfully with countless patients. Ellis has published a great deal of material on his technique

Reprinted from *School Psychologist*, 1965, *9*, the newsletter of the Division of School Psychology of the American Psychological Association. Reprinted with permission of the author.

and has recently written a definitive textbook entitled *Reason and Emotion in Psychotherapy*.

The fundamental premise upon which Rational Therapy is predicated is that thoughts produce emotions. That is, it is impossible to generate a human emotion without a thought or cerebral signal of some kind which triggers off the feeling. Since, for Ellis, thoughts are largely words or sentences which we tell ourselves (implicit verbalizations), we literally talk ourselves into a disturbed condition. Most people believe that when a situation occurs (let us call the situation "A") they automatically respond with various emotions and attitudes (let us call the response "C"). Actually, there is an intervening process, "B," which follows "A" and causes "C." This process usually consists of simple declarative sentences of "self-talk" which an individual makes to himself and which consequently produces emotions and behavior at point "C." Most of us pay little attention to the "B" part because it happens so quickly and so often that we have become habituated to it. We believe, erroneously, that "A" causes "C" when, in fact "A" causes "B" and "B" causes "C."

Perhaps a brief example will make this clear. Let us suppose that, as you are walking down the street, another person very rudely and forcefully bumps into you. Very likely you would react with anger and would attribute your ire to the fact that you were so roughly and impolitely accosted. That is you believe that "A" caused "C." Actually, what really happened (so Ellis tells us), was that after being jostled you very quickly said something to yourself like, "That big oaf shouldn't have bumped into me—he's uncouth, uncivilized, and downright despicable." Maybe these wouldn't be your exact words but you would have to say something fairly similar to this, perhaps even a resort to a vulgar epithet, in order to make yourself angry.

In order to further develop this contention, let's take the example one step further. Suppose you did become angry and suppose you were all set to give this discourteous ruffian a "piece of your mind" when suddenly, glancing at his face, you realized that he was blind, that he accidentally bumped into you. Perhaps you then would react with a feeling of remorse or embarrassment by saying something quite different to yourself like "What a clod I am, how could I be heartless enough to get angry at a poor, helpless blind man?" The important point is that in either case, whether you became angry or contrite, you did so because of the internalized sentences at "B." Similarly, individuals who entertain irrational and highly charged emotional attitudes toward themselves, their parents, their teachers, or the world in general are saying something irrational to themselves at point "B." Rational Therapy and its derivative, Rational Counseling, make the client aware of these "B" statements so that they can be brought to light, analyzed, attacked, and expunged. Thus, with this type of therapy or counseling, the individual's problems are attacked directly and swiftly by dealing with the proximal cause of his disturbances, his internalized sentences. Ellis has listed a large number of typically "neurotic" statements which are common to our culture. For the sake of brevity, these statements can usually be reduced to three categories.

1. Catastrophic sentences, for example, "Isn't it terrible that I flunked my history exam!" (Actually, it is unfortunate but not terrible.)

2. Shoulds, oughts, and musts, for example, "My teacher should treat me more fairly." (Why should she? It would be nice if all teachers were fair, accepting, and adjusted, but why must they be?)

3. Blame—either self-blame (guilt) or other blame (hostility), for example, "My teacher is a dirty rat because she is unfair to me." (Your teacher may be ignorant or disturbed but she is not inherently a blamable person simply because she is unjust or prejudiced.)

During Rational Counseling the client is explicitly asked to pay attention to his sentences. Then, when he recognizes that he does interpret relatively neutral stimuli through exaggerated and emotionally toned internal modifiers, he is helped by the counselor to attack these statements and to replace them with more rational and sensible beliefs. Last, the client is urged to immediately put his insights into practice by altering his behavior in accordance with his new set of implicit sentences.

With certain modifications this rational approach can be directly transferred to the school setting. In fact, Rational Counseling embodies a number of distinct advantages which, in our opinion, makes it superior to any other technique yet devised for use by the school psychologist or school counselor.

Here are some of the advantages of Rational Counseling:

1. Rational Counseling is easy to learn and easy to apply. Our experience has shown that the average school psychologist, having familiarized himself with the literature and listened to representative tapes, can do a respectable job with this technique after a few trial runs.

2. School problems are often pressing and require swift intervention and solution. Questions of transfer, promotion, suspension, and the like are sometimes imperative, and the counselor is not permitted the luxury of the months of therapeutic contacts usually required with analytic or client-centered techniques. Rational Counseling permits immediate intervention and a direct attack on the presenting problems.

3. Rational Counseling teaches the child to live in his environment. The nonblaming attitude which is the essence of this technique helps the child to accept teachers, parents, and peers and to make the best of an imperfect world.

4. The basic principles of Rational Counseling are easy to understand and apply and can be adapted to children of most ages and IQs. It gives the child something concrete to work with and provides immediate environmental reinforcement. The child is not burdened with complicated theories and "dynamics" which he often cannot understand but is given a direct explanation of why he is maladjusted and is shown, in simple terms, how to become adjusted.

5. Children, having lived in this neurotic culture for a shorter period of time than their parents, are usually less indoctrinated than adults and make good subjects for Rational Counseling.

6. Rational Counseling, being shorter than most other techniques, permits greater and more effective use of the counselor's limited time and does not necessarily require the cooperation of recalcitrant or hostile parents. Furthermore, should the counselor fail to help the student it is unlikely that he will hurt him. Rational Counseling makes no dangerous incursions into the unconscious, it militates against irrational antisocial behavior, and it discourages rumination, wool-gathering and preoccupation with historical antecedents or "dynamics."

While Rational Counseling was based on Ellis' Rational Therapy, experience indicated that certain modifications were required. For one thing we soon found that typical "neurotic" verbalizations of children differed somewhat from those of adults. To be optimally effective in dealing with children it is necessary to recognize and even anticipate what a child is saying to himself. While the list is by no means exhaustive, here are some common verbalizations and beliefs found in psychologically disturbed children:

1. It is terrible if parents deny love, play favorites, fight among themselves or behave in other irrational ways. (Instead of realizing

that parents are human and while it is too bad if one's parents are disturbed, it is by no means a catastrophe.)

2. Teachers (principals, counselors) should be perfect, that is, fair, interesting, knowledgeable, understanding. (Teachers are human too and quite often disturbed. It is more rational to accept than to condemn an inefficient teacher.)

3. Self-worth depends on achievement vis-à-vis a particular peer group, for example, one must be good at athletics, popular with boys, good looking, or tops scholastically. (Real enjoyment comes from doing your best and becoming actively involved in life. Achievement is nice but it has nothing intrinsically to do with self-worth.)

4. Sexual misapprehensions, for example, it is wrong to masturbate, it is bad to pet, a male teenager must be a sophisticated Don Juan or a sexual acrobat in order to be a "Man." (Sexual thoughts or acts are never wicked in themselves although, to be sure, certain types of sexual behavior are inefficient because they get you in trouble. Sex in this culture is a learned, complicated set of behaviors and it is natural enough for a young person not to be highly knowledgeable and competent.)

5. It is horrible that grownups do not understand or cater to young people. (Why is it horrible? It is not necessary to always obtain sympathy or to always get the car in order to be happy. Frustration is part of living and growing up.)

In addition to being able to quickly spot the kind of verbalization which lies behind the child's disturbance, experience has shown that it also is advantageous to employ some special techniques or gambits such as:

1. Employing the language level or patois of the child. Don't talk down to him but avoid sophisticated or "grownup" language.

2. Using humor liberally, for example, it is perfectly sound to laugh good naturedly about an obviously disturbed teacher so the child can learn not to take her seriously.

3. Emphasizing the self-defeating aspects of maladjustive behavior and de-emphasizing the moral, social, or disciplinary aspects.

4. Making liberal use of concrete examples.

5. Treating the child as an equal.

6. Using obvious internalized sentences as an ice-breaker, for example, "Most boys your age tell themselves it's wrong to masturbate. Do you feel this way?"

7. Admitting that other people are often inefficient and disturbed instead of rigidly insisting that significant adults are always right.

8. Emphasizing the need for homework and practice. It is useful to compare the development of rational thinking to a series of homework assignments which take time and effort but pay off in the long run.

Summarizing, Rational Counseling consists of first accepting the client as a fallible but not blamable human being. The counselor then explores the internalized nonsense which the youngster is telling himself, keeping as close to the actual verbiage and individual frame of reference as possible. Next, the self-defeating and irrational nature of these sentences are pointed out and the child is urged to replace them with more logical and realistic thoughts. Lastly, the necessity for practice and follow up is stressed with a final objective of eliciting change in behavior. Rational Counseling is thus explanatory, educative, and didactic—very much like teaching.

It is not possible, due to limitations of space, to delve into the intricacies and finer points of Rational Counseling. It is our hope, however, that this paper may have whetted the therapeutic appetite for further study in this area and may stimulate the reader to explore this approach in his own counseling. We think Rational Counseling is ideally suited to the problems and limitations of school counseling. Why not give it a try?

4

Rational Counseling: A Dynamic Approach to Children

Morley D. Glicken

As a by-product of psychoanalytic thought, few treatment groups have quite the mystique of the latency-aged child. One has only to read any number of famous studies by Freud, Ericson, Anna Freud, and other psychoanalytic thinkers to be somewhat awed by their often brilliant "detective" work. The unfortunate result of this complex, difficult approach has been a great deal of illogical, unsupported thinking concerning the latency-aged child with emotional difficulties and an effective treatment for the resolution of his problems.

Psychoanalytic theory suggests that children are often unable to discuss their problems because they tend to repress important material. It further assumes that one can often uncover relevant motives, events, and traumas by providing an atmosphere in which the child can relate freely. We call this atmosphere or approach "Play Therapy." It is assumed that, either in play or in his random dialogue with the therapist, the child will often unconsciously bring to the surface important material. As the child forms a close, healthy relationship with the therapist, he begins to develop insight into his

Reprinted from *Elementary School Guidance and Counseling*, 1968, 2(4), 261-267. Copyright 1968 American Association for Counseling and Development. Reprinted with permission.

feelings. This insight, when properly developed, frees the child of his difficulties and allows changes in behavior to develop gradually.

While few therapists in the school setting rely completely on the analytic approach, many remnants of it remain which tend to decrease the effectiveness of the therapist in his treatment of children.

To begin with, it is, in the author's opinion, fallacious to assume that most children cannot readily and quickly discuss their problems in regard to either school or home. Most children in the author's elementary school social work caseload can and do discuss their difficulties without being coaxed by saccharine words or play therapy.

Too often we overtly or covertly convey to the child the same ego-deflating attitudes of the parent when we assume that, because of his age, the child is incapable of involving himself in a treatment-oriented verbal dialogue. By assuming that we need play objects or other gimmicks with most children, we effectively undermine the child's ability to discuss problems and resolve conflicts and we may often avoid facing important issues by turning the therapy session into a fun-and-games time for clay throwing and paint splashing.

This avoidance of issues seems grounded in our illogical premise that disturbed children are too brittle to face their problems actively. This is just not true. Many disturbed children have undergone years of the most violent psychologically damaging conditioning one can imagine and still function beyond our expectations.

Another psychoanalytic remnant too often inculcated in our treatment of children is the notion that once a child understands his feelings more accurately change will take place. Understanding feelings seldom precipitates change since disturbed feelings are end products of pathological decision making and are in themselves only symptoms. What occurs too often is that the therapist is a "nice" person and the child consciously improves to please the therapist or to gain the therapist's love. Such improvement sometimes is long term, but more often than not it disappears when treatment ends. When treatment fails we often wooden-leggedly assert that the child has only intellectual understanding and lacks the emotional understanding necessary for change, or that the child lacks motivation and doesn't really want to change because he fears losing the attention of his mother, with whom he is still involved.

What should be obvious to most child therapists is that we are woefully inefficient, ineffectual, and inaccurate in our treatment of children. We have neither a very good theory nor a very useful treatment approach in psychoanalytically oriented therapy, counseling, or casework—all of which mean the same. We, particularly those of us who work within the reality confines of a school setting, should be thinking more in terms of an effective, short-term, truly depth-oriented approach.

If the author's experiences are at all transferable to other school counselors, it is suggested that Rational-Emotive Psychotherapy might be just such an approach. The rational approach holds that disturbed emotions, the outward sign of malfunctioning, develop because the child acquires irrational thoughts, beliefs, attitudes, or philosophies about himself and his environment (Ellis, 1962). When a child bases a decision upon an illogical idea the outcome is often a self-defeating emotion or act. It is held that if the counselor can, by aggressively challenging him, help the child see the illogic of his thinking, then the child can often significantly improve his functioning. This means that the therapist must be able to isolate the illogical idea, prove to the child why it might be illogical and what harm it does to him, and then help the child accept a saner view of himself and his world by actively encouraging and supporting the child in his attempt to live more logically.

It might sound at this point as if the rational therapist is a walking logician without feelings or emotions. Not so. He challenges only disturbed ideas, not all ideas. People will always emote and feel no matter how logical or bright. But the healthier the internal logic and self-spoken sentences, the healthier their outward manifestations. This assumes, of course, that people think before they act even if the thought is spontaneous or illogical. If we see a dog at the door we might react a number of ways, usually not violently. However, if the dog is foaming at the mouth, our reaction often indicates fear or panic. We then consciously make choices based upon past experiences before we act.

Probably most helpful to the rational therapist is a good working understanding of common irrational ideas. Most of the children seen by the author use one or more of the following irrational ideas in making self-defeating decisions (Ellis, 1962).

1. It is a dire necessity to be loved or approved by virtually every significant person in our environment.

2. One must be thoroughly competent, adequate, and achieving in all possible respects if one is to consider oneself worthwhile.

3. It is catastrophic when things are not the way one would very much like them to be.

4. It is easier to avoid than to face life difficulties and self-responsibilities.

5. One's past history is an all important determiner of one's present behavior; because something once affected strongly one's life, it will indefinitely have a similar effect.

Along with isolation of illogical ideas must come the counselor's belief, conveyed directly to the child, that the child is capable of resolving his problems with minimal intervention from the therapist. The therapist functions essentially as an educator by teaching the child a new way of looking at himself and his world. In no way does he, as is so common in many forms of therapy, subtly encourage the child to improve by offering the child his love. The child is encouraged to improve for his *own* benefit, *not* the benefit of parents or therapist. Too many children who function well in the school setting mainly to win the approval of their parents face extreme frustration when the parent's interest wanes. The rational approach attempts to help the child learn that achieving to win the acceptance or love of others is often self-defeating. Not everyone can possibly like or accept us. If one attempts to win the approval of virtually everyone, the few who refuse to accept us, particularly if they are parents or other significant persons in our environment, tend to negate the other 98 percent who like us. More important than demanding total acceptance of others is the child's ability to relate more positively toward difficult objects in his life, be they disagreeable parents or a rejecting teacher. The concept of forming healthy working relationships rather than unhealthy "love" relationships should be stressed by the therapist.

Once the child has a fairly good understanding of the rational approach and has been able to isolate his irrational thoughts, the therapist begins assigning homework in the form of practical experiences geared to help the child overcome his school or home difficulty.

A most common type of difficulty in the worker's caseload is the underachiever. Very often the underachiever is a relatively bright child so brainwashed into perfectionist thinking by his demanding parents that school becomes a nightmare of continual defeat. The underachiever often is convinced that unless he can do virtually everything well, he is really a terribly worthless person. If he fails to achieve competence in a subject quickly, he gives up. Effort, he irrationally maintains, might indicate that he really isn't a very competent person. After all, he might really try to master a subject and only get a B or C, and that, he equally illogically declares, would be catastrophic, indicative of the fact that he really *is* the worthless, inadequate person he believes himself to be. Consequently, the defeatist attitude or belligerent facade is often an excellent coverup for his own fears (Glicken, 1967). Not trying but still passing at least gives him the excuse that had he *tried* harder, he would have done better. He easily lapses into lethargy, continues avoiding the issue, and is, to all practical outward appearances, poorly motivated. On the contrary, the underachiever in almost all instances is a terribly ambitious, power hungry, perfectionistic child.

Once the therapist isolates the underlying illogical ideas of the underachiever, he begins to encourage attempts at new behavior by assigning homework. The child might be encouraged to complete his classroom paper no matter how poor a job he does just to prove that part of a job is better than none at all and that improved competence in anything requires practice. The child might also be assigned the task of trying to point out to the parent that the more he (the child) attempts to do all things well, the more difficult it might become, because of his increased internal stress, to do *anything* well. The child attempts to show the parent that he can't become the perfect student overnight and possibly that he never will. He might, however, by continued practice significantly improve with time. The therapist at no time lectures the child on the need to get good grades. Instead, he helps the child see that if he wants good grades for the right reasons (his own feeling of accomplishment, *not* just to please his parents), practice and effort rather than Jehovian thinking are the most realistic means to achieve his goal.

Of course, no child lives in the therapist's perfect world and he sometimes makes mistakes in his attempts to change. The therapist nonjudgmentally helps the child break through these blocks. In most cases children do follow through on assignments, and over the past two years the author has noted significant improvement in about 90 percent of all cases referred using such measurements as pre- and post-therapy personality testing, improvement in grades, teacher reports, and evaluation of parents. (The author's caseload is unscreened and consists of a good number of underachievers, acterouters, predelinquents, neurotics, and even some borderline psychotics.)

To serve the children in the author's caseload more effectively, teachers are seen in group consultation sessions and an attempt is made to help them gain insight not only into the child's problems but also into ways in which the teacher can cope more effectively with the troubled child in the classroom (Glicken, 1968). This often means that teachers must begin questioning their own ideas and attitudes toward teaching, particularly as it relates to the troubled child. The group acts as a stimulating force to educate, to motivate, and often to change the way teachers teach. Many school mental health workers, facing the awesome number of troubled children in the school as compared to static treatment resources, are beginning to see the importance of preparing teachers to cope with children, not necessarily as therapists, but as knowledgeable, helpful adults who are in contact with the child a good part of his day. No thinking therapist should ever underestimate the treatment impact of a good teacher on a child.

Parents too are seen by the worker, and an attempt is made to help them cope with their troubled child more rationally. The author has been impressed with the similarities between the Rational and Adlerian approaches and has been active in developing, for the referral of parents in his school district, a family education facility which uses the Adlerian concept of counseling families before groups of other parents. Such a facility helps parents resolve their child management difficulties by questioning their internal logic as it relates to the child and his behavior and role in the home.

It should be clear to the reader that the rational approach is not effective for all therapists. Its effectiveness is highly dependent upon the therapist's ability to aggressively intervene in the therapeutic dialogue by challenging the child's illogical thinking and then by encouraging new thinking so that improved behavior may result. What must also be stressed is the therapist's acceptance of the *person*, though not necessarily his *behavior*. If properly done it is possible to be therapeutically critical of the child's behavior and thinking and yet convey to him your acceptance of his worthiness as a person.

The rational approach also challenges the premise that one's past behavior is the all-important determiner of one's present and future behavior. It stresses instead changing "here-and-now" thinking. As such, it has been found to be a highly effective treatment approach for use in the school setting with all varieties of pathology.

References

Ellis, A. *Reason and emotion in psychotherapy*. New York: Lyle Stuart, 1962.

Glicken, M. Counseling children: two methods. *Rational Living*, 1967, *1*, 2, p. 36.

Glicken, M. The training of teachers: a mental health issue. *Illinois School Journal*, 1968, *47*(1), 259-261.

5

Rational-Emotive Therapy and Youth: Some New Techniques for Counselors

David W. Roush

Rational-Emotive Therapy (RET), as defined by Ellis (1973, 1974, 1977) and others (Walen, DiGiuseppe, & Wessler, 1980; Wessler & Wessler, 1980), has been used effectively with a wide variety of client populations, including youth (Beckmeyer, 1974; DiGiuseppe, 1975; Hauck, 1967; Knaus, 1974; Maultsby, 1975*b*, McMullin & Casey, 1974; Moleski & Tosi, 1976; Tosi, 1974; Tosi & Moleski, 1973; Young, 1974, 1975, 1977). Furthermore, Tosi (1974) and Young (1977) presented intervention strategies and techniques particularly relevant for counselors working with troubled youth.

Effective RET interventions with youth are frequently contingent on the successful instruction of three basic processes. First, young people must understand the principles of rational thinking (Young, 1977). In other words, they must be able to discriminate between rational and irrational beliefs about themselves and their environ-

Reprinted from *Personnel and Guidance Journal*, 1984, 18, 414-417. Copyright 1984 American Association for Counseling and Development. Reprinted with permission.

ment. Second, they must have a working knowledge of core irrationalities, that is, beliefs expressing self-denigration, intolerance of
frustration, or blame and condemnation of others (Walen et al.,
1980). Third, youth must develop a usable system for identifying and
disputing the components of irrational thinking (Wessler & Wessler,
1980.)

Armed with the previously referenced materials, counselors are
faced with the task of teaching these skills. Although various strategies
are recommended, counselors in institutional settings (corrections,
mental health, and special education classrooms) frequently encounter major problems due to the limited cognitive abilities of the
young people in question. Whether these limitations result from
emotional impairment or learning disabilities, counselors are forced to
translate the didactic principles of RET into understandable strategies for youth with cognitive and perceptual deficits.

Based on experience using RET as a treatment intervention with
emotionally impaired juvenile offenders (Roush & Steelman, 1982),
several practical strategies are offered for youth counselors and teachers that simplify the critical processes of RET. Recommended by Ellis
(personal communication, December 17, 1982), these new or synthesized approaches were designed to increase the youth's ability to
understand rational thinking, recognize core irrationalities, and identify and dispute irrational beliefs.

Rational Thinking

The ability to label one's own biased interpretations of life's events
as rational or irrational is a relative process. Beliefs are rarely cate-
gorized as absolutely rational or irrational in every instance. Rather,
rational beliefs are those values and interpretations that lead to
healthy and self-fulfilling emotions and behaviors. Conversely, irrational beliefs would result in unhealthy and self-defeating emotions
and behaviors. Therefore, counselors need to teach a functional
definition of rational and irrational. This challenge is often aggra-
vated by the commonly encountered difficulty of emotionally impaired youth to engage in consequential thinking.

When deficits occur in consequential thinking, counselor interventions must be immediate so as to link the emotional and behavioral

response with the preceding belief. In institutional and classroom settings, insufficient staff frequently prevents this type of intensive intervention. Therefore, counselors must generate an understandable system for youth that will allow them to predict the probable consequences of their beliefs. When the assessment of beliefs focuses on probable outcomes, youth have a more usable tool for determining rational and irrational thinking.

Maultsby (1975a) outlined a five-step approach for identifying rational thinking. Taking a belief or interpretation of an event, youth are forced to predict the outcome in five general areas. If the predictions are positive, they are encouraged to hold to the belief as rational. If, however, any or all of the predictions are negative, the youth are encouraged to view the belief as irrational. Because of its dual simplicity as a tool for defining rational thinking and a method of getting young people to look at emotional and behavioral consequences, Maultsby's rules for rational thinking are highly relevant.

The usefulness of Maultsby's rules is a function of the youth's ability to remember each component. This has proven to be the major obstacle for cognitively and emotionally impaired youth. Thus a mnemonic device was created. Using one key word to represent each rule, the acronym AFROG (pronounced: A Frog) was developed to assist youth in remembering Maultsby's rules. Shown in Table 1 is the comparison of the AFROG acronym with Maultsby's rules.

AFROG has been used with young people in a state training school, a residential treatment program, a juvenile detention center, special education classrooms, and family counseling. Without exception, youth have been able to recall AFROG to use Maultsby's rules for rational thinking.

Core Irrationalities

After identifying beliefs as irrational, a RET intervention focuses on the type of irrational premise that sustains the belief. These faulty premises have been termed irrational ideas. Through careful identification of irrational ideas, youth can clarify problem situations and better understand the nature of their inappropriate emotions and behaviors.

Table 1. A Comparison of AFROG with Maultsby's Rules for Rational Thinking

AFROG Acronym		Maultsby's Five Rules for Rational Thinking
A (Alive)	Does it keep me alive?	It will enable one to protect his or her life.
F (Feelings)	Do I feel better as a result?	It will enable one to prevent or quickly eliminate significant personal emotional conflict.
R (Reality)	Is it based on reality?	It is based on objective reality or the known relevant facts of a situation.
O (Others)	Does it help me get along with others?	It will enable one to keep out of significant trouble with other people.
G (Goals)	Does it get me to my goals?	It will enable one to achieve his or her goals more efficiently.

Six Irrational Ideas

Ellis (1973, 1974, 1977) has generated a set of irrational ideas characterizing the hundreds of such ideas encountered in therapy. McMullin and Casey (1974) have further distilled these irrationalities into six general categories that more directly address the faulty premises typically held by youth. Although McMullin and Casey provide no rationale or methodology to explain how they derived their six irrational ideas, experience indicates a high level of face validity based on years of feedback from both juvenile offenders and youth counselors. Furthermore, the six irrational ideas represent the core irrationalities defined by Walen and others (1980).

The simplification of irrational ideas makes them more useful for impaired youth. If the number of ideas is reduced and each is given a name, youth can more easily remember the content of the irrational premises. But McMullin and Casey did not simplify the irrational ideas quite enough. Overlap in irrational content exists in several ideas, so much in two instances (Doomsday and Monster) that these ideas can be effectively combined. The resulting five irrational ideas still express some repetition of core irrationalities, but further simplification may produce problems for youth by eliminating minor yet critical distinctions surrounding the impact of irrational self-statements.

A new sixth irrational idea represents the efforts of Steelman (Roush & Steelman, 1982) to generate an irrational idea that addresses directly the recurrent problem of irresponsibility among youth. This new idea, Robot, attacks the erroneous notion that life's events cause one's emotions and behaviors. When youth endorse the Robot idea, they indicate that they have no control over themselves, their emotions, and their behaviors. Without the element of personal control, young people can adeptly abdicate all responsibility for emotions and behavior.

Shown in Table 2 are the six irrational ideas recommended for RET strategies with youth. The ideas are identified by key words, a typical statement of the idea, and a classification of the idea according to core irrationalities defined by Walen and others (1980). The first five ideas are based on the work of McMullin and Casey; the sixth is attributable to Steelman.

Human Worth

At the heart of a RET intervention with youth is the concept of human worth. Expressed as self-esteem, self-concept, or self-worth, the elegance of RET is its focus on the elimination of self-rating or self-evaluation, which are causal to human worth problems. It has been argued that a comprehensive RET intervention with youth is grounded in the development of self-acceptance (Roush & Steelman, 1982; Tosi, 1974; Young, 1977). Yet the ability to give up self-rating and to don the mantle of self-acceptance is the most difficult of all tasks for young people.

A most effective strategy for addressing the problems of human worth concentrates on the separation of the person from his or her behavior. By divorcing the deed from the doer, responses to the appropriateness or inappropriateness of behavior can be made without casting judgments on the worth of the individual. To achieve this seemingly impossible goal, counselors and teachers must have strong control over their emotional reactions to misbehavior. No one is advocating a stifled or cold response to youth when they succeed or exert efforts toward appropriate behavior. Rather, the critical issue in

Table 2. The Six Irrational Ideas

Irrational Idea	Typical Statement	Core Irrationalities[a]		
		1	2	3
1. Namby pamby	I can't stand it		X	
2. Fairy tale	Things should be different		X	
3. I stink	I'm no good	X		
4. You stink	You're no good		X	X
5. Doomsday (Monster)	It's terrible, horrible, awful			X
6. Robot	I can't help it; he, she, it made me do it			X

[a]Core Irrationalities column descriptions:

1. Beliefs expressing self-denigration.
2. Beliefs expressing intolerance of frustration.
3. Beliefs expressing blame and condemnation of others.

addressing the question of human worth is the extent to which adults can internalize a nonjudgmental response to the misbehavior of youth.

The fundamental concept is unconditional neutral regard for misbehavior. Characterized as an emotionally neutral response, this concept reflects a refusal to condemn or judge youth who behave inappropriately. In addition to preventing the inadvertent reinforcement of misbehavior, unconditional neutral regard depersonalizes the intervention process to such a degree that the youth's sense of worth is rarely threatened. The emotional neutrality of this depersonalized approach is a prerequisite for creating the quality of relationships that permit youth to become more self-accepting.

Beyond the modeling of personal control over thinking and behavior, unconditional neutral regard sends two important messages to young people. First, by maintaining an emotionally neutral response that neither condemns nor judges youth, counselors and teachers are clearly stating that, "You cannot make me mad at you, regardless of how inappropriate the behavior." Thus, staff provide a concrete example of a personal rejection of irrational idea 6 (Robot).

Second, the very nature of emotional neutrality symbolizes an unconditional acceptance of the youth's human worth. Although the youth's behavior may be totally unacceptable, emotional neutrality demonstrates a separation between the deed and the doer. Most importantly, it may cause young people to question their irrational ideas about themselves, specifically irrational idea 3 (I Stink). For example, "If adults can accept me as worthwhile when my behavior is totally inappropriate, maybe I am not a worthless person." It would be better for youth if counselors and teachers viewed emotional neutrality as essential for addressing the problem of human worth.

Teaching the separation of deed from doer can be facilitated through the "Do/Are Conflict." Using a chalkboard or piece of paper, the counselor makes two columns, one labeled "Do" and the other "Are." Youth are then asked to describe themselves. Responses are rephrased and recorded so that behavioral characteristics are listed in the "Do" column and fallible human being is written in the "Are" column. For example, if the youth states, "I am a juvenile delinquent," the counselor replies, "You are a fallible human being who has committed delinquent behavior." Thus, the "Do/Are Conflict" forces young people to reframe their evaluations of themselves in a manner that rejects the idea that human essence or worth is equivalent to human behavior.

To enhance this distinction, two extremely effective techniques are also recommended. Both the "fruit basket" approach (Wessler & Wessler, 1980) and the "flat tire" analogy (Young, 1977) demonstrate the difficulty in evaluating the human being (human worth) through an evaluation of its characteristics or properties. Wessler and Wessler summarize this distinction very clearly by asserting, "The whole may or may not be different from the sum of its parts, but one thing is certain—the whole is not any one of its parts" (p. 126). Youth are not their behaviors.

Disputing Irrationalities

Following the processes of recognizing irrational thinking and identifying the concommitant irrational ideas, youth must be persuaded to dispute their faulty interpretations of themselves and life. Three types of disputes are common among RET interventions.

1. The logical dispute attacks the irrational belief and thinking on the basis of the soundness of the argument. When the structure of reasoning is invalid or when the initial premises are false, beliefs are disputed on a logical basis as making no sense.
2. The empirical dispute focuses on the truth of the belief. Emphasizing the evidence behind the belief, empirical disputes demonstrate the absence of the factual data for holding to a particular belief.
3. The functional dispute targets the emotional and behavioral response as the source of motivation for changing beliefs. If these responses are painful and self-defeating, the functional dispute appeals to the basic hedonism of youth by suggesting more rational beliefs (and their new, more appropriate responses) as a means of reducing the discomfort associated with the inappropriate responses from irrational ideas.

For cognitively impaired youth, functional and empirical disputes seem most relevant. In particular, functional disputes are more effective when youth have difficulties with consequential thinking. Without the ability to anticipate the effects of certain irrational beliefs, young people seem surprised and shocked by the emotional and behavioral responses to their thinking. This deficit frequently leads to heightened anxiety about life and perpetuates the notion that youth are inherently worthless. When counselors provide functional disputes, youth view staff as a source of help. It is the helping relationship with youth that makes the RET intervention a humanistic approach.

Again, the teaching process is aided by a concrete technique. For disputing, the Rational Self Analysis (RSA) (Maultsby, 1971) is recommended for youth. This systematic format allows counselors to walk them through the process of disputing irrational ideas. With supervised practice, they soon learn how to complete the RSA independently. For this reason the RSA is seen as a vital component in the self-help orientation of a RET intervention.

Returning to the issue of consequential thinking, the RSA has been expanded by adding a section for identifying environmental consequences. Within institutional settings, inappropriate behaviors usually have additional consequences. Whether originating from peers, staff, or program rules, these environmental consequences present a host of new activating events that compound the intervention. Hence, the new section of the RSA forces youth to attend to the issue of environmental consequences. In addition, the section exploring new reactions to disputed beliefs includes the requirement of listing alternative behaviors. These expansions of the disputing process address the additional institutional problems of youth. Outlined in Table 3 are the components of the Expanded RSA.

Table 3. The Expanded RSA

	Components
A. What happened	Camera check
B. What you told yourself about A	D. Dispute irrational Bs
C1. Your reaction to B: Feelings Behavior	E. New Reaction: Feelings *Alternative behaviors and consequences*
C2. *Consequences of C1*	

Discussion

Because RET postulates that people, including youth, are largely responsible for creating their own emotional and behavioral disturbances, it follows logically that they are also responsible for the work required to solve their problems. For impaired youth, these problems are frequently compounded by inabilities to generate causal, alternative, and consequential thinking deficits and, therefore, an effective problem-solving strategy based on RET must address these issues.

Supplementing the various RET problem-solving strategies, these additional techniques are offered as methods of increasing the effectiveness of the RET intervention with cognitively and emotionally impaired youth. Although more research is needed to validate them, each technique has provided many young people with useful tools for building an effective personal problem-solving approach to life's difficulties.

References

Beckmeyer, G.H. Rational counseling with youthful offenders. *American Journal of Correction*, 1974, *6*, 34.

DiGiuseppe, R. The use of behavior modification to establish rational self-statements in children. *Rational Living*, 1975, *10*, 18–19.

Ellis, A. *Humanistic psychotherapy*. New York: Crown, 1973.

Ellis, A. *Growth through reason*. North Hollywood, Calif.: Wiltshire, 1974.

Ellis, A. *Reason and emotion in psychotherapy*. Secaucus, N.J.: Citadel Press, 1977.

Hauck, P. *The rational management of children*. New York: Libra, 1967.

Knaus, W. *Rational-emotive education: A manual for elementary school teachers*. New York: Institute for Rational Living, 1974.

Maultsby, M. Systematic written homework in psychotherapy. *Psychotherapy: Theory, Research, and Practice*, 1971, *8*, 195–198.

Maultsby, M. *Help yourself to happiness*. New York: Institute for Rational Living, 1975 (*a*).

Maultsby, M. Rational behavior therapy for acting-out adolescents. *Social Casework*, 1975 (*b*), *56*, 35–43.

McMullin, R., & Casey, B. *Talk sense to yourself*. Denver: Creative Social Designs, 1974.

Moleski, R., & Tosi, D. Comparative psychotherapy: Rational-emotive therapy versus systematic desensitization in the treatment of stuttering. *Journal of Consulting and Clinical Psychology*, 1976, *44*, 309–311.

Roush, D.W., & Steelman, B.T. *The intensive learning program: A comprehensive approach to the institutional treatment of juvenile offenders*. Rockville, Mary.: National Criminal Justice Reference Service, 1982.

Tosi, D. *Youth: Toward personal growth—a rational-emotive approach*. Columbus, Ohio: Merrill, 1974.

Tosi, D., & Moleski, R. Rational-emotive counseling: Implications for self-directed behavior change. *Focus on Guidance*, 1973, *6*, 1–11.

Walen, S., DiGiuseppe, R., & Wessler, R. L. *A practitioner's guide to rational-emotive therapy*. New York: Oxford University Press, 1980.

Wessler, R.A., & Wessler, R.L. *The principles and practice of rational-emotive therapy*. San Francisco: Jossey-Bass, 1980.

Young, H. *A rational counseling primer*. New York: Institute for Rational Living, 1974.

Young, H. Rational casework with adolescents. *Journal of School Social Work*, 1975, *1*, 15–20.

Young, H. Counseling strategies with working-class adolescents. In J.L. Wolfe & E. Brand (Eds.), *Twenty years of rational therapy*. New York: Institute for Rational Living, 1977.

Additional Reading

Spivak, G., Platt, J., & Shure, M. *The problem-solving approach to adjustment: A guide to research and intervention*. San Francisco: Jossey-Bass, 1976.

SECTION II

Reality Therapy

Through accepting responsibility for one's own behavior, and acting maturely to constructively change their behavior, individuals find they are no longer lonely, symptoms begin to resolve and they are more likely to gain maturity, respect, love and that most important success identity.

— *William Glasser*

Originally developed for adolescent and adult clientele, reality therapy has recently been successfully applied to young children and to elementary school situations. Reality therapy developed from the psychiatric practice of William Glasser. Working primarily with delinquent adolescents and disturbed adults, he found his approach to be more effective in a shorter period of time than the classical model of psychotherapy. The factor of a typically short duration of time in therapy appears to have increased the appeal of reality therapy for counselors working with children. The relatively uncomplicated theory of behavior and the direct therapy process are undoubtedly additional desirable factors.

The primary propositions of reality therapy involve the following:

1. A focus on present, conscious behavior.
2. An examination of the value system by the client.
3. A concern with the process of need satisfaction in the client.

51

4. An insistence on responsible behavior from the client.

5. No toleration of excuses for unacceptable client behavior.

6. Encouragement of active, directive counselor involvement.

7. De-emphasis of case histories and diagnostic test data.

8. Acknowledgment of the client's freedom to choose responsible or irresponsible behavior.

Thus, the emphasis in counseling is for the client to shed the shackles of past misbehavior and to focus on establishing a future success orientation.

In the first reading, William Appel reviews the writings of William Glasser from 1960 to 1976. He highlights the major concepts in the theory of reality therapy that have developed over the years, and he uses examples to demonstrate their applicability in different counseling settings. Richard Hawes, in the second reading, applies reality therapy to the elementary school. He uses behavioral incidents in the school setting to clarify the counseling process, and he offers several guidelines for anyone wishing to apply reality therapy in school settings. Concluding this section, Borgers applies the principles of this model to gifted children.

6

A Review of the Works of William Glasser

William Appel

Reality therapy is a logical psychotherapeutic orientation based on learning theory and existential philosophy. *Mental Health or Mental Illness?* (1960) was Glasser's first book in which he spoke in basically Freudian terms, but reality therapy can be seen emerging. Glasser's emphasis on ego defectiveness being converted into ego strength with the help of a therapist certainly portends his later notions of involvement and teaching of responsibility by a therapist. Glasser stresses his double lack of emphasis on the history of the client and on insight, both of which figure in his later books.

Reality therapy is one of the newer humanistic therapies that challenge traditional psychoanalytic thought. Reality therapy is based on the assumption that people are innately good and loving as opposed to the Freudian belief that people are repressing sexual frustration and aggression. Glasser suggests that individuals have two basic needs: to love someone whom they respect and be loved in

Reprinted from *Together*, Fall 1977 2, (2), 51–59. Copyright 1977 American Association for Counseling and Development. Reprinted with permission.

return and to do something that makes them feel worthwhile. In order to be happy, people need to fulfill their needs without denying others the right to fulfill theirs. When a person's needs are not fulfilled, he or she begins to behave irresponsibly. There is only responsible (normal) behavior and irresponsible (abnormal) behavior. Glasser (1965) said, "People do not act irresponsibly because they are 'ill'; they are 'ill' because they act irresponsibly" (p. xv). Reality therapy rejects the concepts of neurosis and psychosis, of dementia præcox, paranoid schizophrenia, manic depression, and all the other labels of traditional Freudian psychiatry. Whether the patient thinks he or she is Jesus Christ or has migraine headaches, Glasser attributes the cause to an inability to fulfill the two primary needs. Therefore, in the practice of reality therapy, there is no real difference in the treatment of a myriad of psychiatric problems.

Glasser (1972) stated that the need for love and affection can be traced to cave dwellers who huddled together in tribes against the mostly mysterious, frightening, and cruel world. In her study of chimpanzees, Goodall (1971) observed that grooming, a period during which chimpanzees touch and pat each other for reassurance, may last as long as two hours daily. Goodall demonstrated the obvious need for social grooming when she related her experience with an old male chimpanzee with paralyzed legs who dragged himself sixty yards to try to join a group of grooming males. The need for love, Goodall suggested and Glasser concluded, is programmed into our genes. People, like chimpanzees, do not recognize their need for others and look at the world from their bodies inward. People forget why lovers share a bed and why, in their most intimate moments, they sometimes find it difficult to tell where one body leaves and the other begins.

Before the 1950s, Glasser (1972) reported, people generally pursued the feeling of worthwhileness by attempting, if they were male, to succeed financially and, if they were female, domestically. They sought a goal rather than a role. The goal-oriented person would be the one who wanted to become a doctor, an athlete, a success in business, rich, and famous. A role-oriented person would be one who wanted to do something: heal the sick, play baseball, market a new invention, create, fulfill. Glasser describes society before the 1950s as the survival society and after the 1950s as the identity society. Before the 1950s the major concern was what people were; more recently it has been with who people are. McLuhan (1969) stated, "The students are searching for a role, not a goal" (p. 23).

The mental illness that people usually suffered from in Freud's time was hysteria. In the identity society, most people with mental problems have been labeled neurotic. Logic, therefore, demands a different therapy for the new society. Reality therapy is a unique psychotherapeutic orientation rather than a modification of the Freudian position. Freud claimed that sex and aggression are primary needs. Glasser, in contrast, believes that love and relatedness are fundamental. Glasser (1965) described six differences between traditional Freudian psychiatry and reality therapy:

1. Conventional psychiatry believes that patients are mentally ill or sick, whereas in reality therapy clients are behaving either responsibly or irresponsibly.

2. Conventional psychiatry believes that investigation into a patient's past provides insight into unhealthy patterns of living and what the individual's attitude toward life has been. The patient can change attitudes and subsequently patterns of living. Reality therapy, in contrast, emphasizes working only in the present and the future because nothing can change the past, no person needs to be limited by the past, and the past will become meaningless once the individual learns how to fulfill needs in the present.

3. Conventional psychiatry stresses transference by means of which the patient transfers or projects onto the therapist previous or current feelings about significant people in the past. The analyst interprets this transference to the patient, which theoretically provides the patient with insight into unconscious attitudes and patterns of living. Reality therapy ignores the transference phenomenon.

4. Conventional psychiatry stresses the need to gain insight into the patient's unconscious through the interpretation of transference, dreams, and free associations. Reality therapy rejects an exploration of the unconscious because the client can offer excuses for irresponsible and asocial behavior.

5. Conventional psychiatry avoids the issue of whether a patient's behavior is morally right or wrong. Freudians view patients as being sick and, therefore, as being excused from responsibility for their

behavior. Reality therapy emphasizes constant evaluation by the client of current behavior and recognizes his or her responsibility to maintain a satisfactory standard.

6. Conventional psychiatry does not attempt to teach patients better behavior. The reality therapist actively helps clients to maximize success by finding more ways to behave.

Most patients attempt to deny, to varying degrees, the reality of their environment. Whether the denial is mild (neurosis) or severe (psychosis), denial is present. Reality therapy attempts to help clients stop denying reality, do what is responsible, and make better choices. Reality therapists ask What?, not Why? Traditional psychiatry attempts, through insight, to change attitude, which will help change behavior. Glasser contends that attitudes and feelings are unreliable guides because they cannot be controlled by a person. Behavior may be controlled. It is not possible for people to tell themselves to begin feeling happy. Individuals can do something responsible, however, which will create better feelings.

The traditional psychiatrist maintains a position of superiority and aloofness from patients. A reality therapist recognizes that any person coming for help is lacking the most critical factor for fulfilling his or her needs: a person whom he or she cares about and whom he or she feels genuinely cares about him or her. The psychotherapist initially assumes that the client may be desperate for involvement, which can cause a great deal of pain. The therapist, therefore, becomes involved to help the client cope with reality. Without this kind of human involvement and concern, chances to establish a humanistic therapeutic alliance are minimized. If a client feels a therapist does not care, in all probability no relationship will develop. The therapist must be tough, honest, interested, human, optimistic, and sensitive. The psychotherapist must be able to fulfill his or her own needs and reveal and discuss his or her own struggles so the client can see that acting responsibly is possible though sometimes difficult. The therapist must never be too professional or detached, and if asked a personal question that doesn't invade his or her boundaries of privacy, he or she can respond candidly. The therapist never makes little of what he or she does, stands for, or values. The therapist must be strong enough to have his or her values tested and to withstand a client's request for sympathy no matter how the client pleads or threatens.

The psychotherapist should try never to condone an irresponsible act. He or she must be willing to watch the client suffer if that helps him or her become more responsible.

The therapist can reject and show his or her disapproval of irresponsible behavior without rejecting a client as a human being. Praise may be given for responsible behavior. The therapist teaches that happiness occurs most often when an individual is willing to assume total responsibility for his or her behavior. Once involvement occurs, the client has found someone who cares enough to reject unproductive behaviors that prevent him or her from fulfilling his or her needs. The skill of the counselor is to place the responsibility on the client and to ask why the individual continues in therapy if he or she is not dissastisfied with his or her behavior. If an adolescent boy, for example, cannot stop stealing, no therapy is possible. Many people avoid evaluating their current behavior by emphasizing how they feel rather than how they are behaving. Clients are lonely and usually without friends. The more people discuss their painful memories or current negative feelings, the more depressed and resigned they feel.

Clients should be encouraged to try new behavior patterns. This is accomplished through the therapist's use of positive expectation. Faith is a catalyst that stimulates better performance.

After a client has evaluated his or her behavior and decided to change, the therapist helps make a realistic plan. Once a plan has been determined, the therapist requires a commitment from the client. Glasser suggested that initial goals should be minimal and become progressively more difficult. A person with a failure identity needs some small successes before he or she can tackle difficult goals. Often a plan is written in the form of a contract to strengthen a commitment.

The sincerity of a therapist may be demonstrated by a refusal to accept a client's excuses if a plan is not accomplished and by maintenance of high expectations for improved behavior. If a therapist accepts any excuses, he or she communicates to the client that the plan was unimportant. Punishment for failure to achieve goals is countertherapeutic and reinforces the idea of failure. Glasser explicitly counsels the psychotherapist not to interfere with the natural consequences of any uncompleted contract, that is, a failure in school, being forced from a job, and so forth.

Knowing that many people in therapy consider their problems

unique, the therapist stresses work in groups. It is usually much easier for an adolescent to discuss problems with a group of peers than to relate to a therapist. An effective reality therapist never gives up. The psychotherapist believes that anyone can learn how to become more responsible and productive. Often this process takes time and can occur only after several abortive starts and failures.

In *Schools Without Failure*, Glasser, who applied the principles of reality therapy to the schools, focuses on how the schools can use the need-fulfilling involvement that is basic to reality therapy in the classroom with the goal of helping kids succeed. Glasser contended that "Unless we can provide schools where children, through a reasonable use of their capacities, can succeed, we can do little to solve the major problems of our country" (1969, p. 6). Glasser digressed from the original reality-therapy precepts and expanded into the area of identity. He noted that schools do much to encourage failure through grading systems, emphasizing rote learning, and pretending that there is one right answer for any question. He recommended classroom meetings. The psychiatrist concluded that education today is failure oriented. He faulted punishment as an impediment to involvement (this time between teacher and student). Like Henry James, Dewey, and Whitehead, Glasser believes that the teacher's role is to meet the needs of the student. He does, however, advocate discipline. Among the many innovations he proposes is a grading system that all but eliminates failure but increases motivation. Elementary education is stressed, although not exclusively. Glasser says that blaming poor education on poverty, parents, racial discrimination, and the community removes the student's responsibility for failure. Some of the more salient points of *Schools Without Failure* are:

1. The teacher is urged to become involved with the students and to be a model for them.
2. There should be no record of failure on any permanent transcript. Only courses passed should be recorded. By ignoring failures, the teacher encourages students to change their present behavior. Also, without the threat of failure, students might risk taking more courses. Glasser (1969) contended that grades have become a substitute for learning. Grades are "measures of the student's ability to remember designated facts rather than to think." Students listen only

when the material is relevant and they are not motivated by the payoff of a grade. Grades can label a student a failure and make him or her identify himself or herself as such. Case Western Reserve University Medical School (Cleveland, Ohio) has not used grades for more than twenty years. In national testing, students from Case Western Reserve have performed well. As an alternative to grades, Glasser suggested that constructive comments be placed on papers and tests. He stressed regular oral and written assignments that emphasize thinking. Most teachers dislike grades because they are inaccurate, take time away from teaching, and reduce involvement between teacher and student.

3. Rote learning dehumanizes students and stresses memorizing rather than creative and critical thinking. Problem solving and thinking are minimized in all but a few scientific subjects. Glasser (1969) said, "There is little satisfaction in being right unless thought or judgment go into the procedure or unless there is a great extrinsic payoff, usually money."

Most of what students are required to memorize seems irrelevant to their world. Glasser (1969) said, " 'Smart' children soon learn that what is important in school is one thing and what is important in life is another, and they live this schizophrenic existence satisfactorily." Without relevance there can be no motivation to learning. Glasser suggested that the teaching of relevance in itself be a part of the educational system.

Rather than the letter method of grading, Glasser suggested a system that will eliminate failure yet recognize superior work: S, P, and * for no record of attempting the course. To eliminate the possibility of S becoming a substitute for an A, only one S is allowed per semester. For an S, a student must do extra, superior work on his or her own. In this manner the student can assume responsibility for his or her own education and creatively determine not only his or her standards but also the curriculum. In an effort to avoid labeling students, Glasser suggested that at least twice a year a report such as the following be made:

Reading: Susan seems to enjoy reading short stories from "readers" rather than library books. Her oral reading is fair. She seems to enjoy reading but needs to take responsibility for keeping records of what she reads and reporting on stories. Susan does need to develop better listening skills. She is often disinterested when a story is being read. When she does listen, she can recall main ideas and details.

4. Glasser believes that objective testing emphasizes only the answer and neglects the thought process. His preference would be testing that emphasized discussing or describing situations for which there are no right answers. He believes that better education occurs when the student is taking a risk, broadening his or her outlook, and exploring the unknown. Glasser emphasizes the importance of communication in school by use of the classroom meetings, which are held in a circle to stimulate participation. There are three kinds of meetings: social problem-solving—social behavior in school; open-ended—intellectually important subjects; and educational-diagnostic—students understanding the concepts of the curriculum.

One of the main reasons for these meetings is to help students become involved with the faculty and the administration so that they will be motivated to change. Glasser considers classroom meetings indispensable to achieving schools without failure.

Positive Addiction (1976), Glasser's latest book, seems to have been written in response to one question: What does a reality therapist do if he or she goes through the steps of therapy and a client continues to act in reckless and irresponsible ways? Glasser breaks this problem down in his characteristically logical manner and presents the ideas of positive and negative addictions. Positive addiction is based on the premise that "weakness is the cause of almost all the unfortunate choices we make" (p. 1) and "the best solution for all of us, weak or strong, is to get stronger" (p. 7).

Whether the problem is a lack of self-discipline to stop smoking or the inability to terminate a destructive relationship, the answer is strength. If we lack sufficient strength, we try to reduce our pain by giving up. "Just because the fox said the grapes were sour didn't make them sour. What made them sour was the fact that he couldn't reach them. It hurt less to stop jumping" (p. 8). Glasser calls giving up "the first choice of the weak" (p. 7). The next choice of the weak is "symptom categories" (p. 11). The psychiatrist contends that symptoms such as persistent headaches, overeating, drinking, depression, and phobias are means by which clients avoid facing the reality about which they feel too weak or inadequate to be doing something worthwhile.

According to Glasser, the third choice of the weak is some sort of addiction that reduces pain. It is difficult to stop a negative addiction because in addition to relieving the pain of failure the addiction also provides a pleasurable experience. The pleasure of addiction is more intense than any previous pleasure. Strong people have the ability to find love and self-worth and generally have options to achieve success.

Glasser describes positive addictions as activities such as jogging, meditation, and yoga that, if practiced for approximately an hour a day for six months, become habits that lead to the positive-addiction state of mind. This transcendental, trancelike, often euphoric state in which a person loses a sense of identity has been reached by most people. Glasser suggests that the positive-addiction state of mind will permit individuals to create options for problems for which none seemed to exist. Besides imparting strength, positive addictions benefit people by giving them increased mental alertness, self-awareness, confidence, and a sense of well-being. Positive addictions have no age or activity limitations. The only condition is that people need to do the activity for at least six months.

Much of reality therapy is not new. Eysenck concluded that the so-called symptoms are the illness, and if they are resolved, therapy may be considered successful. In the 1940s Rogers developed client-centered therapy in which he did not consider transference an essential or significant factor in the therapy process, and he stressed the responsibility of the client to direct his or her own life. Skinner has argued that people can be taught how to behave more responsibly. Thomas Szasz, a leading proponent of the Freudians, has said that labeling a client as sick or mentally ill will encourage the individual to behave accordingly. Freud became involved by taking long walks with patients in the park, lending them money, and even permitting them to reside in his home.

One of the strengths of Glasser's work is that he can be understood by any intelligent person who is interested in changing human behavior. Obviously, people other than therapists and paraprofessionals are finding help and substance in Glasser's simple, yet brilliant, concepts.

References

Glasser, W. *Mental health or mental illness?* New York: Harper and Row, 1960.
Glasser, W. *Positive addiction.* New York: Harper and Row, 1976.

Glasser, W. *Reality therapy—A new approach to psychiatry.* New York: Harper and Row, 1965.

Glasser, W. *The identity society.* New York: Harper and Row, 1972.

Glasser, W. *Schools without failure.* New York: Harper and Row, 1969.

Goodall, J. *In the shadow of man.* New York: Dell, 1971.

McLuhan, M. Interview. *Playboy*, March 1969, p. 23.

7
Reality Therapy: An Approach to Encourage Individual and Social Responsibility in the Elementary School

Richard M. Hawes

The technological and cultural forces of today seem to have a separating and depersonalizing effect. This situation causes people to experience the gnawing feelings of loneliness perhaps more frequently and more intensely than in the recent past. As authority, tradition, and conformity lose their potence to solve the problems of the day and to protect us from loneliness and uncertainty, self-esteem (to care for oneself—individual responsibility) and the capacity to love (to care for others—social responsibility) become more necessary for human survival.

In an attempt to *be* loved, many people learn ways to "make" people love them. These desperate power plays are sometimes successful in gaining respect, but respect is only a substitute for love, and the pains of loneliness remain. An alternative method is to learn ways to become more self-responsible (worthwhile) and socially responsible (the capacity to love).

This paper is based on the premise that these conditions (self-worth and the ability to love) are learned, that they are essential learnings for survival, and that the educational system needs to look

Reprinted from *Elementary School Guidance and Counseling*, 1969, *4*(2), 120–127. Copyright 1969 American Association for Counseling and Development. Reprinted with permission.

at them as major educational aims. The following is a description of
an attempt in that direction.

Teaching Self-worth and Ability to Love

At 10:19 A.M. in the third-grade class of the Eastern Elementary
School, Mrs. McHenry has the following discussion with Jimmy, an
eight-year-old boy who has a difficult time completing assignments
even though the school records show him to have above average intelligence. Jimmy, slouched in his chair, is blowing on the edge of his
science book when, with the rest of the class, he should be copying
five arithmetic problems for his homework assignment. Usually, Mrs.
McHenry tells him to get busy, but this time she begins by asking a
question. In this approach, it's more valuable to ask questions than
to make statements or give directions.

Mrs. McHenry: Jimmy, what are you doing?

Jimmy: (Startled, says nothing and shows that he's not sure what to say or
do.)

Mrs. McHenry: Show me—tell me what you are doing. It's important to me.

Jimmy: I—I—I was blowing on the edge of the book like this. (He then demonstrates.)

Mrs. McHenry: (Smiling.) That's right, you were.

Jimmy: (Smiles slightly.)

Their smiles suggest that Mrs. McHenry and Jimmy are experiencing a positive relationship and feeling good about it. A classroom situation that usually ends in a strained or distressful relationship has
ended in a positive one. Mrs. McHenry has helped to make a potential minus into a plus and the therapeutic value is significant—for
both parties. Another similar technique to help create a positive tone
is making a "yes" out of a "no."

Example: A child is raising his hand to ask permission to sharpen a
pencil. The teacher feels this activity would disturb the class. In place
of saying, "No, you can't," she says, "Yes, you may when the bell
rings."

A single incident of this nature is of little value, but when many
people (children and adults) try to make a "yes" out of a "no," the
effect on the school's atmosphere is great.

Mrs. McHenry: (Continues by asking.) Does that help you complete the arithmetic problem?

Jimmy: (Shrugging his shoulders.) No.

Mrs. Mc Henry, without commenting, moves across the room to help another child who has her hand raised, leaving Jimmy with the choice of continuing the behavior discussed, doing something else, or copying the arithmetic problems.

In another classroom, Mrs. Jones' second-grade class is lining up in the back of the room for recess. Tom and Sam get into one of their playful shoving matches, which usually results in a rather serious scuffle. This one is no exception, and one of the girls in the class is slightly injured by an unintentional kick in the shin.

Mrs. Jones: What happened?

The children begin to talk all at once, creating a lot of confusion and noise.

Mrs. Jones: I think we had better bring this up for discussion at our regular class meeting later this morning.

Later, after the class has returned from recess and about twenty minutes before lunch, the class moves into a circle for discussion.

Mrs. Jones: Let's review in as much detail as possible what happened between Tom and Sam earlier this morning.

Tom and Sam reenact or "role play" the situation for the class.

Mrs. Jones: What do you think? How do you feel it worked out?

The children begin to comment, express their opinions, discuss various ideas on how it worked out, judge how valuable it was, estimate the effects the incident had on the class, and suggest how a similar situation could be prevented.

Tom: I guess it wasn't so hot, but we were just fooling around.
Mrs. Jones: We've talked this over pretty well now and we've come up with several ideas on how to solve it. Tom and Sam, what's your plan? (The discussion is always directed toward solving the problem. It is not directed toward finding fault or deciding on punishment.)
Sam: I guess we'll do our own idea of lining up at the ends of the line.
Mrs. Jones: When?
Tom: (After exchanging glances with Sam.) At lunchtime.

It's best to spend as little time as possible on classroom behavior problems. Too much concern can backfire and reinforce what you are trying to eliminate. Time is better used on open-end discussion sessions.

The open-end sessions, the most frequently used and perhaps the most valuable of class meetings, are designed to supplement the academic program by stimulating the children to think and respond. The sessions provide the children with a situation that gives each pupil the opportunity for intellectual success without the possibility of failure. The child makes no mistakes by his answers. Thinking rather than memory is accentuated. These regularly scheduled classroom discussions are the backbone of the program's attempt to encourage individual and socially responsible behavior.

The topic for open-end discussion may be introduced by any class member or the teacher. The topic for one day is introduced by a teacher as she asks the children the following series of questions. Enthusiastic discussion usually follows each question, such as What is play? What is work? Is play or work more important? Would you rather work or play? Is school work or play? Do you learn anything when you play?

Later in the afternoon, several teachers are enjoying coffee in the teacher's lounge. Bill, a sixth-grade student who is well known for disruptive behavior, poor academic attitude, and a low achievement record is being discussed.

As in the class meetings, the teachers accentuate practical, reasonable, and realistic solutions rather than reasons (excuses) for his behavior, fault finding, where he can get help, or methods of punishment. They ask, "What can *I* do to make him feel worthwhile?" "Who has an idea that will help him to be more successful while he is in school?" "Of all the people available, who can work out something with Bill whereby he can begin to be more successful?" "Is school relevant to him?" "What can we do to make his time in school more important to him?" Before long, a specific plan is worked out which possibly will help him to be more successful in school and lead him to more self-satisfying behavioral patterns.

The plan: Mr. Ackley, a third-grade teacher who gets along well with Bill, will ask him to help as a teacher's aide during part of the school day. Bill will be given the responsibility of helping younger children to learn. A responsibility of this nature frequently has a very positive effect on the behavior of the pupil who is giving the help. It is far more effective than when one is lectured or punished.

Applying Reality Therapy

These are a few glimpses of how reality therapy may be applied in an elementary school. Reality therapy has been developed by William Glasser, a Los Angeles psychiatrist who has had considerable experience in private practice, correctional institutions, and as a consultant to various groups, schools, and organizations throughout this country and in Canada. Recently he has shown increasing interest in the schools and their relationship to mental health and human development.

Dr. Glasser's work in the schools over the last few years is reflected in a book entitled, *Schools Without Failure* (1969). His earlier books are *Mental Health or Mental Illness?* (1960) and *Reality Therapy* (1965).

Reality therapy is based on the idea that everyone needs to have an identity. For some, this may be described as a "successful" identity because the person is able to become involved with life in a manner that allows him to fulfill two basic needs: Feeling worthwhile toward himself and others; and to love and be loved. When one is unsuccessful in fulfilling any part of these needs he suffers. One suffers not only if he is unable to be loved but also if he is unable to give love—it's a two-way street.

Dr. Glasser (1966), in a speech to primary reading specialists in the Los Angeles School District, has commented:

These are two-way needs: to love and be loved implies someone to love and someone who loves me. If we don't have this we suffer. For some children the form of this suffering is not learning to read and they won't learn to read until they get the idea that someone is able to care for them and they *can* learn. [P. 1]

Because these suffering children are in the process of developing failure identities by their very experiences, they are unable to make the kind of relationships with *responsible* people that are necessary for them to fulfill their needs. It then becomes the first responsibility of the teacher to make contact with them in a way that is open, transparent, honest, and congruent. One needs to meet them as a human being who cares. Without this type of encounter, their chances of shifting from a failure identity (characterized by delinquency or withdrawal) to a successful identity (characterized by self-esteem and love) will be slim indeed. People need people. As Glasser (1966) puts it:

Children suffer by not learning or they get tired of suffering and cause others to suffer. . . . The teacher's first job is to make contact with these children . . . as a person who cares . . . a person interested in them . . . not as a teacher but as a person. . . . Everyone is doing the best he can at the time. If he could do better he would. You can't convince them they can do better until they relate to you and begin to meet their needs. [P. 1]

By making this authentic and personal contact, involvement is increased while loneliness is decreased. This personal involvement is reflected by the child's increased motivation to learn.

As the discussion so far implies, the first essential step in the application of reality therapy is to get personally involved. With little children particularly, it is important to use personal pronouns as Mrs. McHenry did with Jimmy when she said, "It's important to me" (that you show and tell me what you are doing). It is important for the child to know that you are interested in him as a person, not only as a pupil in the class, a name on the attendance book, a 1.5 reading level, or a 107 IQ score. Casual, interested, and authentic conversation where you get to know one another as people is extremely important. It is important for *him* to know that you enjoy playing tennis, watching "Bewitched," have two boys and one girl, and a husband who sells carpets at Sears. It is important for you to know personal things about him. Spontaneous, casual give-and-take, one human being to another, creates a quality of involvement that causes one to hurt if the child is unable to read.

Our daily newspapers remind us with foreboding that one of our most serious problems today is lack of involvement or social responsibility. Arthur H. Brayfield (1968) suggests that we need to develop an environment ". . . that will foster the sense of personal worth and self-esteem required to sustain the human spirit, give meaning to our lives, and provide the energizing force to forge our personal destinies and to insure the emergence and survival of a humane society."

A second guideline of this approach is to accentuate the present time. Do not get involved in reinforcing the set that Jimmy is always doing something like blowing on the pages of his book when he is supposed to be doing arithmetic, that Tom and Sam have a past history of scuffles, that Bill has always been a behavior problem, or that Johnny was unable to read in the past. Being successful at not succeeding is a certain kind of success, and so we have some very successful failures. Do not reinforce past failure but rather expect Johnny to be successful at reading in the present, expect Jimmy to complete the arithmetic lesson successfully today, expect Tom, Sam, and the class to come up with a solution to their scuffling, expect Bill to be successful in helping a third grader to learn.

A third consideration is to deal with behavior. The purpose is not to search for *why* he is behaving the way he does or *how* he feels about it. The valuable point is to help the child become aware of *what* he is doing that is contributing to his failure. In the case of

Jimmy, Mrs. McHenry was able to help him become consciously aware of his behavior, not by demanding that he stop and get busy (an approach designed to take responsibility for him, rather than his taking responsibility for himself), but by encouraging him in a non-punitive manner to describe, as best he could, his actual behavior. The process of describing helps to bring the behavior to the most optimum conscious level.

These first three points, establishing personal involvement and accentuating present behavior, put the situation clearly in the open and set the stage for a fourth point, which is one of the most important, relevant, and meaningful learning opportunities anyone can experience: The opportunity for one to reflect upon and make a value judgment about his own behavior. The value of this experience of responsible self-evaluation and direction cannot be overemphasized. It is extremely important when working personally with individuals, small groups, or large classroom groups to work toward their making value judgments. This is usually best accomplished by asking questions, not making statements. "Is it worthwhile to blow on the book or complete the arithmetic lesson?" "Is it worthwhile to learn to read?" "Is it worthwhile to help another student?" "Is it worthwhile to kick someone in the shin?" "Is it worthwhile to graduate from high school?"

On this point, Glasser (1966) states, "You can't tell them it is important to learn to read. They must make their own value judgments" (p. 3). When the child decides it is worthwhile to change his behavior, the teacher must work with him in an effort to come up with a specific plan and then encourage him to make a commitment to the plan. Making a plan and getting a commitment are steps five and six. The plan should be such that its fulfillment is guaranteed. Nothing succeeds like success. Once again, questions are important rather than statements or directions: "What can you do about it?" "What is your plan?" "Will you commit yourself to the plan?" "Will you do it?" "When?"

Jimmy could choose to do the arithmetic lesson, Tom and Sam decide to line up at the extreme ends of the line, and Mr. Ackley is going to ask Bill to help in the third grade.

The seventh and eighth steps are to eliminate punishment and not to reinforce excuses. Punishment and excuses are of no value when working with children who already hurt.

As Glasser (1966) remarks:

Discipline is hard because we not only deal with excuses, we ask for them. Discipline is poorly understood—it has nothing to do with hurting or harming children. It is teaching someone that the way he is going is not helping him and getting him to make better choices. It takes a long time for a child to fulfill his commitments. He will check you out. He will try to see if you will take excuses. If you accept excuses, it proves you don't really care and the old failure pattern recurs. If you accept excuses you are saying, "You are worthless." If the assignment is not done say, "When will you do it?" "Can you do it?" "Can you do it in school today?" "After school?" Not "Why didn't you do it?" If you don't ever accept excuses you are saying, "You are a worthwhile person and I'm waiting for you to complete your commitment." [P. 4] .

It should be noted that the cumulative effect of many people becoming personally involved, dealing with present behavior, changing why to what, making plus out of minus or yes out of no, emphasizing thinking and value judgments through techniques such as regularly scheduled classroom meetings, accentuating and expecting successful experiences, eliminating excuses, and not resorting to fear or punishment, creates a distinct environment. This atmosphere itself becomes an added force toward responsible behavior, successful identity, mental health, overall human development, and the capacity to love.

References

Brayfield, A. H. Human resources development. *American Psychologist*, 1968, 23, 479-482.

Glasser, W. How can we help young children face reality and become responsible human beings? Excerpts from a speech made by Dr. Glasser at the ESEA Workshop for Primary Reading Specialists, Los Angeles, Calif., August, 1966.

Glasser, W. *Mental health or mental illness?* New York: Harper and Row, 1960.

Glasser, W. *Reality therapy.* New York: Harper and Row, 1965.

Glasser, W. *Schools without failure.* New York: Harper and Row, 1969.

8

Using Reality Therapy in the Classroom with Gifted Individuals

Sherry B. Borgers

Our educational system has not been highly successful in working with the gifted, although teaching and counseling gifted children are considered important responsibilities for educators. According to Ziv (1977), the educational establishment may be biased, misinformed, or uninformed in relation to working with the gifted.

Because of this misinformation and bias, some educators have been hesitant to work with the gifted. Some believe that since the gifted have superior ability, they have no problems; other teachers may fear that they lack specialized skills that are required in order to work effectively with such children. These statements are often inaccurate. In fact, the gifted may not be able to develop and achieve their highest potential unless they are identified and receive special assistance. Although the same wide range of problems will be found among gifted

Reprinted from *Gifted Child Quarterly*, 1980, *24*(4), 167–168. Copyright 1980 National Association for Gifted Children. Reprinted with permission.

children as among average children, gifted children may also have unique problems that result from being gifted.

Since it is important that teachers and counselors increase their contact with the gifted, the purpose of this paper is to suggest reality therapy (Glasser, 1965) as an example of methods and techniques that educators can use in order to work more effectively with gifted individuals. Reality therapy (RT) has been used successfully by teachers, counselors, and administrators, and has resulted in increased involvement of both teachers and students, reduced disciplinary problems, enhanced school performance, and greater development of a "success identity" for students (Glasser, 1969, 1972; Treat & Bormaster, 1979). In addition, the principles of RT can be learned. One is not required to be a therapist in order to put them into practice (Glasser, 1965).

A fundamental assumption of RT is that the single basic need of every person is the requirement for an identity; all individuals need to believe that they are worthwhile and important. According to Glasser (1969), this successful identity is achieved through love (social responsibility in the school) and self-worth. Since school is a child's major experience in growing up, it should provide a chance to give and to receive love, as well as a chance to become educated, to be productive, and to experience self-worth. If the schools do not provide ways for each child to fulfill this basic need for a successful identity, the student may withdraw and develop a failure identity. This has meaning, for example, in the problem of underachievement, which Ziv (1977) believes to be paramount among the problems of the intellectually gifted.

The basic principles of RT (Glasser, 1972) are involvement, focusing on present behavior, evaluating behavior, planning responsible behavior, commitment, accepting no excuses, and eliminating punishment. Each of these will be discussed briefly in relation to working with gifted students.

The first principle, involvement, is the most essential step. Glasser (1972) believes involvement is a basic need and a prerequisite for a success identity. Teachers are often hesitant to get involved with gifted children because they are threatened by their abilities. Yet teachers must become responsibly involved and communicate caring if they are to be successful in working with these children. This involvement might include the use of praise, a smile, friendliness, and the ability to forgive. Warmth, understanding, and concern are effective cornerstones of growth that the teacher needs to convey as well as the belief that the child has the ability to do well and to function in a responsible manner.

In focusing on present behavior, one deals with what is currently happening in the child's life. The focus is on behavior, not feelings. Feelings are not denied, but neither are they emphasized, since RT is based on the premise that individuals can more easily control their behavior than their thoughts and feelings. "What"-type questions (i. e., What were you doing? What was your part in the incident?) will be more helpful in bringing out behavior then "why" questions (Why did you do it?). There are times when teachers who feel intimidated by gifted students are hesitant to give feedback to them. However, gifted children need to be aware of their behavior so that they can assume responsibility for it and possibly make changes. People do not change behavior unless they first understand it.

The third principle is evaluating behavior. Since RT asks that every student decide if behavior is responsible or irresponsible, it is necessary that students judge and evaluate their own behavior. In order to accomplish this, it may be necessary for the teacher to define responsibility (the ability to care for one's needs without depriving others of their needs) and then ask the student to make a responsible value judgment . The teacher may also need to help the student examine the consequences of certain behaviors. If there is to be effective communication, it is important that the teacher be a good listener and be able to project a sense of hope. Communication between teachers and gifted students may help to combat the lack of understanding, which can lead to conflicts and result in problems such as underachievement.

The fourth principle is planning responsible behavior. Much of the meaningful work of teaching responsibility is the process by which a person is helped to make specific, realistic plans to change failure behavior to success behavior. Plans should be simple and positive. If a plan is written, it is harder to ignore or forget. Apologies, promises, and bargains are not plans. The teacher works directly and closely with the student in formulating the plan and helps to reevaluate it if it does not work. According to Ziv (1977), society loses a great deal of the talent of gifted individuals. Planning can help gifted students to utilize their talents to the benefit of all.

The fifth principle, commitment, is important because it helps individuals to gain a sense of self-worth and maturity. Being gifted does not guarantee the sense of self-worth necessary for successful functioning. Also, gifted students who have many talents may find commitment difficult since learning has generally been easy for them. It may be especially difficult to delineate specific areas of interest. Questions such as "When can you start?" and "How often?" may help a student to reach a commitment. The teacher can assist the student in making reasonable commitments, keeping in mind that these may have to change as reality changes. In addition, opportunities to reinforce students' behaviors should be taken advantage of. It is important to remember to give positive reinforcement when commitments are kept.

The sixth principle is accepting no excuses. Not all commitments will be achieved nor will all plans be successful. When this happens the teacher should not be concerned with why a plan failed, but with the necessity of making modifications or a new plan. It is important that the teacher makes it clear that excuses are unacceptable and also avoids blaming the student. Gifted children will not be helped unless teachers encourage them to become more responsible. The real discipline of teaching responsibility is the ability not to accept excuses but rather to assume that a commitment is always possible.

The last principle is eliminating punishment. The RT approach suggests that students be allowed to suffer the natural or logical consequences of their behavior. Consequences allow the student a choice, whereas punishment does not. Natural consequences are the realistic outcomes that result from a behavior; [for a discussion of] logical and natural consequences, see Dreikurs and Soltz (1964).

Punishment has not generally been successful with students who are irresponsible, who have a failure identity, or who have learned to manipulate the system. Yet these students are likely to be the ones who most need help. Rather than assigning punishment and accepting excuses for failure, teachers can help students to substitute reasonable value judgments, to make plans in accordance with these value judgments, and to make commitments to follow through with their plans. When teachers do this, they are truly assisting students to gain a success identity. The secret of RT is persistence. Once students believe that those around them are not giving up on them, they are more likely to change their behavior.

In conclusion, it is important to remember that RT is not the answer to all problems nor is it always successful; however, it is one workable strategy that has the potential to increase involvement, and it can help individuals to assume responsibility for their behavior. Establishing more meaningful relationships with gifted students can be an extremely important step toward encouraging the individual responsibility that may help gifted individuals to develop more of their potential.

References

Dreikurs, R., & Soltz, V. *Children: The challenge*. New York: Hawthorn, 1964.

Glasser, W. *Reality therapy: A new approach to psychiatry*. New York: Harper and Row, 1965.

Glasser, W. *Schools without failure*. New York: Harper and Row, 1969.

Glasser, W. *The identity society*. New York: Harper and Row, 1972.

Treat, C., & Bormaster, J. C. *Counseling, consulting, coordinating*. Austin: TLC, 1979.

Ziv, A. *Counseling the intellectually gifted child*. Toronto: University of Toronto, 1977.

SECTION III

Behavioral Counseling

*Without doubt, people have feelings, and many have learned an
extensive vocabulary for describing such feelings. I am not against
people feeling they understand and accept themselves. I favor such
feelings just as I favor people loving justice, truth, and beauty.
My point is that, stated as goals of counseling, such subjective
feelings will not prove as useful as more objective statements of
behavior. Being sensitive to the feelings of a client is certainly a
necessary attribute for any counselor. That it is sufficient is
questionable.*

— John Krumboltz

Behavioral counseling is an approach to therapy developed by John
Krumboltz in the mid 1960s. In this model, counseling is viewed as a
learning process. Behavioristic explanations of behavior and behavioristic change techniques form the core of Krumboltz's theoretical
model. These include the importance of environmental factors in
learning, the belief that all behavior is learned and can thus be
unlearned or modified, the belief that modification or manipulation of
the environment can produce change in the client, the focus on
reinforcement and extinction techniques for changing behavior, and
the importance of measurement in the counseling process.

Unlike behaviorism, Krumboltz believes in the importance of the
counseling relationship and its power to affect a client's behavior. In
this relationship, the mutual establishment of goals by counselor and

client is an essential initial step. Once specific behavioral goals have been identified, the counselor can use one or more general techniques in the counseling process. Each of these techniques incorporates the principles of reinforcement and extinction, and each is used once a specific behavior has been identified. The techniques can be summarized as follows:

1. *Operant learning*—Selected behaviors are reinforced, and special attention is given to the timing of reinforcement.
2. *Imitative learning*—Use of behavioral models in the counseling process.
3. *Cognitive learning*—Involves the use of role playing, client contracts, and verbal instructions.
4. *Emotional learning*—Patterned after the techniques of reciprocal inhibition.

Thus, behavioral counseling can be viewed as a process emphasizing specifics: specific identification of behavior, specific goal establishment, and specific changes in client behavior.

The first article is by Carl Thoresen. He uses the case example of a high school student to illustrate his interpretation of behavioral counseling and to present his rationale for its use in school situations. Classroom behavior problems are dealt with in the second selection by Foley and Willson, in which they describe using a contract system. Their step-by-step analysis of the implementation of a contract procedure in consultation with a teacher is particularly helpful.

Charles Bugg, in the third reading, describes the process of systematic desensitization. He explains how it can be readily applied to counseling situations, and he presents several case studies to demonstrate its application in the school.

In summary, behavioral counseling is viewed as a learning process, using behavioristic principles and emphasizing the importance of the counseling relationship. Mutual goal identification is essential to the process, followed by the modification or elimination of specific behavioral incidents using behavioristic reinforcement and extinction techniques.

9

Behavioral Counseling: An Introduction

Carl E. Thoresen

Just what is behavioral counseling? Why should a counselor really give serious consideration to this approach? Let's take an example presented by a student to convey some basic features of behavioral counseling.

The Case of Bob

Bob, a bright high school junior, came into my office to talk about his poor grades. He complained of difficulty in concentrating on his studies, particularly math. "I just seem to go through the motions—I mean I can't remember what I read. . . ." Bob also said that he got very nervous and tense before taking tests, especially in United States history. "Sometimes I get so tied up my mind goes blank!" He brought up his reluctance to participate in class discussions: "I know that Miss Stein really expects us to speak up, but—well, you know, I feel so kinda stupid—and then sometimes other kids say just what I was thinking." Bob pointed out that his parents were very concerned about his grades but felt in general that it was really up to him to try

Reprinted from *The School Counselor*, 1966, *14*(1), 13-21. Copyright 1966 American Association for Counseling and Development. Reprinted with permission.

harder. He expressed great dissatisfaction with his school work, especially his performance on tests, his short concentration span, and his inability to participate. I asked Bob how he felt about involving his parents and teachers in helping solve his problems. He said, "It's O.K. with me. I know they're worried. . . . Well, uh, can you help me?"

Behavior Is Learned

Behavioral counseling uses the adjective "behavioral" to emphasize that counseling seeks to bring about changes in student behavior. In the problem cited, Bob asked for assistance in changing his behavior; that is, he wanted help in improving his ability to concentrate, in reducing tension just before tests, and in increasing his oral participation in class. A basic assumption in behavioral counseling is that most behavior is learned and is therefore potentially changeable. The individual's environment is recognized as being very influential in what is learned and how it is learned. Significant changes in behavior may take place if the individual's environment is systematically modified.

Reinforcing Behavior

How can Bob be assisted in changing his behavior? Let's look first at his problem of concentration. In talking with Bob, I found that he usually studied after dinner. He complained of loss of concentration after about ten minutes of studying, especially with math. After that, the more he tried to concentrate, the less he was able to do so. I suggested that Bob start the next evening with his math and that he study it for only a ten-minute period. If he felt that he had really concentrated during that time, he was free to take a five-minute break and do something that he really enjoyed. Bob said he could look through a car magazine, something he enjoyed immensely, or he could practice his uke or he might get something to eat. He asked if he should try studying his math again after the break. I suggested he try one more ten-minute session and then do something he thoroughly enjoyed.

I asked Bob to stop by my office each morning during the first week to tell me how long he had studied his math. I deliberately made an encouraging comment (e.g., "Bob, that's very good!") when he told me how long he had spent on his math. During the second week I asked him to come by three times and twice during the third week. Over a period of time he was gradually able to build up his "good study time" (as he called it) in math to forty minutes.

In assisting Bob to improve his concentration, I drew upon a demonstrated principle of learning: behavior which is rewarded or reinforced, especially immediately after it occurs, is strengthened and is more likely to occur again. Bob was rewarding himself for concentrating by doing something he enjoyed, immediately after he had successfully studied his mathematics. The counselor was also reinforcing Bob with attention and approval for his changed behavior. By chance, Bob's father also became involved. (It should be noted that the counselor could have deliberately asked the parents to participate.) His father asked him to check with him after studying math each evening. He would praise Bob for his progress in increasing his "good" studying time and also talk with him about other things. In effect, he was specifically rewarding Bob for his progress.

A Variety of Tailored Procedures

Behavioral counseling does not rely on any one set of procedures. In particular, this approach does not expect the counselor himself to function personally as the most important or influential source of change. The following definition of counseling makes an important point: "Counseling consists of whatever ethical activities a counselor undertakes in an effort to help the client engage in those types of behavior which will lead to a resolution of the client's problems" (Krumboltz, 1964, p. 4). The point is that counselors can develop and use a wide variety of procedures, often specifically involving significant persons in the student's life, to assist him in solving problems. Procedures can be tailored to the individual situation. Counselors need not (and should not) place exclusive reliance on the face-to-face, one-to-one interview. It may be that parents, classroom teachers, and peers can be far more influential in helping to bring about desired changes in behavior. Many writers in counseling have recently urged the creation and use of new counseling procedures, procedures which would move the activities of counselors beyond use of the interview per se and which would take the counselor away from his desk and out of his office (Krumboltz, 1965; Magoon, 1964; Robinson, 1963; Truax & Carkhuff, 1964; Williamson, 1962; Wrenn, 1962).[1]

Specific Change as Success

How about Bob's tenseness just before tests? Bob said that this problem seemed to have developed recently, especially in his English and history classes. He said that both teachers used essay tests which have always bothered him. "I really get excited and nervous because I never know how to get started right—I mean, I, uh, always never have enough time . . . can't figure out how to say it." I asked Bob if he knew someone in class who did well on essay tests. My suggestion was that he read over some of his past test papers to get an idea of what the finished product looked like. I also suggested he talk with the student as to how he went about organizing his ideas during the test. My hunch was that Bob's tenseness was in part a function of his poor essay test skills. If he could acquire greater proficiency he might begin to feel more relaxed and therefore less tense about essay tests. Looking over good examples of well-written essay answers could provide Bob with a kind of model to emulate.

I also talked briefly with his English and history teachers, explaining Bob's problem of tenseness and eliciting their assistance. I suggested that these teachers take particular note of Bob in class just prior to taking a test. Specifically, I asked that they make some reassuring comment, coming by his desk before he started the test, or use a nonverbal expression, such as a smile or nod. Such behavior might assist Bob to relax a little more prior to the test. His English teacher suggested that making encouraging remarks could also be done immediately following the test, especially if Bob had appeared more relaxed. I suggested that Bob might actually practice writing essay answers before school in the same classroom, with the teacher present. Experience in writing an essay response in a near-reality setting (i.e., the classroom), with the support and approval of the teacher, would be less anxiety-arousing for Bob. His increased ability to be more relaxed as well as skillful while writing an essay answer would, in effect, counteract his anxiety and tenseness. His increased calmness would then generalize into the actual class situation. (This procedure may be thought of as a way of "desensitizing" Bob to an anxiety situation.) I also agreed to stop by the classroom several times before school to encourage Bob in his efforts.

After three weeks, Bob reported feeling much more relaxed about taking essay tests. In addition, his grade in history had improved by one letter grade. His English grade, due to some problems on grammar quizzes, remained the same, although he was getting higher essay test grades.

The counselor here was effective in assisting Bob to reduce his tension about tests. Counseling effectiveness, as viewed in behavioral counseling, must depend on having specifically defined outcomes. Did the behavior in question—in this case tension about taking essay tests—show any change? Often counseling effectiveness is judged solely from what happens during the counseling interview; that is, how does the counselor conduct the interview and what does the student say? While interview behavior is crucial, especially in establishing a relationship that will permit the counselor to tailor procedures to the individual problem, relevant changes in student behaviors *outside* the interview remain the most significant yardstick of counseling effectiveness.

Modeling Behavior

Bob's third problem, you may recall, concerned his oral participation in history. Since several junior students had recently talked with the counselor about this problem, I asked Bob if he would like to work with a small group of students on this. He and eight other students met with the counselor for three sessions. During each, the counselor played a short, rehearsed audio tape-recording of a student group, which had also been concerned with problems of participation—principles of good discussion, specific steps for improving participation, and expectations for trying them out in class. During the sessions the group reacted to the tapes, talking about how they felt their situation resembled or differed from those presented on the tapes. Their "participation" in the group was encouraged by the counselor with approving comments, smiles, and nods. During the third session an attempt was made to simulate the reality of the classroom by role playing a history discussion.

Most students, including Bob, reported feeling much more comfortable in voluntarily making a comment in class. Bob's history teacher also noted an increase in the number of his voluntary comments in class. In talking with her, it became clear that the teacher was thinking about responding to Bob more positively.

This illustrates an important point: assisting a student in modifying a specific behavior, such as increasing his oral participation, may have several positive consequences; that is, the change in a particular behavior may contribute to changes in other behaviors in the person and in others. Besides the increased feelings of self-mastery and esteem experienced by the student himself, the behavior of others toward him in other situations (including their perceptions and expectations) may undergo change.

The use of tape-recorded peers as "social models" in a group situation, in which students can make comments and immediately experience an encouraging response from the counselor and other members of the group, is based on research and theory in social learning. Behavioral counseling freely and deliberately draws upon social learning principles and experimentation to develop counseling procedures. In this situation, for example, the peer group was employed specifically to provide social reward for participation behavior.

The problem of Bob as presented is admittedly fragmentary and incomplete. With him the procedures described above proved effective. Other procedures might have been equally or more effective. In addition, Bob may still have problems. But he has experienced some success with the counselor in changing certain specific problem behaviors. As a result, he may be more receptive to approaching the counselor in the future with more "dynamic, deep-seated" difficulties or he may have started to learn how to handle and resolve his own problems. Then, too, these procedures may not have a positive effect with a student who is less desirous of changing or with a student from a different subculture. (The dramatic Streetcorner Research Project by Schwitzgebel and Kolb (1964), involving work with "unreachable" delinquents, demonstrates how behavioral counseling procedure can be successfully tailored to the individual problem.

Some Basic Points

Bob's problem as presented does, however, serve to introduce some basic points which characterize behavioral counseling:

1. Most human behavior is learned and is therefore subject to change.

2. Specific changes of the individual's environment can assist in altering relevant behaviors; counseling procedures seek to bring about relevant changes in student behavior by altering the environment.

3. Social learning principles, such as those of reinforcement and social modeling, can be used to develop counseling procedures.

4. Counseling effectiveness and the outcome of counseling are assessed by changes in specific student behaviors outside the counseling interview. Interview behavior per se is not a satisfactory measure of effective counseling.

5. Counseling procedures are not static, fixed, or predetermined, but can be specifically designed to assist the student in solving a particular problem.

What Behavioral Counseling Is Not

Behavioral counseling is not, as Patterson (1963), McCully (1964), and Jourard (1961) have recently suggested, cold, impersonal, or manipulative counseling. It does not consider the counseling relationship as totally irrelevant, nor does it seek to "dehumanize man" or to manipulate the client subtly against his will. It has not created, nor does it seek to create, mechanical, technique-ridden counselors or slavish clients. "A behavioral approach to counseling and guidance does not consist of a bag of tricks to be applied mechanically for the purpose of coercing unwilling people" (Michael & Meyerson, 1962, p. 382).

I think the alarm of some may stem from these sources: (1) misinformation about behavioral counseling; (2) the connotation and semantic confusion about certain psychological terms; and (3) perceived philosophical implications of the scientific method in counseling, that is, counseling as a behavioral science.

Pigeons and Patients

Aware of the successful work of B. F. Skinner at Harvard with pigeons and other animals, some categorically condemn behavioral counseling as "Skinnerian . . . pigeon-oriented." While Skinner does offer established principles and provocative ideas about the learning of human behavior (Skinner, 1963, pp. 503-515), behavioral counseling can and does draw upon the experimentation and principles of *several* learning theories as well as other behavioral sciences.

Others, aware of the research in behavior modification with severely disturbed persons, in which abnormal behavior has been dramatically changed with the use of social learning procedures (Eysenck, 1964; Frank, 1965; Krasner & Ullman, 1965; Ullman & Krasner, 1965; Wolpe, Salter, & Leyna, 1964), may err in generalizing to the school setting these special situations in which the client does not necessarily request help in changing certain behaviors. In these studies, psychotic patients have, for example, been "taught" to pick up utensils before entering the dining room and to eat properly in a few weeks, after years of being "unreachable." Procedures developed to do this were based on reinforcement learning principles, where patients were consistently verbally and nonverbally reinforced for their successive approximation of relevant behaviors. Their cooperation was not necessarily elicited in advance. In the school setting, on the other hand, the behavioral counselor does *not* arbitrarily and secretly influence the student against his will. Instead, he uses what is known about how learning occurs and how it can be changed to help the student modify his behavior in directions desired by the student himself.

Manipulation

The emotional and very negative connotation for some of the commonly used scientific and psychological terms creates problems. Consider the term "manipulation." As used in psychological research, for example, it means management of certain factors to control a particular situation. To many, however, the term suggests some devious activity, perhaps with a questionable ulterior motive. Therefore, when the phrase "manipulate the environment" is encountered, many react negatively. The same may be said for such terms as "conditioning" and "programming." Actually, as Patterson (1963, p. 683), a proponent of client-centered counseling, recently pointed out: "We must recognize that anything we do in or out of counseling, has some influence on others, that it is not possible, in this sense, to avoid some control or manipulation of the behavior of others . . . everyone, including the client-centered counselor, manipulates."

The Individual in Control

I think counseling can move toward becoming a behavioral science, using methods scientifically developed, without dehumanizing the client (or the counselor). Some seem to believe that the increased use in counseling research and practice of social learning principles and experimentation ignores basic human values and philosophical questions in counseling. This does not follow. The counselor will always be confronted with value judgments and ethical issues. He cannot function, as several studies have demonstrated, without involving in some way his perceptions of what is desirable. Making the counselor more effective in solving problems by, for example, having clients view a videotape, does not mechanize him or make him impersonal. Using the methods of science, testing hunches derived from principles of social learning, studying the client's environment and how he interacts with it—these do not ignore man as a complex entity or leave him ". . . sitting off in a corner, quite alone" (Arbuckle, 1963).

Actually, clients will come to exercise more self-control and self-direction by learning specifically how factors in their environment influence their behavior and how to modify their own behavior in desired directions. The shy girl, for example, who after working with a behavioral counselor feels more comfortable in a group situation such as the classroom and is able to take part in discussions, has acquired greater freedom. She can now choose to participate or not. "Really, man becomes free only when he has attained self-mastery" (De Rougemont, 1956). One might say that the client's potential for exercising freedom and responsibility is greatly enhanced. He sees his own behavior as learned, as a product of his environment, and as subject to change by himself.

Behavioral counseling in many ways is very demanding on the counselor. He must constantly study the environment and social learning history of students and try out hunches. He does not know the complacent security of one set of fixed procedures. He experiences the inevitable frustrations and failures. Yet he has the satisfaction at times of observing the consequences of his procedures: changes in the behavior of students. The extent of his ingenuity, openmindedness, and creativity may be the only limitation in his developing more effective procedures. Perhaps the real limitation is what John Gardner (1964, p. 56) recently termed the tyranny of tradition and "proper procedures," which often become encased in a hard, almost impregnable change-defying shell.

Recommended Readings

The following introductory list of readings is suggested for counselors and others who wish to learn more about behavioral counseling.

John D. Krumboltz. Behavioral counseling: rationale and research. *Personnel and Guidance Journal*, 1965, *44*, 383-387. Discusses how goals of counseling can be determined for each client, how behavioral counseling can achieve them, and what are the limitations on counselor activities. Several counseling research studies are presented.

John D. Krumboltz. Parable of the good counselor. *Personnel and Guidance Journal,* 1964, *43,* 118-123. Presents a counseling problem and how two counselors— "behavioral" and "client-centered"—might handle it. Discusses similarities and differences in assumptions and procedures between behavioral and client-centered counseling.

John D. Krumboltz & Carl E. Thoresen. The effect of behavioral counseling in group and individual settings on information-seeking behavior. *Journal of Counseling Psychology,* 1964, *11,* 324-333. Reports an experimental counseling study (11th grade students) in which a fifteen-minute audio tape and encouraging comments by counselors were found effective in helping students seek information relevant to their future plans.

Jack Michael. Guidance and counseling as the control of behavior. In E. Landy and P. Perry (Eds.) *Guidance in American education: backgrounds and prospects.* Cambridge, Mass.: Harvard University Press, 1964, 71-83. A more readable treatment than the Michael and Meyerson article of a behavioral approach. Defines reinforcement learning terms with many good examples. Good discussion of implications of behavioral approach to educational practice.

Jack Michael & Lee Meyerson. A behavioral approach to counseling and guidance. In Ralph L. Mosher, Richard F. Carle, & Chris D. Kehas (Eds.) *Guidance on examination.* New York: Harcourt, Brace and World, 1965, pp. 24-48. Also in *Harvard Educational Review,* 1962, *32,* 382-402. Presents the behavioral approach to many problems faced in counseling, using the sometimes confusing terminology of the experimental learning psychologist. Defines several learning terms such as operant conditioning, positive reinforcers, and aversive stimuli. Stresses use of environmental changes to modify behavior.

Thomas Magoon. Innovations in counseling, *Journal of Counseling Psychology,* 1964, *11,* 343-347. Offers several novel ideas about how counselors can develop more effective procedures in such areas as occupational information and career planning.

Albert Bandura. Psychotherapy as a learning process. *Psychological Bulletin,* 1961, *58,* 143-159. Appears in O. Milton (Ed.), *Behavior disorders.* New York: Lippincott, 1965, 185-207. Thorough discussion and review of attempts to use principles of learning in psychotherapy. Discusses some objections to a social learning approach.

Israel Goldiamond. Justified and unjustified alarm over behavioral control. In O. Milton (Ed.), *Behavior disorders.* New York: Lippincott, 1965, 237 ff. Provocative, stimulating and well-written discussion of misunderstandings and confusions about a behavior approach to human problems.

Leonard Ullman & Leonard Krasner (Eds.) *Case studies in behavior modification.* New York: Holt, Rinehart and Winston, 1965. Examples of how counseling and psychotherapeutic procedures based on social learning can be designated to change specifically a wide variety of problem behaviors.

Ralph Schwitzgebel & D. Kolb. Inducing behavioral change in adolescent delinquents. *Behavior Research and Therapy,* 1964, *1,* 297-304. Forty "unreachable" delinquent boys are given part-time jobs which involved talking into tape recorders, learning how to read, etc. Counselors successfully used a variety of rewards (positive reinforcers) to encourage nondelinquent behavior.

John D. Krumboltz, Barbara B. Varenhorst, & Carl E. Thoresen. Nonverbal factors in the effectiveness of models in counseling. Paper read at American Educational Research Association Convention, Chicago, February, 1965. Experimental counseling study used two videotaped counseling interviews (woman counselor and junior year girl) to help girls with their future planning. Differences in counselor attentiveness and prestige were involved. Available from authors, c/o School of Education, Stanford University, Stanford, California.

Arthur Bachrach (Ed.) *Experimental foundations of clinical psychology*. New York: Basic Books, 1962. Several chapters cover such topics as verbal conditioning, operant behavior, and small groups. Excellent source of references to research literature.

Footnote

1. I am reminded here of recent articles by Schwebel (1964), Wrenn (1962), and Lifton (1963) on "counselor encapsulation"; that is, how counselors have become, among other things, trapped in the exclusive use of traditional techniques.

References

Arbuckle, Dugald S. Foreword to Carlton Beck, *Philosophical foundations of guidance*. Englewood Cliffs, N.J.: Prentice-Hall, 1963.

De Rougemont, Denis. *Love in the western world*. New York: Pantheon, 1956.

Eysenck, Hans J. (Ed.) *Experiments in behavior therapy*. New York: Macmillan, 1964.

Frank, Cyril M. *Conditioning techniques in clinical practice and research*. New York: Springer, 1965.

Gardner, John W. *Self-renewal*. New York: Harper and Row, 1964.

Jourard, Sidney. On the problem of reinforcement by the psychotherapist of healthy behavior. In Shaw, Franklin (Ed.), *Behavioral approaches to counseling and psychotherapy*. Montgomery: University of Alabama Press, 1961.

Krasner, Leonard, & Ullmann, Leonard P. (Eds.) *Research in behavior modification*. New York: Holt, Rinehart and Winston, 1965.

Krumboltz, John D. Parable of the good counselor. *Personnel and Guidance Journal*, 1964, *43*, 118–123.

Krumboltz, John D. Behavioral counseling: Rationale and research. *Personnel and Guidance Journal*, 1965, *44*, 383–387.

Lifton, Walter. The culturally encapsulated counselor faces reality. Paper read at Annual Meeting of American Psychological Association, Philadelphia, August, 1963.

McCully, C. Harold. The two secrets of the gods. Paper read at Iota Alpha Banquet, Pennsylvania State University, May, 1964.

Magoon, Thomas. Innovations in counseling. *Journal of Counseling Psychology*, 1964, *11*, 342–347.

Michael, Jack, & Meyerson, Lee. A behavioral approach to counseling and guidance. *Harvard Educational Review*, 1962, *32*, 382–402.

Patterson, Cecil H. Control, conditioning and counseling. *Personnel and Guidance Journal*, 1963, *41*, 680–686.

Robinson, Francis P. A cubist approach to the art of counseling. *Personnel and Guidance Journal*, 1963, *41*, 670–676.

Schwebel, Milton. Ideology and counselor encapsulation. *Journal of Counseling Psychology*, 1964, *11*, 366–369.

Schwitzgebel, Ralph, & Kolb, D. Inducing behavioral change in adolescent delinquents. *Behavior Research and Therapy*, 1964, *1*, 297–304.

Skinner, B.F. Operant behavior. *American Psychologist*, 1963, *18*, 503–515.

Truax, Charles B., & Carkhuff, Robert R. The old and the new: Theory and research in counseling and psychotherapy. *Personnel and Guidance Journal*, 1964, *41*, 108–111.

Ullman, Leonard P., & Krasner, Leonard (Eds.) *Case studies in behavior modification.* New York: Holt, Rinehart and Winston, 1965.

Williamson, E.G. The counselor as technique. *Personnel and Guidance Journal*, 1962, *41*, 108–111.

Wolpe, Joseph, Salter, Andrew, & Leyna, L.J. *The conditioning therapies.* New York: Holt, Rinehart and Winston, 1964.

Wrenn, C. Gilbert. The culturally encapsulated counselor. *Harvard Educational Review*, 1962, *32*, 444–449.

Bandura, Albert. Psychotherapy as a learning process. *Psychological Bulletin*, 1961,

Additional Readings

Ayllon, Theodoro, & Michael, Jack L. The psychiatric nurse as a behavioral engineer. *Journal of Experimental Analysis of Behavior*, 1959, *2*, 323–334.

Bachrach, Arthur (Ed.) *Experimental foundations of clinical psychology.* New York: Basic Books, 1962.

Bandura, Albert, Psychotherapy as a learning process. *Psychological Bulletin*, 1961, *58*, 143–159.

Goldiamond, Israel. Justified and unjustified alarm over behavioral control. In Milton, O. (Ed.), *Behavior disorders.* New York: Lippincott, 1965. Pp. 237–261.

Krumboltz, John D., & Thoresen, Carl E. The effect of behavioral counseling in group and individual settings on information-seeking behavior. *Journal of Counseling Psychology*, 1964, *11*, 324–333.

Krumboltz, John D., Varenhorst, Barbara B., & Thoresen, Carl E. Non-verbal factors in the effectiveness of models in counseling. Paper read at American Educational Research Association Convention, Chicago, February, 1965.

Michael, Jack. Guidance and counseling as the control of behavior. In Landy, E., & Perry, P. (Eds.), *Guidance in American education: backgrounds and prospects.* Cambridge, Mass.: Harvard University Press, 1964. Pp. 71–83.

Patterson, Cecil H. Comment on John D. Krumboltz, Parable of the good counselor. *Personnel and Guidance Journal*, 1964, *43*, 124.

Wrenn, C. Gilbert. *The counselor in a changing world.* Washington: American Personnel and Guidance Association, 1962.

10

Contracted Behavioral Counseling: A Model for Classroom Intervention

Wayne E. Foley
John W. Willson

Students who exhibit various forms of maladaptive academic or social behavior are frequently referred by teachers to counselors. In response to such referrals, counselors usually assume independent responsibility for diagnosis and treatment. They prepare case studies that may include individual and group test scores, family histories, and anecdotal teacher impressions and classroom observations. Rarely included, however, are specific workable suggestions as to how to plan and implement a program of behavioral remediation for such students.

Although the referring teacher may gain a greater understanding of a student's problem from a comprehensive case study, she is nevertheless primarily concerned with seeing improved classroom performance in the problem student.

A relatively new methodology, contracted behavioral counseling, adapted from the works of Lloyd Homme (1969) and John D. Krumboltz (1966), provides counselors with a specific and expedient program for intervention. Contracted behavioral counseling is a systematic application of the "laws of learning," providing incentive for

Reprinted from *The School Counselor*, 1971, *19*(2), 126–130. Copyright 1971 American Association for Counseling and Development. Reprinted with permission.

students to learn new kinds of adaptive behaviors. This procedure requires that the teacher share joint responsibility with the counselor
as an active participant in behavioral change rather than a recipient
of counseling outcomes. This model of intervention assumes that the
referred problem is being controlled or maintained by consequences
operative in the classroom environment; therefore, the remediation
takes place in the classroom or environment from which the problem
generates. Each contract is individually designed to meet the specific
needs of a particular problem student.

Implementation of such counseling follows these steps:

Step 1. Referral of maladaptive behavior. The counselor and teacher
jointly define the referred problem in behavioral terms. The referral
is stated so as to identify the actual behavior or actions that constitute the problem (Vance, 1967).

Step 2. Selection of terminal behaviors. The desired adaptive or
terminal behaviors are identified by the teacher and counselor as
mutually expected counseling outcomes or goals. Also identified are
those intermediate behaviors or successive approximations that lead
to the terminal behavior.

Step 3. Construction of a reinforcement menu. A list of positively
reinforcing consequences or events is compiled from the counselor's
and teacher's observations and conversations with the student. The
student is allowed to select his own reinforcer from the reinforcement menu.

Step 4. A token economy is developed. The counselor assists the
teacher in developing a point system or token economy and demonstrates how to dispense positive reinforcers (i.e., points and teacher
praise) in formulating and shaping adaptive student behaviors
(Ayllon & Arzin, 1968).

Step 5. Initiation of a contractual agreement. The counselor and
the teacher discuss the maladaptive classroom behavior with the
problem student. The student is asked if he would like to participate
in a program designed to improve his performance. If the student
chooses to participate, the program's contingencies and consequences
are discussed leading toward contractual agreement.

Step 6. Specification of contractual terms. The terms of the contract are completed when the student agrees to perform certain social
or academic behaviors, while the teacher agrees to award a specified
number of points. The student and the teacher mutually agree on the

number of points needed before free time may be spent for any item on the reinforcement menu.

Step 7. The contract is formalized. The exact behaviors and contingencies to be carried out by the teacher and the student are explicitly stated in a written document. The contract (cosigned by the student and the teacher) serves to remind the signees of their cooperative efforts to solve the problem. The teacher initials the contract only after the student's behavior has met the contractual requirements (see Figure 1).

Step 8. Contractual pay-off. As the student performs successive approximations to the terminal behaviors, points are accumulated that are cashed in at specified times. Points are converted for minutes of free-time activities listed·on the reinforcement menu (Premack, 1959).

Step 9. Renegotiation of the contract. Since the objective of contracted behavioral counseling is to produce behavioral change in small steps or successive approximations, the contract must be renegotiated and increased as the teacher and the student accomplish the intermediate behaviors. The same procedures are followed in the renegotiation process.

Summary

Usually by the time a teacher requests the counselor's assistance with a problem student, he has already attempted a variety of approaches to improve the student's academic or social performance. At this point he has experienced failure and, probably, so has the student.

Contracted behavioral counseling provides a method of intervention that removes the conflict from centering directly between student and teacher. The counselor as a neutral to both parties may offer his skills in behavioral contracting in securing their cooperative effort to resolve the impasse or conflict situation that they have reached.

Communication problems existing between student and teacher expectations are minimized by the use of behavioral statements written into the formalized contract. Also, the terms of the contract are mutually negotiable and acceptable; therefore, the contractual arrangements are viewed as fair and honest.

*Figure 1. An Example of a Contract Used in Increasing
        Academic Behaviors*

Student: John B. Goode

Terminal Behavior: John will complete each written Math assignment in the
    allotted time with a minimum of 90% accuracy.[a]

Behavior Contract

Terms of the Contract: (Contract One—beginning requirements)

1. John is to complete each written Math assignment in the allotted time with
   a minimum of 50% accuracy.[b]
2. John must only complete written Math assignment in the allotted time
   with 50% accuracy to gain the teacher's signature.
3. By completing each assignment as stated above, John gains 10 points. The
   contract is issued daily and signed by both the teacher and the student.
4. Total points necessary for cash-in is set at 30.

Period	Subject	Teacher's Initials	Room
1			
2			
3	Math		23
4			
5			
6			

Teacher

Student

a. That point which the student and the teacher have mutually defined as
the eventual behavioral goal.

b. As John is able to consistently meet the requirements of this contract,
the percentage of accuracy will be systematically increased. As one academic
subject comes under control, others may be added.

An important aspect of contracted behavioral counseling is that as a result of the teacher's participation in the planning and execution of the intervention program, he gains useful skills in dealing with this and future classroom behavior problems. Teacher training in problem identification and intervention procedures is a necessary and intrinsic element of this model. Further, since the referral identifies the precise observable behaviors that constitute the problem it is compatible with measurement requirements. That is, empirical data may be collected on the frequency of occurrence of the referred problem and used to evaluate the success or failure of the intervention program. The actual written contract may be constructed to provide a daily written summary of performance data, as well as serve as a constant reminder of the student's and teacher's cooperative efforts to remediate the problem. Even without the collection of empirical data, the specific identification of the terminal behaviors and those intermediate behaviors (successive approximations) provide observable and objective criteria for evaluating behavioral change.

The utilization of contracted behavioral counseling gets the counselor out of his office and in direct contact with teachers and students in arranging effective classroom environments to meet individualized student problems.

References

Ayllon, T., & Azrin, N.H. *Token economy.* New York: Appleton-Century-Crofts, 1968.

Homme, L., Csaryi, A. P., Gonzales, M., & Rech, J.R. *How to use contingency contracting in the classroom.* Champaign, Ill.: Research Press, 1969.

Krumboltz, J. D. (Ed.) *Revolution in counseling.* Boston: Houghton Mifflin, 1966.

Premack, D. Toward empirical behavior laws: I. Positive reinforcement. *Psychological Review,* 1969, *66*, 219-233.

Vance, B. The counselor—an agent of what change? *Personnel and Guidance Journal,* 1967, *45*, 1012-1016.

11

Systematic Desensitization: A Technique Worth Trying

Charles A. Bugg

During the past four years, I have noted that a substantial proportion of children's self-referrals for counseling concerns problems in
which anxiety related to specific events or situations is the major
causal element. One particularly common reason they seek counseling is test anxiety. Another is stage fright associated with public-
speaking situations (e.g., making reports, reading in class, speaking in
student election campaigns, performing in plays and talent shows). I
assume that other working counselors encounter similar client problems and therefore in this article I will briefly describe the technique
of systematic desensitization and then relate my own experiences in
using a modified form of this technique in a public school setting.

Although the experiences reported here occurred in a school setting, systematic desensitization is a general technique and may be
useful to many persons, regardless of age or setting, whenever minor
specific anxieties are causing some debilitating effect. Counselors in
settings other than the schools should be able to extend and generalize the experience reported here to their own clients in their own
settings.

Reprinted from *The Personnel and Guidance Journal*, 1972, *50*(10), 823–828. Copyright
1972 American Association for Counseling and Development. Reprinted with permission.

Systematic Desensitization

Systematic desensitization is one limited-purpose form of behavior therapy based upon the principle of reciprocal inhibition. Wolpe (1961) describes reciprocal inhibition:

If a response inhibitory to anxiety can be made to occur in the presence of anxiety-evoking stimuli so that it is accompanied by a complete or partial suppression of the anxiety response, the bond between these stimuli and the anxiety response will be weakened. [P. 189]

The essential principle of reciprocal inhibition is that an organism cannot make two contradictory responses at the same time. Behavior therapy assumes that anxiety responses are learned (conditioned) behaviors and may be extinguished by reconditioning. If the response that is contradictory to anxiety results in a more pleasant state or more productive behavior for the subject, the new response to the anxiety-evoking stimuli will gradually replace the anxiety response.

Wolpe (1961, 1966) restricted his use of systematic desensitization to cases involving minor neurotic anxieties, simple phobias related to specific situations and objects (fear of high places, fear of dogs, etc.) and those not resulting from interpersonal relations. He claims 90 percent effectiveness in treating patients when he uses systematic desensitization.

Systematic desensitization consists of three steps: (a) training in deep muscle relaxation, the primary anxiety-inhibiting response; (b) construction of anxiety hierarchies for the patient (ordered from stimuli that produce slight anxiety to those that produce great anxiety); and (c) counterposing relaxation and anxiety-evoking stimuli from the hierarchies. Usually the patient is hypnotized. (Other researchers have demonstrated that hypnosis is unnecessary in the settings and for the clients with which most counselors deal.) Wolpe (1961) describes the process in these words:

In brief, the desensitization method consists of presenting to the imagination of the deeply relaxed patient the feeblest item in a list of anxiety-evoking stimuli—repeatedly, until no more anxiety is evoked. The next item of the list is presented, and so on, until eventually, even the strongest of the anxiety-evoking stimuli fails to evoke any stir of anxiety in the patient. It has consistently been found that at every stage a stimulus that evokes no anxiety when imagined in a state of relaxation will also evoke no anxiety when encountered in reality. [P. 191]

Wolpe's Method

To illustrate the technique developed and used by Wolpe, I will use as an example a patient with an irrational fear of cats. First, a hierarchy is constructed. The greatest anxiety is evoked by a scarred, ugly alley cat hissing and snarling in the walkway as the patient goes down the street. A pet cat in a friend's house causes great anxiety, but not so much as the alley cat. Little kittens cause anxiety, but not as much as grown cats. Pictures of cats evoke fear, but not so much as real cats. A picture of little kittens playing with a ball of yarn causes just noticeable tenseness.

Second, the patient is taught the method of deep muscle relaxation.

Third, the therapist relaxes the patient and begins to describe the picture of little kittens—the item producing the most feeble anxiety reaction. When the patient signals that he feels tense or anxious, he is ordered to relax. After a few seconds' relaxation, the stimulus is described again until the patient again signals anxiety and is relaxed. These steps are repeated until the stimulus finally evokes no anxiety in the patient. Then the process is repeated with the second weakest stimulus, and so on up the line. The process works very rapidly, and it is not unusual for a patient to have two or more sessions with the therapist per day.

Nonmedical Research

A number of recent studies have involved modifications of Wolpe's method of systematic desensitization. Two of these are of particular significance to those who work in nonmedical settings.

Emory (1967) found desensitization effective in reducing test anxiety in college students, and, very importantly, his results indicated no significant differences in reduction of test anxiety between students treated with individually developed hierarchies and students treated by the use of a standardized hierarchy for relief of test anxiety.

Paul and Shannon (1966) worked with college students whose anxiety about public speaking restricted their academic success. Their study compared group desensitization, insight-oriented therapy (with psychoanalytically oriented therapists), attention-placebo treatment, and individual desensitization. They found that both group and individual desensitization techniques proved to be effective and both were superior to insight-oriented therapy and attention-placebo treatment in reducing anxiety. Group desensitization was not significantly different in its effect from individual desensitization. Furthermore, Paul and Shannon used a modified form of deep muscle relaxation requiring less training than Wolpe's method, and none of the subjects was hypnotized. The results of a study by Dixon (1966), however, reported no difference between a group method of desensitization and conventional group therapy in reducing test anxiety.

In the School Setting

Almost every day the working school counselor encounters students whose educational, social, and personal development and success are hampered by some specific anxiety, usually in a testing or public speaking situation. In my work during the past four years, I have observed that a modified form of systematic desensitization can help counselees with such problems, provided that the following two conditions exist:

1. The counselor must spend enough time listening to the student, reflecting his feelings and concerns, and helping him describe and clarify his problem situation to determine that anxiety is in fact the culprit and to gain some reasonable idea of the counselee's hierarchy. (A student may flunk tests because he plays around and is not prepared rather than because anxiety causes him to tense up and forget everything he has learned.)

2. The counselee must conscientiously apply the techniques of systematic desensitization at every opportunity in both imagination and reality.

As I use it, systematic desensitization is a technique taught to and applied by the counselee. Ordinarily, one or two half-hour sessions are sufficient for the counselee to learn the basic principles of the technique and how to apply it. I discuss the principle of reciprocal inhibition and the technique of systematic desensitization in nontechnical language until I feel that the counselee understands them. Then we discuss the counselee's specific problem until he understands not only the major situation that causes him anxiety and problems but also a number of related situations (his hierarchy) in which the technique should and can be applied to alleviate the problem. The basic test of the counselee's understanding is to have him describe in his own words the technique and how it can and will be applied to his personal situation.

The student learns to relax himself by using three basic steps in words to this effect. "First, whenever you are in the situation or imagine yourself in it, take a deep breath and let it go suddenly. This forces relaxation for a split second. Second, tell yourself to be calm and relax. Third, think of something very pleasant for a few seconds before bringing yourself back to the problem situation and repeating the whole process."

The student is instructed to imagine himself in situations related to his strongest anxiety-evoking situation and to relax. He is told to do this over and over again, hundreds of times if necessary. Gradually, he works himself through his hierarchy in imagination. He also practices the techniques of relaxation and desensitization whenever he finds himself in such a situation in reality. I stress that if the technique is to work, the counselee must apply it repeatedly at every possible opportunity in reality and imagination, both in the problem situation and in related situations.

Examples

The following case studies from my own experience illustrate the use that has been made of systematic desensitization.

William, a seventh-grader, came into my office just before semester exams and declared that he had a serious problem in math. He anticipated failing the quarter test two days hence and getting a D for his quarter grade. He expected to follow that up by flunking the semester exam a few days later and getting a D for the final semester grade. The result would be that his parents would place him on restriction for the next nine weeks or until the grade went to C or above. William was known to be a strong, conscientious student. He diagnosed his own case, stating that he studied math regularly, sometimes with his father who knew math well, and that he was certain he understood the material. He added,

I always get good grades for homework. I can answer any question or work any problem in class that the teacher wants me to do, but I just can't pass a test. I get all excited and nervous and then make stupid mistakes or just completely forget how to work the problems. When he gives the test back, I can work any of the problems that I have missed without any help at all.

I explained systematic desensitization to William and told him that the method might not work as quickly as he needed in order to pass the tests, but that at least it could help him get off restriction by the end of nine weeks. Two days later he said, "Man, what you told me to try sure works. I made a B on the test and got a C for my quarter grade." A few days later he repeated this high performance, getting a B on the semester final.

Because he wasn't much concerned about his other subjects and felt confident that he basically knew the math, William had devoted almost full time during those two days to desensitizing himself for the math test. He imagined himself in the math room and relaxed. He imagined himself speaking with the math teacher and relaxed. As he studied math, he relaxed himself. He imagined himself taking tests in other subjects and relaxed. He imagined taking the math test and relaxed. When he finally took the test, he relaxed himself as much as possible beforehand and then took the test one problem at a time, relaxing in between. He kept telling himself, "Just be calm and relax. You know this stuff, and if you don't get shook, you'll make a good grade." After resolving his test anxiety, William continued in counseling to discuss concerns that he had about dating and sexual behavior and values.

Rita, in second grade, presented a problem that combines test anxiety and fear of public speaking. She said that whenever the teacher called on her to work something on the board she got upset, started crying, and couldn't do the work. Like William, she knew how to do the work. There was just something about being asked to do it on the board that upset her so much that she couldn't do it. She practiced the same techniques prescribed for William in both imagination and reality and added a wrinkle of her own.

When she came back for her second meeting a week later, Rita reported that on that very morning the teacher had asked her to go to the board to work a math problem and that she had felt nervous about it but had done it without crying. She said that she had been working very hard that week on trying to relax herself. Then she added,

Last weekend, I had three of my best friends over. I told them about my problem and what you had told me to try to solve it. We played school almost all day. They played the teacher, and they called on me a lot to go to the board and work. I was nervous, but I just kept taking deep breaths and relaxing. That helped me a lot.

John, in ninth grade, was an outstanding student and a natural leader. Although he hadn't sought either office, he had been elected as a student council representative and as the top officer of another major school activity. Just before the deadline for filing as a candidate for one of the four major student council offices, he was asked why he hadn't signed up to run for one of them. His reply was:

I would love to serve in one of the offices, but I couldn't possibly run, because I would have to make a speech to the student body. I can't even read out of a book in class when the teacher calls on me. I know the material perfectly, but I get so nervous that I either start stuttering or else just can't get anything to come out at all.

Assured that his problem could be overcome, John agreed to run for one of the offices. Two weeks later, he made an excellent speech to the student body and was elected. Afterward, his office required him to speak to a number of groups to explain student council plans and policies. He spoke successfully on every occasion.

To achieve this result, John imagined himself engaged in spontaneous debate with his peers in student council (this caused only slight anxiety) and relaxed himself. He imagined himself reading in class and relaxed. He relaxed himself as he wrote his speech. He practiced in front of the mirror and relaxed. He practiced in front of his parents and relaxed. He practiced in front of his friends and campaign managers and relaxed. Called upon to read or speak in class, he relaxed himself and did the best he could. In both imagination and reality, he found and practiced opportunities to employ the techniques of systematic desensitization during the two weeks prior to his election speech.

Systematic desensitization is a technique that has worked for a substantial proportion of the pupils who have come to me for help. It is a technique with which all counselors should be familiar. One of its distinct advantages is the time it saves for the counselor to devote to other cases that require other approaches. With most counselees whom the technique can help, only one or two short sessions are needed. It can also be used in group counseling, and students who have been taught the technique can teach it to others without the intervention of the counselor. On many occasions, a student has approached me and said:

I had planned to make an appointment with you, but I was talking with my friend. He told me why he saw you and what you suggested. My problem was the same, so I tried the same thing and it worked. I don't need to see you now.

In Other Settings

No great stretch of the imagination should be required for counselors in settings other than the schools to apply the principles of systematic desensitization to their own clients. Sooner or later most counselors are likely to encounter clients who are afflicted by specific anxiety to some degree and for whom desensitization may contribute to more effective functioning. The client who is well qualified for a position but who becomes so nervous during a job interview that he is judged unfavorably is a prime candidate for desensitization. Another example of someone who would benefit from the technique is the person who becomes so anxious while being taught the responsibilities and techniques of a new job that he fails to learn properly or makes mistakes that may cause him to lose the job or not advance in it in accord with his true abilities. A toning down of the stage fright associated with public speaking in both large and small groups would enable people to communicate their ideas more effectively, would free them to utilize more of their basic talents as human beings, and would enable them to live more effective, more productive, and more rewarding personal, civic, business, and social lives. Whatever the counselor's setting, whenever he encounters a client whose functioning is hampered by some specific minor anxiety, he might use systematic desensitization to help his client overcome the negative effects of the anxiety and achieve his goals and potential.

Relax and Try It

Do you get a little worked up about using something from the behavioral school? Imagine yourself hearing a counselee describe his problem and thinking that you know what is wrong. Just before that puts you into a catatonic seizure, take a deep breath and let it go. Relax. Think about something less threatening for a moment. Now, repeat that until you stop feeling tense and nervous about having such a thought. Next, imagine yourself saying, "I think I know what your problem is, and I know what you can do to solve it." When that makes you feel uneasy, relax. Keep trying this in your imagination until you feel comfortable with it, then try it out on a real live counselee. Chances are good that it will help him and save you time for others whose concerns are of a different nature and require a more extended application of your reflective skills.

References

Dixon, F. S. Systematic desensitization of test anxiety. *Dissertation Abstracts,* 1966, *27* (4-b), 1301-1302.

Emory, J. R. An evaluation of standard versus individualized hierarchies in desensitization to reduce test anxiety. *Dissertation Abstracts,* 1967, *27* (7-b), 2510-2511.

Paul, G. L., & Shannon, D. T. Treatment of anxiety through systematic desensitization in therapy groups. *Journal of Abnormal Psychology,* 1966, *71,* 124-135.

Wolpe, J. The systematic desensitization treatment of neuroses. *Journal of Nervous and Mental Disease,* 1961, *132,* 189-203.

Wolpe, J. The conditioning and deconditioning of neurotic anxiety. In Spielberger, C. D. (Ed.), *Anxiety and behavior.* New York: Academic Press, 1966, 179–190. 179-190.

Suggested Reading

(These two chapters provide an excellent brief overview of Wolpe's work and of the principles and techniques of systematic desensitization.)

Ford, D. H., & Urban, H. B. *Systems of psychotherapy.* New York: John Wiley, 1963, 273–303.

Patterson, C. H. *Theories of counseling and psychotherapy.* New York: Harper and Row, 1966, 154–178.

SECTION IV

Adlerian Counseling

A new professional discipline has emerged: child psychiatry. It is based on an assumption we cannot share, that children who need help are "emotionally sick." Few of them are really sick; most are misguided. Who is best qualified to help them—the teacher, the parent, the counselor, the psychiatrist, the social worker, the minister, or any adult friend or relative? In our experience, any one of them can be effective in influencing.the child and helping him to adjust. The disturbed child has wrong ideas about himself and life and uses socially unacceptable means to find his place. Anyone who can win his confidence, who understands him, who can show him alternatives, can redirect the child.

— Rudolf Dreikurs

Adlerian psychology as we know it today is a direct result of the work of Alfred Adler at the beginning of this century. A colleague of Sigmund Freud, Adler eventually rejected the tenets of psychoanalytic thought and developed his own system that he termed *individual psychology*. This system is more widely known today as Adlerian counseling.

The basic theoretical concepts of Adlerian counseling focus on the following:

1. *Teleoanalytic goals*: Behavior is seen as a movement toward future goals. The counseling process involves an analysis of these future goals.

105

2. *Striving for superiority*: All individuals are attempting to become better than they are at present. This striving carries a person from one level of development to the next.

3. *Inferiority feelings*: These feelings arise from a sense of incompletion or imperfection. These feelings are normal and are the cause of all improvement in a person's life.

4. *Social interest*: Each individual possesses a natural interest in the welfare of society. By working for the common good, a person compensates for his or her individual weakness.

5. *Style of life*: This concept is the sum total of an individual's attempts to be superior and to overcome his or her basic inferiority feelings. The style of life is unique for each individual.

6. *Creative self*: Individuals create their own personality. They creatively search for experiences that fulfill their unique styles of life.

7. *Consciousness*: Each individual is capable of planning and guiding his or her behavior with full awareness of its meaning for his or her self-realization.

Rudolf Dreikurs extended the work of Adler to include, more specifically, the family constellation. Most of Dreikurs's work has been concerned with the development and management of children and adolescents. He titled his approach *family counseling*, since the focus of therapy was the family constellation. He readily adopted the Adlerian concepts of inferiority feelings, superiority striving, style of life, birth order, and teleoanalytic goal orientation. The latter concept he translated into the four goals of a child's disturbed behavior.

More recently, Donald Dinkmeyer has extended the work of Adler and Dreikurs. He has incorporated their concepts into the counseling approach that he terms *developmental counseling*. Dinkmeyer begins this section of readings by briefly yet comprehensively surveying Adlerian psychology and its application to school counseling. A description of the stages in the counseling process could be especially helpful for practicing counselors. Rudolf Dreikurs, in the second article, focuses more specifically on the four goals of a child's misbehavior and their remediation by counselors and parents. In the final article, Dinkmeyer applies the philosophy of Alfred Adler to developmental counseling.

12

Contributions of Teleoanalytic Theory and Techniques to School Counseling

Don Dinkmeyer

School counseling demands competency in a variety of psychological areas in the dimensions of educational, vocational, and personal-social problems, and in the area of consulting teachers and parents.

The most noticeable deficiency in some counselor-education experiences is the lack of familiarity with a theory demonstrated to be effective in school counseling. The purpose of this paper is to present the contributions of Adlerian psychology to school counseling.

An Overview of Personality Theory as Related to Counseling

Adlerians perceive man as an indivisible, social, decision-making being whose psychological movement and actions have a purpose. The fundamental assumptions for understanding personality are:

1. *Human personality is best understood in its unity or pattern.* This is the holistic approach, which views man as a unified organism, a unity moving by definite life patterns toward a goal. He is seen as a total unit and regarded as an irreducible whole. From this vantage point, we do not add to our understanding by fragmentary analysis,

Reprinted from *The Personnel and Guidance Journal*, 1968, *46*(9), 898–902. Copyright 1968 American Association for Counseling and Development. Reprinted with permission.

but instead are required to see the pattern and relationship between the data.

2. *Behavior is goal directed and purposive.* A contrast is apparent here. There are theorists who adhere to the view that behavior is caused and can always be explained in mechanical terms. From this point of view, motivation can be understood in the light of its goal-directed nature; such goals give direction to man's striving, which becomes the final cause or final explanation. In contradistinction, Adlerians look forward to determine the cause; they comprehend the goal as the cause.

Furthermore, the goals are recognized and treated as subjective, creative, and unconscious goals that may be only dimly perceived by the individual. It is recognized that they direct the person's selective responses in two areas: in the cognitive life (revealing his private logic) and in the emotional life wherein emotions may be employed as social tools.

3. *Motivation can be understood as the striving for significance or the movement to enhance self-esteem.* Striving for significance receives its direction from the individual's unique, subjectively conceived goal of success (self-ideal). This search for significance emerges when man experiences the subjective feeling of being less than others and then engages in various attempts to compensate. His inferiority feelings are often due to a faulty self-evaluation. This situation suggests that we seek a master motive, a concept common in organismic psychology. It has sometimes been called self-actualization, self-expansion, or competence (Dreikurs, 1950; Rogers, 1951; Maslow, 1954; Combs & Snygg, 1959; White, 1959).

4. *All behavior has social meaning.* Man is primarily a social being; and his behavior is understood in terms of its social context. The significance of behavior really lies in our interaction and transaction with others. Social striving, from this point of view, is primary, not secondary. Behavior is highly influenced by the consequences of the reactions of other persons. Behavior often makes sense in terms of an ironic social regard, for example, a child's bothering the teacher and forcing her to deal with him so that he can have a special place among the peers of the class and the school.

5. *Each individual has the creative power to make biased interpretations.* Biased apperception influences our every process. Behavior is not only reactive, it is creative. The individual has the power of choice. His uniqueness ultimately rests in this creative power. Behav-

ior is thus understood not only within the purview of stimulus and response but also in terms of the intervening variable of the organism or person who makes a creative decision about that stimulus (S-O-R).

6. *The individual is understood in terms of his phenomenological field.* The individual, being always understood in terms of his subjective point of view, impels us to be concerned with the meaning that a given event possesses for him.

7. *Belonging is a basic need.* Man has the desire to belong to someone or something. His social significance derives from belonging. He is not actualized without belonging. Many of man's fears and anxieties arise out of the fear of not belonging or of not being acceptable.

8. *The emphasis is on idiographic, not nomothetic, laws.* There is a greater concern with finding laws that apply characteristically to the individual in relation to his style of life (idiographic) than in the development of nomothetic laws that apply generally but include many exceptions.

9. *The psychology of use has priority over the psychology of possession.* We are concerned with determining the conclusions the person has drawn from his experiences. The individual at any moment does that which is most useful or best accomplishes his purposes and strivings at that moment. That which interferes with his goals is not done. This principle is noted in the varying ways in which individuals make use of their heredity or their environment.

10. *The development of social interest is crucial for mental health.* Social interest is based on our capacity to give and take. It is demonstrated by a readiness to demand less than one is able to offer and in the desire to cooperate. Social interest becomes a criterion of mental health. This method of counseling places as much emphasis on cognitive change as it does on affective change.

Counseling Procedures

The foregoing assumptions, fundamental to Adlerian psychology, lead naturally into a set of procedures.

Counseling is seen as a learning process that provides a re-educative bridge for solving the tasks of life. Counseling involves communications for the purpose of modifying concepts, convictions, and attitudes.

The counseling process is divided into four parts: (1) the relationship; (2) the investigation of dynamics and motives; (3) insight; and (4) the reorientation phase.

The Relationship

There is an emphasis upon an alignment of the goals of counselor and counselee. Effective counseling cannot take place unless the counselor and the counselee are working within a framework of similar purpose. This type of relationship transcends rapport.

Since school counseling often involves contact with children who are not self-referred, the aspect of goal alignment becomes crucial to the relationship from the very start. A bridge to such alignment can be found, more often than not, through the development of intermediate goals. The counselor may ask, for example, "Would you like to find out why you feel that way?" Or he may choose to work with the counselee on a current problem which may lead to the major concern.

Indispensable to the relationship is mutual trust and respect. The child is treated with respect even when his ideas are diverse and opposed. It is axiomatic that one of the functions of the counselor is to listen and to understand. A child seldom has situations in which adults show that they really care about what he says. It is this unique understanding that leads to and provides a therapeutic relationship. Empathy in this relationship is the result of being understood. Stated another way, when the child is in contact with an adult who shows he understands how that child feels and can guess his private logic, the highest form of empathy is achieved. It becomes important, through motivation, to win the child, and gain his confidence, revealing enough to convince the child that the counselor does understand, anticipates success, and that the child has found an individual with whom he can align his goals.

The Investigation

The counselor begins by exploring the current situation and the way in which the child approaches social relationships and responsibilities as they appear, first in the home and then at school. The counselor might systematically raise certain questions and investigate them further by listening attentively to what is said and what is not said. It is seen that the investigation begins with "here" and "now" problems, and always with focus on determining "for what purpose?"

The family constellations and the relationship between siblings are important in this system also. The individual's ordinal position in the family can show how he uses his situation to create his style of life, while a systematic study of the relationship between the siblings is made to derive the psychological position of the child in the family.

Early recollections provide another method of understanding individual goals and mistaken assumptions about life. The first incidents in life that a person can recall are consistent with the pattern of life as seen by the individual (Mosak, 1958; Ferguson, 1964). Adlerian clinicians using early recollections can develop a type of diagnosis that might be made by a clinical team. Therefore, early recollections are used as an aid in comprehending individual life-style (Hedvig, 1965).

Adler placed emphasis on utilization of hunches and the ability to guess correctly the psychological movement of the individual. Dreikurs developed a technique that he calls the "hidden reason." This technique is effective in understanding what transpires in a person's private logic. It is used when the person does something out of the ordinary that is puzzling. Thereafter, when he is quizzed about it, he does not seem to understand why he did it. The person is really not aware of the reason. The "hidden reason" technique attempts to determine the individual's rationale for his behavior; it involves guessing what he is thinking. The counselor attempts to determine under what circumstances certain behaviors make sense. The counselor asks the individual if he wants to change, and then asks him to cooperate by telling what goes on in his mind. If one can get the exact words that were on his mind at the time, then he immediately will acknowledge it (Dreikurs, 1966).

Techniques such as these are devised to assist the counselor to understand how the client thinks and how he came to hold these convictions. The understanding, in this procedure, often exists in the counselor first and then is transferred to the counselee's awareness so that he ultimately develops self-understanding. These techniques are concerned with understanding the life-style and self-image.

Insight

During this phase the counselor should be concerned with making the individual aware of why he chooses to function in the manner he does.

Interpretation, when used within this frame of reference, places emphasis upon the goals and purposes of the symptoms that are seen. It is usually based on a tentative hypothesis, for example, "Could it be . . . ?" or "Is it possible . . . ?" In this way the individual is actually confronted with his goals. The private logic which he may not see for himself is mirrored for him. During the confrontations the child will often produce a "recognition reflex." This reflex has been described by Dreikurs (1957, p. 47):

This automatic reaction consists of a roguish smile and a peculiar twinkle of the eye, a so-called "recognition reflex." The child need not say one word or he may even say "no" but his facial expression gives him away.

The proper sequence in disclosure involves: (1) asking "Do you know why you are doing this?" "Would you like to know why you are doing this?" (2) If there is a willingness for such discussion, interpretation in a tentative manner is also involved, such as: "Could it be . . . ?" or "I have the impression . . . ."

This procedure is referred to as the "mirror technique." The individual is confronted with his goals and his intentions.

Empathy in this form of counseling involves making the individual aware of his private logic and showing interest in helping him change. Little time is spent in description of feelings or straight reflection of feelings. The emphasis is focused on the purpose of the feelings.

It is important to find one point or place where the counselee may want to change. If the counselor cannot find the place, as in the case of a difficult child, then in all probability the counselor cannot change him at all. In some instances the child has been referred to counseling because of a conflict with a teacher or parents; perhaps the child really does not choose to change. However, in a case wherein the child would like to get along better with his peers, this may be the proper point or place to begin the attempts toward change.

Reorientation

In this phase of counseling the counselor and counselee think the situation through together. The counselor's basic responsibility is to help the individual see the alternatives in attitude and behavior. But mere awareness of alternatives is not enough. It is still necessary to develop the courage to try to change. Encouragement restores the individual's faith in himself (Dinkmeyer & Dreikurs, 1963). Encouragement helps one to realize his own strengths and abilities and develops a belief in his dignity and worth. If a person is discouraged, neither insight nor change is possible.

It is in the reorientation aspect of counseling that the counselor strives to help the counselee become aware he is functioning in a way that inevitably will cause problems of his own choosing. Eventually he is confronted with choice, one of the most important therapeutic agents of all. He can then decide the way in which he will choose to function.

There is an investigation of values involved in these premises. It is vital to the counseling relationship that the counselor does not moralize. The "oughts" and "shoulds" are to be discreetly avoided. Most certainly the therapeutic experience can help to provide some success experiences within and external to the counseling process.

In other situations the counselee will be helped by a setting of tasks. If he does not get along well with his peers, for example, perhaps he can learn to deal effectively with just one child. In some instances children have been helped by learning to act as if they were aggressive, as if they were happy, and so forth.

Adlerian psychology contributes to school counseling theory by establishing certain assumptions about personality and providing unique procedures in the counseling process. The "compleat" counselor will want to become well acquainted with Adlerian theory and practice as he develops his personal theory of counseling.

References

Combs, A. W., & Snygg, D. *Individual behavior.* New York: Harper and Row, 1959.

Dinkmeyer, D., & Dreikurs, R. *Encouraging children to learn: The encouragement process.* Englewood Cliffs, N.J.: Prentice-Hall, 1963.

Dreikurs, R. *Fundamentals of Adlerian psychology.* Chicago: Alfred Adler Institute, 1950.

Dreikurs, R. *Psychology in the classroom.* New York: Harper and Row, 1957.

Dreikurs, R. The holistic approach: Two points of a line. In *Education, guidance, psychodynamics.* Chicago: Alfred Adler Institute, 1966. Pp. 21–22.

Ferguson, E. D. The use of early recollections for assessing life style and diagnosing psychopathology. *Journal of Projective Techniques,* 1964, *28,* 403-412.

Hedvig, E. Children's early recollections as basis for diagnosis. *Journal of Individual Psychology,* 1965, *21*(2), 187-188.

Maslow, A. *Motivation and personality.* New York: Harper and Row, 1954.

Mosak, H. Early recollections as a projective technique. *Journal of Projective Techniques,* 1958, *22,* 302-311.

Rogers, C. R. *Client-centered therapy.* Boston: Houghton Mifflin, 1951.

White, R. Motivation reconsidered: The concept of competence. *Psychological Review,* 1959, *66,* 297–333.

13

The Four Goals of the Maladjusted Child

Rudolf Dreikurs

Every action of a child has a purpose which is in line with his effort toward social integration. A well-behaved and well-adjusted child has found his way toward social acceptance by conforming to the rules governing the social group in which he lives. He senses the requirements of the group and acts accordingly. He is active when the situation warrants it and passive if need be; he talks at the proper time and knows how to be quiet. He can be a leader or follower. A perfectly adjusted child—if there ever was one—would hardly reveal any individuality of his own, since he would reflect only the social needs of his environment. Only in the slight deviation from perfect adjustment does he reveal his individual personality through the characteristic approaches which he has found and developed for himself.

Accordingly, individual behavior is already a slight deviation from absolute conformity. We cannot consider such deviations as maladjustments because the needs of any social group are not static. The social group requires improvement, growth, and evolution. The individual who imposes his own ideas on the group acts as impetus for development. If his ideas are beneficial for the group and his method

Reprinted from *Nervous Child*, 1947, *6*, pp. 321-328.

constructive, he is still—and only then—well-adjusted, although not completely conforming. Mere conformity can be an obstacle to social development and thereby become an expression of social maladjustment.

Maladjustment may be defined as behavior which disturbs the functioning of the group and its development. The psychological dynamics underlying maladjustment are very complex in adults. It takes time and great effort to unveil the variety of factors at work beyond consciousness and the mask of adulthood. Adults have the same fundamental attitudes which they had as children; but in the process of adolescence they learn, for appearance's sake, to subordinate them to the pattern set by society. The successful accomplishment of covering up one's real intentions and motivations is then called maturity. The child who has not yet reached this stage of "maturity" may openly demonstrate his attitudes. It is possible, therefore, to recognize the goals of child behavior by mere observation.

All disturbing behavior of the child is directed toward one of four possible goals. They represent his interpretation of his place within his group. He tries either to:

(1) gain attention;
(2) demonstrate his power or superiority;
(3) punish or get even; or he
(4) gives up in complete discouragement.

The same child may display a certain behavior pattern in one group, while under special circumstances he may behave according to another goal. However, it is possible to establish in most cases the predominant classification of his behavioral goals.

The attention-getting mechanism (A.G.M.) is prevalent in most young children. It is the result of the way in which children are brought up in our culture. Young children have few opportunities to establish their position by socially useful contributions. Older siblings and adults do everything that has to be done. The only way a young child can feel accepted and a part of his family group is by means of the older members of the family. *Their* contributions bestow value and social status on him. As a result, the child seeks constant proofs of his acceptance through gifts, demonstrations of affection, or at least through attention. As none of these increases his own feeling of strength, self-reliance, and self-confidence, he requires constant new proof lest he feel lost and rejected. He will try to get what he wants in socially acceptable ways as long as possible. However, when he loses confidence in his ability to use socially constructive means effectively, he will try any conceivable method of putting others into his service or of getting attention. Unpleasant effects like humiliation, punishment, or even physical pain, do not matter as long as the main purpose is obtained. Children prefer to be beaten rather than to be ignored. To be ignored and treated with indifference is the worst thing that can happen to a child; then he feels definitely left out, rejected, and without any place within the group.

The desire for attention can be satisfied through constructive methods. The child is naturally inclined to be constructive as long as he feels able to succeed; but if his requests become excessive, or if the environment refuses to meet his demands, he may discover that he gets more attention by disturbing. Then the struggle starts. For a while the parents may succumb to the provocation without getting too angry and annoyed. Pleasant and unpleasant episodes are held in balance: the child's desire to occupy them with himself is met and a workable equilibrium is maintained. However, there may come a time when the parents decide to subdue the child, to stop him from being annoying and disturbing. Then the child changes his goal, and the child and the parents become deadlocked in a struggle for power and superiority. The child tries to convince the parents that he can do what he wants and they will not be able to stop him. Or he may demonstrate in a passive way that they can not make him do what they want. If he gets away with it, he has won a victory; if the parents enforce their will, he has lost and the next time perhaps uses stronger methods. This struggle is more fierce than his fight for attention. His maladjustment is more obvious, his actions are more hostile, and the emotions involved more violent.

This struggle between parents and child for power and dominance may reach a point where the parents try every conceivable means to subjugate the culprit. The mutual antagonism and hatred may become so strong that no pleasant experience is left to maintain a feeling of belonging, of friendliness, or cooperation. Then the child moves into the third group. He no longer hopes for attention, his ability to gain power seems hopeless, he feels completely ostracized and disliked and finds his only gratification in hurting others and getting even for being hurt by them. That seems for him the only way to play a part. "At least I can make them hate me," is his despairing motto. In groups where he can still gain personal superiority and power, his actions may be less violent and cruel than in those where he has lost all status. Children of this type are the most violent and vicious; they know where it hurts most and they take advantage of the vulnerability of their opponents. Power and force impress them no longer. They are defiant and destructive. As they are sure from the beginning that nobody likes them, they provoke anyone with whom they come in contact to reject them. They regard it as a triumph when they are considered horrible; that is the only triumph they can obtain, the only one they seek.

A passive child will not move in the direction of open warfare. If his antagonism is successfully beaten down, he may be discouraged to such an extent that he cannot hope for any significance whatsoever. He then may become completely passive and give up any participation. This complete passivity may be limited to certain activities and groups if the child's discouragement is only partial; it may lead to complete inertia if the discouragement is total. As the hostility is not displayed openly, he may provoke less antagonism; but this lack of acute disturbance should not make us consider this maladjustment as less grave than the one of the child in the third group. Both have reached extreme forms of antisocial attitudes. (In certain cases we can actually speak of "violent passivity.")

Maladjusted children may be classed as active and passive and they may use constructive or destructive methods. The choice of constructive or destructive methods depends on the child's feeling of being accepted or rejected by people or groups; his antagonism is always expressed in destructive acts. This feeling of belonging or the lack of it is a decisive factor for the switch from constructive to destructive methods. Active or passive behavior, on the other hand, indicates the amount of courage. Passivity is always based on personal discouragement. The combination of the two pairs of factors leads to four types of behavior patterns:

1. Active-constructive,
2. Active-destructive,
3. Passive-constructive,
4. Passive-destructive.

The sequence as presented is based on the actual progression of maladjustment. Many parents and educators are inclined to regard an active-destructive child as much worse than a passive-constructive one. However, this is not necessarily true. If the child's antisocial attitude has not developed too far, as in cases of attention-getting, he can be induced with relative ease to change his destructive methods into constructive ones; but it is extremely difficult to change a passive child into an active one. The passive-constructive child is less unpleasant, but needs more assistance for the development of self-confidence and courage.

A short discussion of the four types of attention-getting mechanism may illustrate the significance of these four patterns. The *active-constructive* A.G.M. resembles a very cooperative and conforming behavior. These children are the sheer delight of parents and teachers. But they actually are not as good as they seem to be. They merely try very hard to make an impression of excellence in order to gain praise and recognition. Their deficiency becomes apparent if they fail to get it, for then they generally start to misbehave. Their social relationships within their groups are often disturbed; they cannot be equals—if they do not excel they feel lost. Their desire to be perfect, to be correct, to be superior is often stimulated by parents who encourage such traits, either because they themselves are over-ambitious and perfectionistic, or because they play up this one child against the other children. Competition with another sibling is a frequent factor in this striving for applause. In order to maintain his superiority over a younger brother or sister, or to catch up with and possibly surpass an older sibling, the child tries to become good, reliable, considerate, cooperative, and industrious, seeking and accepting any possible responsibility. The excellence of the model child is only too frequently achieved at the expense of the problem child who becomes discouraged and frustrated in this competition.

It is this group of over-ambitious children who develop *active-destructive* methods when their efforts to attract attention with socially accepted methods fail. They may try the most bizarre means to put themselves forward when they are discouraged in the field of tangible and useful achievement. They may show off, clown, be obtrusive, keep others occupied with constant questions; they may become "enfants terribles" and in many other ways force parents and teachers to pay attention to them. They may resemble the children who seek goals two and three; but they differ from them by the lack of violence and antagonism. Their goal is still attention-getting, and their misbehavior stops when this goal is achieved; while the child who wants to demonstrate his power (goal two), and still more the child who wants to punish (goal three), is not satisfied with mere attention and continues his provocative behavior after this is achieved.

A very significant group consists of the children who use *passive-constructive* methods for attracting attention. Many parents and teachers do not recognize these children as misbehaving. Their pleasantness, charm, and submission cause the observer to overlook the discouragement in their passivity and dependence on others. In the masculine culture, passive-constructive behavior patterns are deliberately stimulated in women and almost required from them. For this reason the passive-constructive A.G.M. is found more frequently in girls than in boys and is considered in the latter as effeminate. The passive-constructive child is certainly less unpleasant than the active-destructive one, but requires more efforts for adjustment.

A child who seeks attention with *passive-destructive* methods is generally so much discouraged and feels so much rejected—mostly through the methods which are used with him—that he may very easily reach the fourth group of completely discouraged children (goal four) whom he resembles anyhow. His bashfulness, instability, untidiness, lack of concentration and ability, self-indulgence and frivolity, his fearfulness, his eating difficulties, and his backwardness in taking care of himself and in developing skills, make him the most difficult child in this group.

The distinction between the various groups in which a child belongs can be made by mere observation. It may require some training to evaluate properly the behavior patterns of a child. Such training is essential, as the establishment of a correct psychological diagnosis is a prerequisite for the proper way of dealing with a child. Any one disturbing behavior may serve for several or for all four goals. In each child it may have a different function in his relationship to others; and the specific dynamics of a disturbing behavior must be recognized in order to evaluate its significance. Laziness, for instance, can be a passive-destructive A.G.M., serving to occupy the parents and to make them pay attention and give assistance. But it can also be used by the child as a tool in the struggle for power, by demonstrating his helplessness to a forceful and determined parent or teacher. Regardless of threats and punishments the child will not move or do anything. In certain instances laziness has been used as a specific means to punish an over-ambitious parent. And finally, laziness may indicate complete discouragement; the child just gives up because he has no hope of succeeding.

The function of a certain behavior becomes obvious when correction is attempted. The following example may illustrate this. A child is brought to a new group of children and stays outside, refusing to join the group. The teacher tries to draw him in. If his first hesitation was an attention-getting device, he will probably respond readily to the teacher, because he was only waiting for special attention. If his reluctance to join is based on his desire to demonstrate his power, he will act differently. He may run away as soon as the teacher approaches, inviting the teacher to chase him and putting up some active resistance to being drawn in. On the other hand, if the child is set on revenge because he is sure to be disliked and rejected, he may look defiantly at the approaching teacher and scratch, bite, or spit at anybody who tries to get him. The completely discouraged child may accept the teacher's hand and join the group, but will remain passive and stay where he is left.

The trained observer has no difficulty in recognizing the child's goals and in classifying the category in which a particular behavior belongs. The reaction which the child provokes generally indicates what he expects and wants. In case of doubt a very simple technique can be used to determine with absolute accuracy the goal which the child pursues. This technique affords a reliable diagnosis, verifying the impressions based on observations.

The child does not know why he behaves in a certain way. It is futile to ask a child, "Why did you do it?" When he answers, "I do not know," it is generally true. The child follows his impulses without clear realization of his motives. If he tries to give an explanation for his behavior, his explanations are mostly rationalizations and excuses, but not the real reasons. Instead of asking the child why he did something, one must explain it *to him.* Such disclosures, however, should not refer to the *cause* of his behavior, but only to the *purpose* of it. Reasons such as being jealous, having no self-confidence, feeling neglected, dominated, or rejected, feeling guilty or sorry for himself, regardless of how correct they may be in explaining the child's behavior, are accepted by him at best with friendly indifference. His reaction is quite different when his purposes and goals are disclosed to him. Such interpretation, when correct, evokes immediately a very definite and characteristic reaction. This reaction is automatic as a reflex; for this reason I call it the "Recognition Reflex." It indicates with certainty the correctness of an interpretation. It consists of a roguish smile and peculiar twinkle of the eye. The child need not say one word, or he might even say "no"; but his facial expression gives him away. Disclosure is not only of diagnostic value; it leads often to an immediate change in the particular behavior, especially in a young child. Psychological interpretations are understood even by very young children, as soon as they comprehend the meaning of the words. If the interpretation is correct, they show the typical reflex and are inclined to change their attitudes when they are made aware of them, as they are not reconcilable with the already established conscience. This does not imply a complete change of the life-style, but only a change of methods.

To evoke the reflex the child must be approached in a friendly way without humiliating or belittling him; the disclosure should never impress the child as fault-finding and criticism. It is advisable not to make a definite statement but to start the remarks as a vague conjecture, "I wonder whether you don't want to get attention" . . . "to show your power" . . . "to be a big boss" . . . "to punish your mother?" Or, "Could it be that you want to . . . ?" Such discussions can never do any harm. If the interpretation was wrong, there is no reaction. Then another conjecture can be tried and the child's reaction will indicate which one was correct.

A five-year-old boy repeatedly threatened to hit and bite other children, especially a little girl cousin. Our first impression was that he felt neglected and wanted to hurt them, to get even. Our voiced interpretation encountered a blank face. We went on probing. Maybe he wanted to show how strong he was. Again no reaction. "Could it be that your mother gets very upset about such threats, and you want her to make a fuss over you, to talk to you about it, and tell others what you have done?" His face beamed (Recognition Reflex). He was in his glory. The same behavior in another child would have meant something different. For him, it was only a tool to keep mother concerned with him.

A nine-year-old boy had his hair hanging over his right eye. I met him with his mother. In his presence I asked her why she thought he wore his hair over his eye. She did not know; neither did he. My surmise was that he probably wanted his mother to keep reminding him to push his hair back. She could not understand how I knew that she constantly had to remind him. Very simple—if he could not gain her attention in that way, he would not like to have his hair always getting into his eyes. He beamed. That was all that was said. The next day she called me up, quite excited. The boy had asked for money to have his locks cut by the barber.

Two boys, nine and ten years old, annoyed their mother by using bedtime for fighting in their beds. The mother could not stop it and did not know what to do. I had a talk with the boys. I asked them why they went on fighting after going to bed. I did not expect the correct answer to this question, but wanted to hear what they had to say. They both explained that it is so much fun to fight in bed when it does not hurt to be thrown down on the pillows. That was their rationalization. I asked them whether they would mind if I told them the real reason. Of course, they wouldn't mind. Then I ventured, "Maybe you do it just so that mother will come several times to remind you to be quiet." The younger one said indifferently, "Could be." The older one said nothing, but beamed. One should know that the older one was the favorite of the mother and depended upon her, while the younger one felt somewhat excluded and relied upon himself for his position in the world. Generally he was the one who started the fights, but in this particular situation the older brother obviously had instigated the fights for the sake of getting his mother's attention, bringing her back to the bedroom ever so often. Nothing more was said or done about it; but after our short discussion the evening fights stopped and never were resumed. That does not mean that the older boy suddenly became independent of his mother. But this particular method was no longer useful once he recognized his purpose.

The recognition of the child's goal is the basis for his treatment. Children who drive for attention must learn to become independent, by recognizing that *contributing* and not *receiving* is the effective instrument for obtaining social status. Within the four groups of A.G.M., the attempt should be made to help children to become active and to change destructive methods into constructive ones, until the child is able to overcome the need for any special attention. Children who drive for *power* should no longer be exposed to power and pressure against which they have successfully rebelled and still rebel. Acknowledging their value and even their power is essential for making them self-confident so that they no longer need verification of their power. Children who want to *punish* and to get even are usually those who are convinced that nobody likes them or ever will like them. Helping them involves a long process of demonstrating that they are and can be liked. Children who *give up* in discouragement have to be brought back slowly to the realization of their abilities and potentialities.

The recognition of the child's goal is an important prerequisite for any educational effort. However, knowing, and even changing, the goal of a child does not necessarily affect his fundamental concepts of life, his life-style (Alfred Adler). Understanding and altering the conclusions which a child drew from his experiences with the world around him, his outer environment, and with his hereditary endowment, his inner environment, requires a more thorough analysis of the child. It implies an exploration of his family situation, the dynamics of his relationship with parents and siblings, the methods by which he was brought up, the economic, religious, racial, and national conditions which influenced the atmosphere in which he lived.

For this reason, efforts to reach the deeper levels of the personality structure must be reserved for special child guidance work. Teachers, group workers, physicians, and others who want to influence children will rely mostly on their ability to understand and evaluate the child's goals, which they can determine without involved investigation. The knowledge of a child's goal permits a better approach and, above all, prevents unwitting acceptance of the child's provocation which only increases his maladjustment and misbehavior. Doing what the child expects confirms his belief that his wrong approaches are effective.

14

Developmental Counseling in the Elementary School

Don Dinkmeyer

With the greatly increased extension of counseling and guidance services to the elementary school level, counseling theorists have become aware of a greater need for a theory of developmental counseling with children. This theory must take account of such basic factors as the nature of the child, the elementary school setting, and the goals, techniques, and process of the counseling. Furthermore, those who would counsel in the elementary school must become aware of the research in the broad area of child development and child psychiatry.

Nature of the Child

The most obvious difference between secondary school and elementary school counseling stems from the nature of the child. The elementary school child is still in the process of becoming—physically, socially, emotionally, and as a total personality. He is in a process of unfolding and there are still certain developmental changes that will come about as the result of this growth process.

Reprinted from *The Personnel and Guidance Journal*, 1966, *45*(3), 262-266. Copyright 1966 American Association for Counseling and Development. Reprinted with permission.

Research in child development points to the importance of considering developmental changes. Thus, the counselor would need to be aware of "normal developmental problems" as contrasted with serious adjustment difficulties. He should know that there are wide individual differences in developmental patterns that are due to basic differences in rate of development. These developmental differences create adjustment problems for the child both in the tasks of school and social life.

The counselor, therefore, should have available developmental data that tell him about individual rates of development and enable him to infer something about the child's feelings about himself in the peer group.

Mussen and Jones (1958), in their study of the self-concept in late and early maturing boys, have indicated a variance in the self-concepts and motivation of these two groups.

It is important that each counselor be familiar with the basic needs of the child. The child has specific needs that relate to the guidance process. He needs to mature in self-acceptance, in his understanding of self, and in his comprehension of his assets and liabilities. The child needs to develop a more realistic self-evaluation and the counselor can help in this process. The counselor can also assist the child to develop, to mature in social relationships, to belong, and to identify. The child needs to develop independence, to take on responsibility, to make choices, and to be responsible for these choices. He needs to mature in his ability to plan. The counselor provides an environment in which the child is independent, makes choices, and becomes responsible for his decision. The child also needs to mature in understanding the role of work in life as it first appears in educational achievement and then as it appears in the environment as related to jobs and employment opportunities. The child needs to develop a realistic self-appraisal of his capacities, interests, and attitudes as they relate to the work tasks.

The counselor, at the elementary school level, will recognize that he needs to work with the significant adults in the child's life. This includes the teacher and the parents. With the teacher he will encourage intensive child study that takes into account developmental information and the developmental factors significant in comprehending the way in which the child approaches the developmental tasks of living. He will help the teacher to have available cumulative records that provide information about rate instead of status,

dynamics of behavior instead of descriptions of the past. The cumulative record should show the pattern of development both physically and psychologically.

Behavior is purposive, and acquires its meaning in the social setting. Beyond the understanding of need, the counselor must understand the purposes of behavior in specific children. Purposes are the
directive forces in the child's life, even though the child may not be
aware of these goals and purposes. We need to look at the purposes
of misbehavior as they are illustrated in attention-getting, the seeking
to be powerful, to get even, or to demonstrate inadequacy (Dreikurs,
1957). As we become cognizant of the individual's purposes, we are
able to deal with the child's private logic, and become aware of the
basic style of life and concept of self and others. Psychological
growth is patterned, and we must focus on the unity of behavior and
the style of life, avoiding the collection of fragmentary data and
instead looking at the direction of psychological movement.

Recent research tends to indicate that the early elementary years
are much more significant than any of us have been truly able to
determine prior to now. The research of Bloom (1964) indicates the
significance of the first three grades in predicting the total pattern of
achievement. Kagan and Moss (1962) at the Fels Research Institute
recently released a study indicating that many of the behaviors ex-
hibited by the child during the period from six to ten years of age,
and a few during the period from three to six, were moderately good
predictors of theoretically related behavior during early adulthood.
This study indicated that the child who was achieving well early in
school will generally continue to achieve well. There is a need to
provide early encouragement for the academic achiever, and to identify those who are not meeting the academic tasks at this stage of
life.

The elementary counselor should also be aware of the developmental task concept as first formulated by Havighurst. He needs to
recognize that the pertinent tasks of middle childhood involve learning to get along with age-mates, and participating in the give and take
of social exchange.

Most human problems are interpersonal problems, and these problems increase as the child moves into a peer society. The research of
Piaget (1929), which has increasingly attracted the attention of
American psychologists, shows that during preadolescence the child
begins to develop a concept of self quite distinguishable from the

outer world. This is the time when the clarification of feelings, concepts, attitudes, goals, and an understanding of self would be most significant.

The development of conscience, morality, and values begins early in the elementary school. The child is in the process of developing this internal moral control and set of values. The child learns that rules are necessary and thus develops what Piaget calls the morality of cooperation. Piaget believes that middle childhood is a crucial period for the development of this cooperation. The counselor could be available to help the child through this stage as an awareness of values and goals emerges. The child will frequently need help in reconciling his values, his ideal self, and his actual performance. However, the child needs to learn to make plans, and to act in the present and immediate future independent of other parents and other adults. Counseling can provide the opportunity to assist in the making of choices, planning, and deciding.

Caroline Tryon and Jesse Lilienthal (1950) have provided an interesting presentation of the developmental tasks and their importance for the counselor. They indicate that these might be used as guideposts that permit us to assess the rate at which the child is developing in regard to the tasks of life. They suggest that the counselor might be aware of some of the following pertinent tasks:

a. achieving an appropriate dependent-independence pattern;

b. achieving an appropriate giving-receiving pattern of affection, learning to accept self as worthwhile, learning to belong;

c. relating to changing groups, establishing a peer group, and learning to belong and behave according to the shifting peer code.

Counseling in the Elementary School Setting

The counselor cannot counsel without an awareness of the elementary school setting, and the fact that he is part of an educational team. He should be aware of the philosophy, objectives, and practices of the school. He should be familiar with the curriculum and the opportunities within the curriculum for the student's development. He must be cognizant of the teacher's crucial role in classroom guidance. The teacher should be encouraged to provide regular guidance activities, to identify problems, and to provide guidance through the teacher-counselor role.

Developmental counseling, which can be contrasted with adjustment or crisis counseling, is not always problem oriented in terms of
assuming that the child has some difficult problem. Instead, the goals
are the development of self-understanding, awareness of one's potentialities, and methods of utilizing one's capacity. Developmental
counseling truly focuses on helping the individual know, understand,
and accept himself. This type of counseling, then, becomes personal-
ized learning, not individualized teaching. The child learns not only
to understand himself but to become ultimately responsible for his
choices and actions.

Unique Factors

The type of counseling we are considering Hummel (1962) has
referred to as ego counseling. This implies that it may be a short-term
service in which the relationship is basically collaborative and the
child works on problems that are of concern to him. The counselor
helps the child investigate, analyze, and deliberate to solve more
effectively certain developmental problems. Thus, exploration, examination, and resolution are basic techniques. There is mutual survey
of the facts, clarification of feelings, consideration of alternatives,
development of problem-solving techniques, and arrival at decisions.

The counselor provides a nonevaluative relationship and offers his
collaboration. His job is to clarify, to reflect, to restate as precisely as
possible the meanings he perceives to be implied in the counselee's
statements. However, the counselor, at times, will interpret, confront, question, and thus facilitate the child's capacity to solve his
own problems.

The elementary school child is in the process of formulating a style
of life and self-concept. There is a considerable body of evidence that
indicates that the child with a poor self-concept, compared with
those who have more positive self-concepts, will be more anxious,
less well-adjusted, less popular, less effective, less honest, and more
defensive (McCandless, 1961). One of the tasks of the school counselor is to assist each child to feel accepted as he is. The counselor
seeks to help the child discover his potentialities, to acquire a realistic appreciation of his assets and limitations, and to set certain goals.
This should enable the child to accept himself rather than seek to
conform to standards that are out of harmony with what he is or
would hope to be.

Principles in Child Counseling

What, then, are the fundamentals we need to be aware of in child counseling?

1. Counseling is a learning-oriented process carried on in a one-to-one social environment. It must utilize the best that we have available from learning theory.

2. The relationship is crucial in the counseling process. It should be one in which there is mutual trust and mutual respect, enabling the counselee to become more open to communication and more motivated to change. Change is always more possible in a nonevaluative, nonjudgmental atmosphere.

3. The counselor helps the client to understand and accept what he is, and to use his newly acquired knowledge about self to realize his potential, to change in attitude, behavior, and, eventually, style of life.

4. The child is frequently not a volunteer. There is a real need for common purpose and a motivation for counseling. It is important that the goals of counseling be mutually aligned between counselor and counselee. It is important to understand the individual's objective viewpoint, to be empathic, to recognize his private logic.

5. We need to listen not only for the words, but what is behind the words. We need to become skilled in guessing the child's psychological direction. Behavior is purposive and has social implications. We need to make the child more aware of his purposes, goals, convictions, and attitudes. As the child becomes aware of his faulty assumptions, he can "catch" himself.

6. There are certain dependency factors that will restrict the child from changing certain things in his environment. His choices may be limited in terms of restrictions placed upon him by adults such as parents and teachers.

7. There is a necessity for working intensively both with parents and teachers if we are to change the child's environment. Contact with the significant adults is directed at changing the adult's behavior and thus the child's perception of self and human relationships. The counselor most of all must become aware of the goals and the unity in the pattern of the counselee's behavior. Maladjustment is characterized by increased inferiority feelings, underdeveloped social interest, and uncooperative methods of striving for significance (Dreikurs,

1950). These dynamics help the counselor to explain and understand the child's behavior.

8. Because the child may not be as verbal as the adult, there is need for sharper sensitivity on the part of the counselor in working with nonverbal cues and nonverbal factors. We need to listen with the child's ears and observe to determine what is behind the total psychological movement. Our observation of a recognition reflex in his facial expressions sometimes enables us to comprehend his goal. Disclosure of the child's goals and purposes when given in appropriate fashion can be a most significant technique.

9. The counselor provides encouragement as a major therapeutic technique. He enables the client to accept himself so that he has the courage to function (Dinkmeyer & Dreikurs, 1963).

10. Some children have a minimal ability to relate their feelings. They may not always be sensitive to reflection, and they need a tentative statement in regard to feelings such as: "Could it be you feel the children are against you?"

11. The individual's perceptions are more important than the objective reality of the situation.

12. People will move in positive directions when they are really free to choose. We need to provide the atmosphere that permits them to make these choices.

13. The feeling of basic trust between counselor and counselee opens the channels of communication. The mutual alignment of goals also assists this development.

14. Counseling is looked upon as a reeducative process directed towards the development of self-understanding, the changing of convictions, and the development of increased social interest. It is not heavily oriented toward vocational guidance; instead it deals with the developmental tasks, problems, and needs of the child. Through self-understanding, self-acceptance, and clarification of feeling the greatest growth can occur.

15. The cognitive and conceptual development of the child is not always as advanced as we might hope and, hence, the counselor must be certain communication is meaningful. Children have limited experiences and, hence, will have a limited ability to comprehend certain concepts.

16. The counselor becomes aware that he needs to empathize so closely that he can guess what it is that the client is thinking, and that he can put this into the client's words. The effective counselor is

one who understands the way in which the individual strives to be significant and helps the individual to accept himself. He sees the developmental problems as interpersonal problems. His communication with the client helps the client to understand new ways of relating to others.

Developmental counseling provides the child with an opportunity to explore his feelings, his attitudes, his convictions. The counselor starts with the problems that the child perceives and helps him to solve them. The counselor in this situation provides a relationship that accepts, understands, and does not judge. It provides the counselee with constant clarification of his basic perception of life. This relationship enables the counselee to become increasingly self-directed so that the goal is one of enabling the counselee to deal with both the developmental tasks and the general problems of living. This type of developmental counseling suggests that counselors would not only be problem oriented, but would be concerned about all students in the school population.

The goal is to take certain grade levels and to offer assistance to each student by providing an opportunity for some four or five contacts devoted to the specific objectives as they have been presented. When we can provide this form of counseling at the elementary school level, we can probably insure a greater productivity academically and hopefully much more effective social relationships between children and also between children and the significant adults in their atmosphere. Thus, we can see that elementary school counseling may need a new theory and a new set of practices. Developmental counseling might provide a direction quite different from that of typical secondary school counseling.

References

Bloom, B. *Stability and change in human characteristics*. New York: John Wiley, 1964.

Dinkmeyer, D., & Dreikurs, R. *Encouraging children to learn: The encouragement process*. Englewood Cliffs, N.J.: Prentice-Hall, 1963.

Dreikurs, R. *Fundamentals of Adlerian psychology*. New York: Greenberg, 1950.

Dreikurs, R. *Psychology in the classroom*. New York: Harper and Row, 1957.

Hummel, R. Ego-counseling in guidance: concept and method. *Harvard Educational Review*, 1962, *32*, 463-482.

Kagan, J., & Moss, H. *Birth to maturity*. New York: John Wiley, 1962.
McCandless, B. R. *Children and adolescents: Behavior and development*. New York: Holt, Rinehart and Winston, 1961.
Mussen, P., & Jones, M. The behavior inferred motivation of late and early maturing boys. *Child Development*, 1958, *29*, 61-67.
Piaget, J. *The child's conception of the world*. New York: Harcourt, Brace, 1929.
Tryon, C., & Lilienthal, J. Developmental tasks: The concept and its importance. *Fostering mental health in our schools*. 1950 Yearbook, Association for Supervision and Curriculum Development. Washington, D.C.: The Association, 1950.

SECTION V

Gestalt Counseling

The Gestalt school of counseling began as a philosophical movement around the turn of the twentieth century. It was studied empiri-
cally several decades later and became popular as a method of
therapy during the 1950s and 1960s. Fritz Perls was its leading and
most widely recognized lecturer, writer, and therapist. A German
word, "gestalt" means whole. Gestalt counseling focuses on the whole
person, and emphasis is placed on an individual's perception of events
in the context of the total environment. In therapy, the counselor
attempts to increase the client's immediate awareness of the environment in order to increase the number of practical alternative feelings
or behaviors. There is a distinct emphasis on "here-and-now" events
and behavior.

Gestalt theory may be encapsulated as follows:

Man exists in a world of experience. These experiences create individual needs, which
in turn cause disequilibrium and tension in the personality. Individuals attempt to
satisfy needs by an awareness of alternatives, which eventually leads to more efficient
problem-solving. The healthy individual trusts in his ability to find solutions. The
unhealthy person is blocked in awareness and can't satisfy needs. There is a
dependency on others for fulfillment and a state of unfinished business. As incidents
of unfinished business accumulate, there is a diminished capacity to solve new
problems.

Gestalt therapy is active and confrontive. The counselor does not focus on the past and continually directs the client to the present. Gestaltists favor dramatic techniques that force the individual to confront obstacles in his or her personality, and consequently the individual achieves greater awareness of himself or herself. Common techniques are the "empty chair" (the client's personality is projected into the empty chair), personalization (use of "I" statements), and role playing.

The first two selections in this section explore the theory and technique of Gestalt therapy. Marcus and Melnick expand on this introduction's brief description and demonstrate the major techniques by using dialogue and case examples. The third reading, by Childers and Basse, discusses the application of the model to a school setting. Using a program built on Gestalt principles, they attempt to increase the self-understanding of teachers and students.

15

Theoretical Foundations for Gestalt Practice

Stephen Marcus

Introduction

Fritz Perls had three goals in mind in his proposed revision of psychoanalysis: (1) to "replace the psychological by an organismic concept," (2) to "replace association psychology by gestalt psychology," and (3) to "apply differential thinking based on S.F. Friedlander's "Creative Indifference" (in Perls, 1969a, pp. 13–14). Items 2 and 3 in particular involve theoretical bases for a variety of Gestalt techniques. These constructs will be outlined in the first two sections of this article along with descriptions of the practices related to the constructs. The third section discusses Gestalt therapy's nonverbal dimension and presents examples of how this aspect is realized in the therapeutic setting. The fourth section comments on the use of dream material in Gestalt therapy. In general, the intent of the total discus-

Reprinted from *The Gestalt Journal*, 1980, *3* (2), 57–70. Reprinted with permission of the author. Stephen Marcus, Ph.D., is Associate Director of the South Coast Writing Project, Graduate School of Education, University of California, Santa Barbara, CA 93106

sion is to indicate how Gestalt practice is consistent with and deriv-able from the theoretical groundwork provided by Perls and other seminal figures in the Gestalt literature.

Holistic Thinking

Perls (1969a, chapter II) attributes his therapeutic approach in part to the psychology of Koehler and Wetheimer. He distinguishes their formulations from traditional scientific and psychoanalytic thinking:

The "field" conception stands in direct opposition to that of traditional science, which has always seen reality as a conglomeration of isolated parts—as a world made up of innumerable bits and pieces.

Even our mind consists, according to this (traditional) concept, of a great number of single elements. This theory is called association psychology and is based on the assumption that in our minds one idea is attached to another as if by a string, and that one idea after another will break surface if, and when, the string is pulled.

Actually, associations are mental particles, artificially isolated from more com-prehensive items, which we may call spheres, situations, contexts, categories, and such like names. . . .

The value of associations lies not in the associations themselves but in the existence of specific spheres of which they form a part. [Pp. 26–27]

As an example, Perls refers to a set of thirty-two chess pieces. Collected in a box, they are independent and relatively uninteresting. When used in a game, however, "their interdependency and the permanently changing situation keep the players fascinated. In the box the chessmen represent the isolationist outlook—in the chess 'field,' the 'holistic' conception" (p. 28, author's emphasis).

Fagan (1970), in describing Gestalt therapy's "global" approach, has emphasized that the "therapist is first of all a perceiver and constructor of patterns" (p. 88). To express the dynamic quality of patterning in human functioning—especially in awareness—she uses the analogy of a mobile, "in which a variety of pieces or systems are interconnected into an overall unity and balance" (p. 89).

Gestalt therapy defines human functioning, health, and growth in terms of the formation and completion of these fields, patterns, configurations, or gestalts (Perls, 1951, 1969a, 1969b). The Gestalt clinical literature is replete with transcripts of sessions that indicate a translation of this theory into practice. Two related strategies are employed: (1) attending to details of behavior that indicate an existent (although nonexplicit) context of which they are a part and (2) attending to an overall context to make more evident the gaps left by omitted elements. In both cases, it is the conscious attendance to the relationships between observed phenomena and their existing—if only implied—contexts that ground these strategies in the holistic thinking Perls describes.

An example of the first strategy is provided by Enright (1970). He describes a therapeutic setting in which a man ("constricted, overinhibited") denies that his continued finger-tapping on a table reflects any concern with a woman in the group who has been talking at great length.

He is asked then to intensify the tapping, to tap louder and more vigorously, and to continue until he feels more fully what he is doing. His anger mounts quickly and in a minute or so he is pounding the table and expressing vehemently his disagreement with the woman. He declares that she is "just like my wife. . . ." [P. 110]

In this instance, the often-used Gestalt techniques of repetition and exaggeration (Levitsky and Perls, 1970) make explicit the "field" or configuration, which includes the man, his self-imposed restraints, his wife, the woman, the woman's talking, and so forth. The phrase "feels more fully what he is doing" suggests completing the picture, rounding out the phenomenological environment in which the man is operating.

Naranjo (1980) provides a related example:

Therapist: What do you experience now?
Patient: Nothing special.
Th: You shrugged your shoulders.
P: I guess so.
Th: There, you did it again (Shrugs shoulders).
P: I guess it is a habit.
Th: Please do it again.
P: (Complies).
Th: Now exaggerate that gesture.
P: (Shrugs, grimaces, and makes a rejecting gesture with elbows and hands.) I guess I am saying "don't bug me"—Yeah, leave me alone. [Pp. 39–40]

Here again, a physical expression (the shrug), which was congruent with the initial verbal response ("nothing special") was also—and

more significantly—an element of a totally different context. This one
included the therapist and patient interacting, the patient's desires
with regard to the therapist, and again, perhaps, the constraints the
patient felt against stating his needs directly. In contrast to the
previous example, the movement here constituted a kind of psycho-
motor "pun," a single "word" which fit two contexts simultaneously.
The therapist, attuned to "complex, possibility-loaded situations"
(Enright, 1970), was able to assist the person in completing the gestalt
implied by the movement.

The second strategy referred to above, that is, noting omissions, is
consistent with Perls' emphasis on "keeping our eye on the context or
field or whole in which a phenomenon is embedded. . ." (1969a). Such
attention allows the therapist (and patient) to notice "what's missing
in our lives, what we avoid doing and living. . . ."

In the course of our development we put up a game, a role, instead of actualizing
ourselves, and during the process most people develop holes in their personality.
Most people have no ears. At best they only listen to the abstractions, to the meaning
of the sentences. . . . Many have no eyes. They have their eyes projected. They always
feel they are being looked at. Other persons have no heart. Many people have no
genitals. And very many people have no center, and without a center you wobble in
life. [P. 80]

An example from one of Perls' dream seminars will illustrate this
strategy (1969b, pp. 95–100). A woman, Nora, recounts a dream in
which she is in "an incomplete house and the stairs have no rails."
Perls first asks her to speak as if she were the incomplete house, to
describe the dream from its point of view. He later asks her to become
the stairs and to "have an encounter with the nonexistent railings."
Later he asks her to speak as if she were everything that's missing in
the house: "Okay, can you be all the supplement—all of what's
missing, and talk to the incomplete house. 'I'm here to complete you,
to supplement you.' "

In his remarks after the working session, Perls explains the Gestalt
strategy of working with the relationships between "wholes" and their
missing elements.

Let me say something more about the dream altogether. You see, the whole idea of
repression is nonsense. If you look, everything is there. . . . Every dream or every
story contains all the material we need. . . .

Now Nora's projection is the incomplete house. . . . It is projected as if she is living in this house. But she herself is the incomplete house. What's missing is warmth and color. As soon as she becomes the house, she admits that she has solid foundations and so on. If you're capable of projecting yourself totally into every little bit of the dream—and really become that thing—then you begin to reassimilate, to re-own what you have disowned, given away. . . . If I have a staircase without railings, it's obvious that the railings are somewhere in the dream but they're missing. They're not there. So where railings should be, there's a hole. Where warmth and color should be, there's a hole. [Pp. 98–99]

Differential Thinking

In his introduction to the 1969 edition of *Ego, Hunger, and Aggression* (originally published in 1947), Perls emphasized the importance of his first chapter, "Differential Thinking," in attaining the "adequate perspective, without which a therapist is lost from the beginning" (1969*a*, p.6). Perls considered it one of the "basic concepts pervading the whole of this book" and stressed its importance in understanding the unique character of Gestalt therapy (pp. 5–6).

Perls distinguishes differential thinking from "cause-and-effect" thinking.

It is . . . productive of excellent results to forgo causal explanations of events and to restrict oneself to a description of them—to ask "how?" instead of "why?" (author's emphasis)
Causal explanation . . . applies only to isolated strings of events. In reality we find over-determination . . . or coincidence—many causes of greater or lesser significance converging into the specific event. [P. 21]

Differential thinking, on the other hand, is presented as a way of understanding human beings as systems rather than as "isolated strings of events." Perls identified three aspects of differential thinking that he considered indispensable to this perspective: opposites, pre-difference (zero-point), and degree of differentiation. In differential thinking:

(Every) event is related to a zero-point from which differentiation into opposites takes place. These opposites show in their specific context a great affinity for each other. By remaining alert in the center, we can acquire a creative ability of seeing both sides of an occurrence and completing an incomplete half. [P. 15]

Differential thinking may thus be construed as a special case of holistic thinking. Perls' emphasis here is on a special type of "field," defined by virtue of a unique relationship between two of its elements. With regard to opposites, Perls notes that within the same context they are "more closely related to each other than to any other conception" and recalls Freud's observation that an element in a dream "may stand for itself, for its opposite, or for both together" (p. 17).

The differentiation into opposites is in part determined by the context, in part by the character of the opposites themselves, and at times by the arbitrary selection of the zero point, where the differentiation begins. The "branches" of a differentiation are considered to develop simultaneously and with equal extension. Perls speaks of a point of balance (not identical with the zero-point) at which an individual demonstrates not uninterested detachment but "creative indifference," which is "full of interest, extending towards both sides of the differentiation" (pp. 17–20).

Several Gestalt therapy techniques derive from this theoretical ground. Perls notes that "by having the 'field,' the context, we can determine the opposites, and by having the opposites, we can determine the specific field" (p. 30). In the clinical setting, it is usually the patient's verbal expression or other behavior that gives the therapist a starting point for determining the polar extremes, and eventually the field, of the patient's dilemma.

Naranjo (1980) notes that

The opposite to the person's attitude is likely to be a part of him too, yet a less developed side of his personality. . . .

The principle of reversal can be applied not only to feelings but also to physical attitudes. Opening up when in a closed posture, breathing deeply as an alternative to a restraint in the intake of air or exhalation, exchanging the motor attitudes of left and right, and so on can eventually lead to the unfolding of unsuspected experiences. [P. 38]

Naranjo provides an example in which a therapist notices that a patient habitually interrupts his own speaking to swallow or sniff. Asked to do the opposite, the patient produces "forceful and prolonged exhalation through the nose and mouth" and reports an "unfamiliar and surprising feeling":

... somewhat as if I were sobbing, but also pushing against a resistance, and my muscles are tense, as when I stretch in yawning: I enjoy the tension when trying to exhale to the very end of my breath, which also feels somehow like an orgasm. [P. 38]

The therapist recounts the patient's discovery that he "had been living with this feeling for a long time: " 'It is like waiting to burst . . . , tearing down a sort of membrane in which I am wrapped and limited. And I am at the same time this strait jacket and I am squeezing myself' " (p. 38).

This example indicates the usefulness of the technique of reversal (see Levitsky & Perls, 1970) in attempting to make opposites explicit. The nature of the field (a dimension of the patient's own personality) thus was defined by, and produced, the opposites. His explosive energy was to a great degree balanced by the energy of muscular contractions. His development proceeded from this initial awareness of the polar nature of this expressive and suppressive dynamic (see Naranjo, 1980).

In the exploration of opposites, several stages may be identified. First, one aspect of the polarity is observed. It is made more explicit, and its opposite is then elicited. Confrontation between the two is often encouraged so that their relationship may be clarified and their usefulness to the person examined. This is characteristically done using a variety of role-playing and acting-out techniques, which Naranjo and others have found of special utility in the clinical repertoire (Naranjo, 1980; Enright, 1970; Levitsky & Perls, 1970; Greenwald, 1972).

A strategy related to the exploration of opposites is that of identification of divisions or "splits" in the patients. These may be of a physical type (e.g., between the left and right, top and bottom, or halves of the body) or of a more symbolic nature (e.g., between a forest and a city in a patient's dream). The working tactic is similar to that involving opposites, with identification, elaboration, confrontation, and (potential) integration resulting from the acting out of each side of the split to fulfill the total gestalt.

Perls (1969b) provides several examples of the attention paid to the relationships between one half of the body and the other (for example, pp. 117, 124, 128, and 254). Downing and Marmorstein (1973, chapter 10) introduce their transcript of a Gestalt session of a skier's dream with the combined themes of body splits and polarities.

Most particularly, notice the left-right split in all its dichotomous glory, appearing first as a physical hand signal, then turning into more obvious struggles: sleepy withdrawal versus energy split; reluctant skier versus erratic skis; got to prove myself a big man versus let's play safe weak woman; upper half versus lower half or head versus body split. [P. 122]

Nonverbal Dimensions

It is common for writers to stress the nonverbal focus of Gestalt practice (Naranjo, 1968, 1980, p. 42; Enright, 1970, p. 111; Fagan & Shepherd, 1970, p. viii; Greenwald, 1972). This follows directly from Perls' (1969b) dicta:

. . . self-expression comes out . . . in our posture, and most of all in our voice. A good therapist doesn't listen to the content of the (verbiage) the patient produces, but to the sound, to the music, to the hesitations.

So don't listen to the words, just listen to what the movements tell you, what the posture tells you, what the image tells you.

Everything a person wants to express is all there—not in words. But the voice is there, the gesture, the posture, the facial expression, the psychosomatic language.

Movements like—you see how much this young man here expresses in his leaning forward—the total personality as it expresses itself with movements, with posture, with sound, with pictures—there is so much invaluable material here, that we don't have to do anything else except get to the obvious . . . (In Gestalt) we see the whole being of a person right in front of us, and this is because Gestalt therapy uses eyes and ears and the therapist stays absolutely in the now. [Pp. 53–54]

Perls and other Gestalt therapists do demonstrate a concern for words themselves—witness the emphasis on appropriate ego-language (Perls, 1969b, pp. 65, 70–71, 99–100, 106–107; Naranjo, 1980; Greenwald, 1972, pp. 6–7, 8). Nevertheless, Gestalt is charac-terized (and differentiated from traditional psychoanalysis) by a "distrust" of intellectual insights, cognitive theories, history taking, or interviewing (Fagan, 1970). As sources for promoting growth, Gestalt depends on the patient's and therapist's awareness of here-and-now behavior, of "movements, tones, expressions, word choice, and so on" (Fagan, 1970, p. 91; see also, Naranjo, 1980). Verbal encoding is used for communicating this awareness, not as the primary therapeu-tic medium.

Perls' own work provides ample evidence of his attention to a patient's tone of voice. (All quotations are from Perls, 1969b): "Did you hear the tears in your voice when you said. . ." (p. 141); "Did you listen to your voice? If you were the wheel, would this voice stop the wheel?" (p. 192); "(mimicking a patient's whining tone) Nyahnyahnyahnya. . . ." (And later) "Oh, this is his voice. Come on, switch. I want to hear what he says" (p. 136).

Naranjo (1980) has described a particular technique that focuses attention on oral but nonverbal expression: "unstructured vocalization, or gibberish."

Gibberish has the uniqueness—at least for some individuals—of allowing for a spontaneity of expression that their words . . . would not allow. Sometimes the person may censor all anger from his statement, voice, and awareness, and yet produce gibberish that he acknowledges as angry beyond doubt. Or, his ordinary voice and stance will become collected while his gibberish will be pleading, and this may inspire further work on his suppressed needfulness. Whatever the patient has said in gibberish he may experiment in saying in words later, and this is most likely to lead to expanded awareness. [P. 36]

The following example combines gibberish with repetition and exaggeration (and illustrates differentiation):

P: I don't have any marked feeling. I don't see the point of enumerating my physical sensations. . . .
Th: Please go on speaking with the same voice but without the words.
P: Da da da da da da da da da da da da. (With an expression of hopelessness.)
Th: Exaggerate that expression in your voice.
P: (Goes on; this time with more apparent sadness.)
Th: Still more. Exaggerate it and see what develops.
P: (His voice becomes a melody, sad and majestic, and with increasing potency.) This is what I wanted to do all my life! To sing! (Tearful.) That was truly me, more than in all my words! How wonderful! I don't want to stop! ! (Goes on singing.) P. 36]

A related technique employs the suggestion to provide a sound to accompany a posture, a bodily movement, or a gesture (e.g., Perls, 1969*b*, pp. 172 and 196; Downing & Marmorstein, 1973, p. 36). This may be understood as one part of the process that Naranjo (1980) describes as the "translation from one expressive modality to another" (pp. 45–46). The sound adds expression and nuance, helping complete or realize the emerging event.

Naranjo also describes a technique that may be considered the

opposite of using sounds instead of words. In what he terms "explica-
tion," the patient may be asked to translate into words some form of
nonverbal expression: "Give words to your nodding"; "If your tears
could speak, what would they say?"; "Give a voice to your loneliness." The following transcript illustrates this technique, along with
attention to a tone of voice, and gibberish:

Th: What do you have to say to Martha?
P: (With a very dead voice.) I don't have much to say to you. I like your
expression and what you have said today but I am a little afraid of you. . . .
Th: Speak to her in gibberish.
P: (Turns very animated while doing so, leans forward, smiles and gesticulates
with his hands.)
Th: Now translate that into English.
P: Martha, you're lovely; I'd like to caress you, kiss you, take care of you. I feel
very tender toward you. You are like a beautiful flower and I always like to be near
you.

Most of the techniques described above are attempts to "make the
implicit explicit" or to "point out the obvious," two of Gestalt's
clinical maxims. Attention may be directed to precise behavioral cues
(e.g., fingertapping), to a visual or oral configuration (e.g., facial
expression, posture, or tone of voice), or to a pattern of total behavior
(e.g., "You seem to be playing innocent" or "I think you are looking
for the limelight") (Naranjo, 1980). The general strategy may be
described as an attempt to elicit the existential message that the
patient is presenting. The goal, as always, is to foster the patient's
own awareness utilizing that of the therapist's.

The nonverbal orientation of Gestalt practice highlighted in this
section lends itself to both the general strategies outlined above. On
the one hand, manifest details of behavior—movement, posture,
sound—may be explored for the purpose of eliciting implicit fields in
which these specific behaviors are embedded. The behavior may itself
be significant (e.g., a shrug), or it may be of import by virtue of its
opposite (a hopeless tone of voice being transformed into a majestic
melody). On the other hand, the therapist may observe the patient's
total presentation of self in order to reveal missing or inappropriate
elements. In either case, it is the interaction between part and whole
which invests meaning. As a basically noninterpretive approach,
Gestalt therapy tends not to attribute specific meanings based on
preestablished symbolic or theoretical constructs.

Utilization of Dreams

In Gestalt therapy, dreams often provide the context for a coherent and unified use of a variety of techniques. In this sense, the use of dreams for a therapeutic purpose constitutes what Naranjo describes broadly as a Gestalt "strategy" (1980). Perls considered dreams as primary therapeutic material (1969*b*).

We find all we need in the dream, or in the perimeter of the dream, the environment of the dream. The existential difficulty, the missing part of the personality, they are all there. (Dream work is) a kind of central attack into the midst of your nonexistence. [Perls, 1969*b*, p. 70]

Dreams are approached from both the perspectives described in the section above on holistic thinking. As a collection of disowned elements, these may be used to determine the overall pattern of the dreamer's existence; as a global statement of the dreamer's existence, the dream-as-a-whole may give meaning to the elements of the dream, whether actually present or conspicuous by their absence. The citations below illustrate these two approaches:

I believe we are all fractionalized. We are divided. We are split up in many parts, and the beauty of working with a dream is that in a dream every part—not only every person, but every part is yourself.
. . .
(Spoken to a woman whose dream took place in a carnival.) Always look at the beginning of the dream. Notice where the dream is taking place. . . . This always gives you immediately the impression of the existential background. Now you start your dream out. "Life is a carnival." Now give us a speech about life as a carnival. [Perls, 1969*b*, pp. 89, 263]

Perls rejected the Freudian tradition of purely verbal dream analysis (Perls, 1969*b*, pp. 66–69). Instead, he stressed the individual's responsibility for producing every facet of the dream experience and attempted to make more explicit the dream's (i.e., the person's) statements and internal, primary process logic. All the role-playing and acting-out techniques mentioned in this chapter, all the use of holistic and differential thinking, may be found in transcripts of dream work led by Perls and other Gestalt therapists (e.g., Perls, 1969*b*, 1973; Downing & Marmorstein, 1973).

Conclusion

The above discussion has identified a basic theoretical orientation in Gestalt therapy, that of holistic thinking, and has subsumed under it the special case of differential thinking. Associated with this theoretical ground were two clinical strategies: (1) attending to parts in order to determine wholes and (2) attending to wholes in order to make evident missing parts.

A central concern, theoretically and therapeutically, is "meaning": Of what does meaningfulness consist and how is meaningfulness derived? In the context of Gestalt psychology theory, meaning is "equivalent to organization. It is the relationship between the whole and its parts" (Allport, 1955, p. 544). In addition, the meaning attributed to wholes and the meaning attributed to parts "are always found together; we have no evidence for concluding that one is logically or causally prior to the other" (p. 553). "(0)rganization and the meaning that accompanies it must be considered as operating in the part as well as the whole and must be pursued . . . in every whole-part relationship . . . that enters into the situation with which we are dealing" (p. 559). Thus, the theoretical bases for Gestalt therapy discussed above, as well as the general strategies and specific tactics, are grounded in Gestalt psychology and in Kurt Lewin's field theory. (See Allport, 1955, Chapters 5, 6, & 19.) Gestalt therapy provides an arena for the application of the principles of perception, structure, and learning identified by major theorists in these psychological traditions.

Gestalt shares many of its values, working assumptions, and techniques with other therapeutic approaches. Nevertheless, as a somewhat unified system, Gestalt retains an identifiable methodology for increasing an individual's awareness of the self, of the environment, and of the interaction between the two. The intent of the preceding discussion has been to relate some characteristic Gestalt practices to theoretical constructs in the Gestalt literature. By thus identifying how theory informs practice, some guidelines are clearer for generating new practices and for refining existing ones.

References

Allport, F.H. *Theories of perception and the content of structure.* New York: John Wiley, 1955.

Downing, J., & Marmorstein, R. *Dreams and nightmares.* New York: Harper & Row, 1973.

Enright, J.B. An introduction to gestalt techniques. In Fagan, J., & Shepherd, I.L. (Eds.), *Gestalt therapy now.* Palo Alto, Calif.: Science and Behavior Books, 1970.

Fagan, J. The tasks of the therapist. In Fagan, J., & Shepherd, I.L. (Eds.), *Gestalt therapy now.* Palo Alto, Calif.: Science and Behavior Books, 1970.

Fagan, J., & Shepherd, I.L. (Eds.). *Gestalt therapy now.* Palo Alto, Calif.: Science and Behavior Books, 1970.

Greenwald, J.A. The groundrules of Gestalt therapy. *Journal of Contemporary Psychotherapy*, 1972, *5* (1), 3–12.

Levitsky, A., & Perls, F.S. The rules and games of Gestalt therapy. In Fagan, J., & Shepherd, I.L. (Eds.), *Gestalt therapy now.* Palo Alto, Calif.: Science and Behavior Books, 1970.

Naranjo, C. Contributions of Gestalt therapy. In H.A. Otto & J. Mann (Eds.), *Ways of growth.* New York: The Viking Press, 1968.

Naranjo, C. *The techniques of Gestalt therapy.* Highland, N.Y.: The Gestalt Journal Press, 1980.

Perls, F.S. *Ego, hunger, and aggression.* New York: Vintage Books, 1969 (*a*).

Perls, F.S. *Gestalt therapy verbatim.* Lafayette, Calif.: Real People Press, 1969 (*b*).

Perls, F.S. *The Gestalt approach and eye witness to therapy.* Palo Alto, Calif.: Science and Behavior Books, 1973.

Perls, F.S., Hefferline, R.F., & Goodman, P. *Gestalt therapy: Excitement and growth in human personality.* New York: Dell Publishing Co., 1951.

16

The Use of Therapist-Imposed Structure in Gestalt Therapy

Joseph Melnick

Among Fritz Perls' major talents was his genius for structuring the therapeutic hour in novel and inventive ways. As Zinker (1974) points out, the Gestalt procedures known as the hot seat, empty chair, and top dog–under dog first began as the creative expression of Perls' momentary insights. However, what originated as personal phenomena have since been translated into Gestalt techniques.

These transformations represent the evolution of Gestalt therapy from innovation to institutionalization. First came the period of growth and change, a time of peaceful anonymity for both Perls and Gestalt therapy. Insights were utilized to illuminate the moment and then quickly discarded as other structures, which better fit the tension of the "now," were invented to take their place. Then began the popularization and codification of these insights by the human potential

Reprinted from *The Gestalt Journal*, 1980, 3(2), 4-20. Reprinted with permission of the author.

and encounter group movements. It was also during this time that these momentary insights became frozen into techniques.

Respectability became insured with the adoption of these procedures by hungry therapists feeling limited by the nondirectiveness of Rogers and the noninvolvement of Freud. These techniques were powerful and provided an active way of working that led not only to rapid but also to observable changes in client behavior. No longer did therapists have to rely on clients' testimonials to assess progress and outcome. Therapeutic work could instead be evaluated as it occurred in the "here and now." These experimental structures not only were effective eliciting agents, but they also added excitement and liveliness to the therapeutic hour.

The popularization of Gestalt techniques has served to focus attention on a debate that has been taking place for many years: namely, whether structured experiences, introduced by the therapist during the counseling session, are of value in furthering the therapeutic process. Traditionally, the avoidance of therapist-induced structure (i.e., increased ambiguity) has been alleged to encourage client self-direction and exploration and to enhance transference. This belief system stands in marked contrast to some of the newer, more structured therapies such as Transactional Analysis, which provides a cognitive direction; behavior modification, which explores behavioral and environmental textures; and Gestalt therapy, which guides through the use of experiments.

This article examines the debate as it relates to Gestalt therapy and draws heavily from other therapeutic areas in an attempt to expand ways of conceptualizing and utilizing Gestalt procedures. It is divided into four sections. The first discusses structural issues from a historical vantage point, as they emerged from the human potential movement. The remaining three sections present a more scientific perspective, introducing data from group research relevant to the structure controversy, discussing the concept of experiment from a scientific as well as from a Gestalt viewpoint, and categorizing some of the major Gestalt experiments.

Historical Correlates and Antecedents

Gestalt therapists have long been aware of the effects of the clinician on the ongoing therapeutic interaction: "The therapeutic situation, for instance, is more than just a statistical event of a doctor plus a patient. It is a meeting of a doctor and a patient" (Perls, Hefferline, & Goodman, 1951, p. xi). Yet this currently unquestioned interaction and mutual influence was not easily accepted in the 1950s. In fact, much debate centered, at that time, around the psychoanalytic notion of "therapist as mirror." According to this formulation, the therapist, after having worked out much (all?) of his or her unfinished business in psychoanalysis, became a pure, unblemished mirror upon which portions of the client's assumptive world were projected and, ultimately, reflected back. The primary technique used to elicit these projections was free association, and the primary method for reflection was interpretation.

Behavior modifiers, in the 1950s, began discovering that values (Rosenthal, 1955) as well as behavioral repertoires (Greenspoon, 1951) could be influenced via operant conditioning techniques (cf. Kanfer & Philips, 1970). Other research, supportive of the power of client-therapist interaction (intended or otherwise) derived from the work on placebo effects (cf. Kintz, et al., 1965). Data generated from these studies indicate that clients do not react to the therapist as a blank screen but rather make assumptions about the wants and needs of the therapist and then respond accordingly. It also supports what most clinicians have experienced firsthand: that is, client-therapist behavior, vocabulary, dreams, dress, and so forth usually move toward greater congruence as therapy progresses. The data are also consistent with Gestalt theory:

> The attitude and character of a therapist (including his own training) determine his theoretical orientation, and his method of clinical procedure springs from both his attitude and his theory; but also the conformation that one gets from one's theory springs from the method employed, for the method (and the expectation of the therapist) partly creates the findings, just as the therapist was himself oriented as a trainee. [Perls, Hefferline, & Goodman, 1951, p. 244]

Once the notion was accepted that therapist and client do exert a strong mutual influence (at least in terms of their attitudes and expectations), the next debated issue concerned whether maximal structuring was beneficial. Could the therapist, by intentionally using his or her influence in the form of specific structuring, produce a more facilitative atmosphere for positive change than by ignoring or minimizing this influence? Data relevant to this question emerged out of research conducted with groups.

The group movement not only generated important studies but was primarily responsible for popularizing Gestalt therapy as well as structural approaches to growth. One branch of this phenomenon, known as T (training)-Group, or sensitivity training, was begun by social scientists (cf. Bradord, Gibb, and Benne, 1964). These experimental training groups, originally designed to explore small group interaction, soon evolved a methodology, replete with a series of interventions designed to help members focus on and deal with emerging interpersonal group issues. These procedures became known as exercises and quickly found their way into the methodological bags of more traditional group practitioners (cf. Pfeiffer & Jones, 1969).

It is important to note that as sensitivity training gained popularity, the focus shifted from experimentally oriented, data-collecting groups called laboratories to therapeutically oriented growth groups functioning to implement individual change. As the group's function shifted, so did the rationale for introducing structured exercises. The "What would happen if?" question of the scientist became the "You'll learn _____ if you _____" statement of the teacher-technician.

At approximately the same time that T-Groups were becoming popular on the East Coast, a West Coast version of this phenomenon was emerging in California. Fritz Perls and his new brand of Gestalt therapy, simplified and streamlined, was finally discovered, and the truly experimental approach, which he had so carefully helped to create (cf. Perls, Hefferline, & Goodman, 1951), was adapted and routinized to produce instant insights and cures. Furthermore, Gestalt techniques were implemented often with only a cursory understanding of the client's external support system and intrapsychic characteristics and with little concern for the long-term effects of abrupt shifts in boundary experiences.

The assertion of the analyst that she or he was just background and the client always figural had been totally reversed. Now the therapist with her or his bag of techniques was figural, with the group's task being one of supportive ground for the therapist's interventions. The negative consequences of structuring the therapeutic situation without regard for client boundaries or the provision of support for change have been recently documented (Lieberman, Yalon, & Miles, 1973). These authors found that groups led by "charismatic" leaders had higher casualty and dropout rates than those led by more cognitively oriented, slower-moving guides. Leaders who forced and imposed their own figure-ground process on the group placed clients at greater risk than those therapists who were willing to allow figure-ground formation to occur at a rate that could be integrated more easily into each client's experiences. Technique and coercion had ultimately overtaken inventiveness and creativity.

Client Characteristics and Structure

It is not surprising that responsible scientists can reach such disparate theories if we bear in mind that for various reasons of personality and reputation different schools of therapists get different kinds of patients, and those prove to be empirical verifications for their theories and the basis for further hypotheses along the same line. [Perls, Hefferline, & Goodman, 1951, p. 280)

The relative benefits of therapist-imposed structure do not lend themselves to easy analysis. The contradictory theoretical positions of those advocating minimal structure or ambiguity (Rabin, 1970) and urging greater use of therapist-induced structuring (Melnick, 1974) are not easily reconciled.

Because Gestalt therapy was in many ways a reaction to traditional, history-oriented, personality trait-labeling therapies, it has not often spoken to client characteristics of an enduring nature. Yet, it appears that a client's characterological disposition can and does interact with the therapist's personality, treatment approach, and a whole host of other variables to produce the gestalt we call psychotherapy. By taking account of client characteristics (largely ignored by Lieberman, Yalon, & Miles, 1973), one has data with which to begin evaluating and integrating the diverse theoretical stances.

Analyzing the research for composition of psychotherapeutic and growth-oriented groups, Melnick and Woods (1976) concluded that group members with "more desired attributes" (i.e., internal orientation, high social risk-taking propensity, low social anxiety, good interpersonal skills, etc.) make greater gains in treatment than do clients with less desirable attributes, regardless of the amount or degree of therapist-induced structure present. Furthermore, high structure tends to be facilitative for participants with less desirable member attributes, while possibly inhibiting development in groups whose members have achieved higher interpersonal functioning. It should be noted that the structural conditions reported in this research were primarily low risk in nature and were not presented by a "charismatic leader."

Translated into Gestalt terms, these findings support the notion that clients who are able to create and destroy their own figures and who are able to provide much of their own support (internal orientation, high field independence, etc.) do best in therapy regardless of the degree of structure. Resistance can be explored and worked through with minimal therapeutic guidance. Furthermore, too much therapist input can interrupt this process, thereby decreasing gain. Since psychoanalysts tend to see this type of client, it is not surprising that their stance of staying primarily in the background, as well as of discouraging interpersonal contact and figure formation, has led to successful client growth. On the other hand, behavior modifiers, who have worked primarily in university settings with young, therapeutically naive college students, achieve excellent success with highly structured, highly directive therapeutic techniques and conditions.

Perls tended to work with "high-level" clients who had the ability to benefit, regardless of the amount of structure present. He minimized the potentially negative effects of his high-structure–high-frustration form of therapy by selecting out many potential clients who could not benefit from his therapeutic style. Also, as he became famous, many of his clients preselected themselves. It is questionable whether his high-structure–high-frustration approach would be as successful with the majority of people seeking therapy.

Group research on explicit, therapist-imposed structure provided prior to the start of the group situation (pregroup preparation) or at the beginning of therapy suggests that it serves an orienting, anxiety-reducing function that lowers drop-out rates and casualties and increases cohesiveness (Bednar et. al., 1974; Woods & Melnick, 1979). Other research suggests that clients tend to respond more positively to behavioral rather than cognitive structuring (Bednar & Kaul, 1979), thus supporting the Gestalt philosophy of "doing rather than talking about."

The data, taken as a whole, indicate that clients who have difficulty with figure-ground formation, or who are stuck at different points in the experience (awareness) cycle (Polster & Polster, 1973), need specific structuring that will provide training in awareness, contact, repertoire expansion and refinement, and withdrawal. It is not surprising that exercises that deal with these topics make up much of the structured learning cookbooks.

In sum, the research indicates that a therapist needs to diagnose prior to and during the application of structured interventions in order to provide an accurate "fit." Furthermore, evaluation of the more long-term as well as the immediate impact of therapeutic interventions is essential. Such an assessment must be grounded in a larger body of knowledge, whether it be a Gestalt approach (figure-ground formation, experience cycle, resistances, etc.); interpersonal perspective (social anxiety, risk-taking propensity, intimacy, power, and control needs, etc.); behavior modification (stimuli, response repertoires, reinforcers, etc.); or other serious therapeutic system.

That Perls was a master of intuitively sizing up potential clients is borne out by the many testimonials of his refusal to work with certain people. The "here-and-now—I-do-my-thing" orientation, and the weekend workshop-demonstration form of much of his later work obscured the need for long-term, furture-oriented considerations. Therapy is more than just a moment of heightened awareness conducted in a vacuum. It is, by definition, wed to the past as well as to the future, and it is this relationship that helps give the now its present form.

The Gestalt Experiment and Science

Therapist-directed structure exists in Gestalt therapy as experiment. Experiment derives from *experiri*, to try. An experiment is a trial or special observation made to confirm or disprove something doubtful, especially under conditions determined by the experimenter; an act or operation undertaken in order to discover some unknown principle or effect, or to test, establish, or illustrate some suggested unknown truth; practical test, proof. [Perls, Hefferline, & Goodman, 1951, p. 12]

That Gestalt therapists would have adopted such a value-laden word, *experiment*, might at first appear surprising, since most Gestaltists align themselves more with the artist than the scientist. However, it must be remembered that Gestalt therapy had its roots in Gestalt psychology (Smith, 1976), a highly scientific endeavor. Thus, the Gestalt conceptualization of experiment draws heavily from scientific usage.

Before embarking, however, on a discussion of experiment, it is pertinent to deal briefly with the term *science*. The therapist–scientist controversy is of long standing and has been described and articulated elsewhere (cf. Barker, 1971; Berenda, 1957). It is not the purpose of this paper to enter the debate, except to contend that one can be both scientist and therapist. Much of the confusion and controversy rests on an inaccurate definition of science as method. Science is rather an attitude; it is a point of view (Barker, 1971) directed towards exploring the relationships between phenomena. Scientific method consists of a series of techniques that are situational and vary according to different conditions (Conant, 1952).

An experiment begins to be formed when the therapist-scientist uses his or her observational skills and notices some act of interest. It is this ability that is the basis of both science and therapy. The observational skills of master Gestalt clinicians are well known and have been analyzed at length by Zinker (1977).

As an object or stimulus act captures the therapist-scientist's curiosity, an attempt is made to gather knowledge for the purpose of achieving some clarity and form. The name given to this attempt is *experiment*. It involves the temporary interruption, or transformation, of an ongoing act so that we may "see" or perceive it in a new or different way. The tools we use to help us investigate as well as to arrange and clarify our observations are called techniques. They are highly specified procedures for structuring behavior, thus allowing us to tease out and attend to certain figures.

Experiments are driven by the creative question, "What would happen if?" Therapist-scientists are not interested in outcomes in the sense of their being good-bad or successful-unsuccessful, but rather in that they provide the basis of future work. Like any true scientist, Perls was not wed to specific purposes or objectives when embarking upon a new experiment. The cardinal principle of experimentation is that one accept the results (Kaplan, 1964).

Before conducting an experiment, one must have methodology, which provides the theoretical and operational underpinnings of one's work. Sound methodology permits one to make explicit the rules under which the therapy/science game is to be conducted, allowing for the translation of theoretical insights into more concrete and workable forms. Moreover, an articulate methodology implies an overall experimental structure which signals the data to be attended to, as well as the categories for codification, analysis, interpretation, and feedback.

Methodology incorporates techniques. However, no series of techniques is owned by any one scientific or therapeutic school, despite the tendency of some to discover, name, and declare ownership. For example, psychodrama has much in common with role playing, assertiveness training, and behavioral rehearsal, especially if one views these techniques apart from their methodological context.

A major problem in the experimental approach of some Gestalt therapists can be traced to the confusion between methodology and techniques. Gestalt methodology, which deals largely with figure-ground relations and boundary exploration and articulation, suggests and gives birth to Gestalt techniques such as the empty chair or top dog–under dog. A "Gestalt technique," when used by a TA therapist coming out of a TA theoretical base, becomes a "TA technique," although it was originally created by a Gestalt therapist. For a technique to be truly Gestalt, it must evolve out of and be tied to sound Gestalt methodology, which, in turn, must be solidly grounded in Gestalt psychology and therapy. Any less results in the learning and performing of isolated tricks. Form should not be confused with, or mistaken for, essence.

The stance of the therapist in conducting an experiment is similar to that of the scientist. At first she or he is active in helping to design and construct the experimental situation but then often retreats to the role of consultant or director. During the experiment proper, as well as during the "making something of it," the level of therapist participation varies. Tuning into process as opposed to content, the therapist becomes concerned with rhythm, speed, energy, clarity, and so forth.

Like Ferlinghetti's poem, the therapist is a "mirror walking down a strange street," (1955, p. 6) or to use Zinker's (1977) term, manifests "detached involvement." By detached, we mean that the therapist's mind is yielding and receptive as well as free from attachment to the experimental material and procedures. The therapist neither needs to succeed nor needs the data to conform in any way to expectations, hunches, or hypotheses. The data simply are.

Classification of Experiments

Throughout this paper the term *experiment* has been used as Perls used it in his published work and as it is employed in most scientific journals. However, this refined and polished level of experimentation does not reflect the smaller explorations that are the norm of most laboratories as well as therapeutic hours. In this last section, experiences that have been subsumed under the rubric *experiment* are broken down into more clearly delineated categories. The purpose of this attempt at classification is to lend some clarity to what has previously been a confusing oversimplification of terms. By understanding the purpose prior to the initiation of the experiment, one can sharpen process as well as better evaluate outcome. Borrowing heavily from the work of Kaplan (1964), five types of experiments will be described. They include exercises, methodological experiments, simulated experiments, heuristic or exploratory experiments, and boundary experiments.

Exercises

Exercises are therapeutic directives that are applied in a largely predetermined manner. They are devoid of experimental roots in that their structure does not grow out of the moment but is, instead, prefashioned. As such, their creation and form resemble teaching rather than science or art. The relationship of exercise to experiment is similar to that of an off-the-rack coat to a custom-made garment. Utilization involves a type of "fitting" of the exercise to the ongoing therapeutic experience. As such, outcome as well as therapeutic creativity is limited. Misapplication can result in learning that is of a hit-or-miss variety.

The primary advantages in using exercises are economic. Savings of time, client money, and therapeutic energy can result. Exercises can be used with large groups of people, with the therapist needing to pay only minimal attention to client dynamics. Furthermore, exercises can be initiated prior to the start of treatment as well as conducted without the presence of a therapist. Examples include "homework" assignments to be completed between sessions, audiotaped group exercises, and numerous self-help books filled with directive formulas.

The successful implementation of therapy exercises is only minimally dependent on clinician-client rapport and relationship, thus decreasing client dependence on the therapist. One benefit of this decreased dependence is that clients are able to take greater responsibility for their learning. Furthermore, they are more likely to attribute gains made in treatment to themselves rather than to the magical interventions of the therapist.

Exercises, as vehicles for transmitting learning, are essential to the work of the clinician. Clients are taught a language as a means of providing a common ground for communication and are also helped to establish and expand behavioral and conceptual repertoires. Because of the nature of the therapeutic enterprise (most clients enter therapy in some form of crisis), this teaching is seldom conducted separately or systematically. It is rather interwoven as needed, while the therapist attends to more urgent matters.

Exercises can be broken down into two primary categories: process exercises, which are used to explore the hows of our existence, and content exercises, which teach facts, skills, and behaviors. Process exercises have been most often created and utilized by Gestalt therapists (Perls, Hefferline, & Goodman, 1951; Stevens, 1971), and when used properly can open up many areas for examination and expansion. Examples include exercises designed to help explore body awareness and boundaries ("touch your partner in two distinct ways and observe his or her nonverbal responses") and introjects ("make a list of ten shoulds and should nots").

Content exercises have been used most systematically in group treatment. For example, groups may begin with a series of exercises that are purposeful in nature and designed to teach such skills as self-disclosure, feedback, paraphrasing, and behavioral description (Melnick, 1974). As such, these exercises are canned. The concern is that members have the tools and skills necessary to survive in treatment, and since group research indicates that this type of approach leads to fewer casualties and drop-outs, such skills become the foundation for the group experience (Woods & Melnick, 1979). Certainly, legitimate experiments sometimes grow out of these exercises; however, that is not the primary goal or purpose.

It is important that therapists be able to differentiate between content and process exercises. Content exercises have their roots in traditional teaching and, as such, generate data that can be evaluated along a right–wrong continuum. For example, "paraphrasing" is a skill that can be graded as to accuracy, but "trust" is a highly subjective, nonquantifiable experience that varies as a function of a multitude of personal and environmental conditions.

The successful implementation of exercises requires the skills of a trained technician rather than those of an artist or a scientist. It is a difference similar to that between a draftsperson and an architect. To successfully utilize exercises, one should have a wide repertoire to draw from as well as a talent for matching exercises to therapeutic situations. Furthermore, one must be aware of the limitations of exercises. Transformation into experiments requires a creative, artistic perspective that is not needed for the application of exercises.

Problems arise in that experiments can sometimes appear to the naive observer as exercises, and the role of the creative clinician is similar to that of the trained technician. Client damage can result when technicians with minimal therapeutic skills use exercises as if they were experiments. It is during these moments that exercises, stretched beyond their appropriate focus and purpose, can miss the growing edge of experience, resulting in either boredom and triviality or the anxiety and terror of a not-me awareness.

Methodological Experiments

Scientists undertake methodological experiments in order to develop particular techniques as well as to assess the fit of the experimental structures to the experiment proper. In Gestalt work, a technique that fits is one that helps implement a piece of work so that the client is able to experience and articulate some bit of learning as well as to integrate it into his or her ongoing existence.

The success of experimental techniques rests largely on an assessment of the client's skills, values, repertoires, and abilities. Thus, the therapist needs to learn to hand-tailor procedures to specific clients as well as to environmental situations. For instance, one might conduct a methodological experiment to discover whether a client can image his dead mother sitting in an empty chair. Difficulty in following the directive to "talk to your mother" might be a function of resistances, cultural injunctions, or, quite possibly, a certain difficulty in imaging (Bandler & Grinder, 1975). If imaging is indeed the primary problem, this experiment will fail, not because of an incorrect hypothesis or inappropriate focus, but because the vehicle chosen to implement the therapeutic work does not fit the passenger. Thus, if a client's difficulty is assessed as poor imaging ability, the therapist would have the option of sitting in the chair and playing the mother, of having the client verbally or physically write a letter or bring in pictures, or of selecting some other way of working that would be more in line with the client's therapeutic resources. Later, at a future point in time, the client's difficulty in imaging might be explored as a therapeutic issue in itself. This exploration could then result in the initiation of a series of exercises designed to help him or her learn to better visualize and imagine.

Simulation Experiments

Simulation experiments are designed to provide information concerning what would happen under certain conditions that are difficult, if not impossible, to create or duplicate. From a Gestalt perspective, all experiments are to some degree simulated, in that they are "safe emergencies" designed to help us reexperience unfinished work from the past or to deal with catastrophic or anastrophic expectations concerning the future.

The neurotic state has been described as a "response to a nonexistent, chronic low-grade emergency" (Perls, Hefferline, & Goodman, 1951, p. 288) that lingers on from a once-real dangerous situation. Much therapeutic work revolves around simulating these old situations in such a way that the client can experience or reexperience a high-grade emergency, while at the same time feel safe enough to cope with the situation.

Although all experiments are predictive to some extent, simulation experiments are even more so. This type of work is invoked when more realistic experiments are:

1. Too costly ("What would you do if you had a million dollars?");
2. Physically impossible ("I wonder what it would be like to be a dog?; speak to my dead mother?; etc.");
3. Morally impossible (exploring the theme of murder).

Heuristic or Exploratory Experiments

Heuristic experiments generally begin as a response to language or body movements. Examples include: (1) Playing off of metaphors communication. They also serve a diagnostic function. Since they emerge from only a minimal data base, hypotheses, if present at all, are poorly formed and articulated. These experimental probes do not grow out of a firm foundation, but out of an intuitive sense. Because the investment in finishing them is small, they often meld into other, more elaborate, pieces of work.

Heuristic experiments generally begin as a response to language or body movements. Examples include: (1) Playing off of metaphors suggested by the client ("I feel like a pumpkin—I have a large head with nothing in it") or the therapist ("As you talk, I fantasize a helpless little bird"); and (2) exaggerating or accentuating what already exists ("Would you say that louder?").

Boundary Experiments

Researchers in behavioral sciences use boundary experiments to define or fix the range of any set of laws in order to more fully specify their limits. Examples include work with perceptual thresholds and sensory deprivation. Boundary exploration is one of the primary goals of Gestalt work, and boundary experiments are the fundamental tools for such.

Gestalt therapists explore contact and withdrawal at various boundries to ascertain how clients block out as well as permit awareness of these points. Polster and Polster (1973) talk at length about body, value, familiarity, expressive, and exposure boundaries. They maintain: "The Gestalt experiment is used to expand the range of the individual, showing him how he can extend his habitual sense of boundary where emergency and excitement exist" (p. 112).

By exploring boundaries, the client becomes more limber and flexible, increases his or her alternatives and options, and reworks old entrenched themes in novel and exciting ways. Most polarity work deals with boundary exploration. However, this form of experimentation includes any work through which one risks being awkward and insecure in order to explore the edge of his or her being.

Conclusion

In this paper, the concept of structure has been explored as it relates to psychotherapy in general and to Gestalt therapy in particular. In actuality, there exists a wide array of conditions, which, prior to the initiation of therapy, narrows possibilities and provides a general direction and framework for our work. These "background structures" include not only the theoretical orientation and skills of the clinician but also the personalities, histories, wants, needs, and expectations of all participants, the physical environment in which the therapy takes place, and numerous other variables. The more one is aware of these background considerations, the more one is able to usefully incorporate them in the shaping of the therapeutic hour.

The historical controversy regarding the relative, therapeutic benefit of more or less structure has been traced. This "more-or-less" dichotomy is, in essence, a false one. The issue is more correctly viewed in terms of explicitness versus implicitness and of specificity versus ambiguity of structure. Moreover, the art of therapy involves an ability to notice how one is structuring so that one can craft a specific frame to fit and highlight the contours of the current situation.

A primary form of explicit structuring discussed in this paper involves the use of therapeutic techniques and, in particular, the experiment. To borrow a metaphor (Barrett, 1979), one can think of techniques as carpentry tools such as hammers, screwdrivers, and saws. Give a box of tools to someone who has limited theoretical and practical knowledge concerning their utilization and the tools become, at best, inefficient instruments; at worst, deadly weapons. Give the same tools to a skilled carpenter and their use takes on a creative and artistic form.

This is not to imply that only a skilled carpenter or a master therapist should use powerful tools. When implemented within the limits of one's skills and resources, techniques become facilitative instruments. Problems emerge, however, when the power of the technique exceeds the craftsman's knowledge and good sense.

And above all, one must not confuse technique with therapeutic artistry:

> Genuine creation is precisely that for which we can give no prescribed technique or recipe; and technique reaches its limits precisely at that point beyond which real creativity is called for in the sciences as well as the arts. [Barrett, 1979, p. 22]

References

Bandler, R., & Grinder, J. *The structure of magic I*. Palo Alto, Calif.: Science and Behavior Books, 1975.

Barker, E.N. Humanistic psychology and scientific method. *Interpersonal development*, 1971, *2*, 137–172.

Barrett, W. *The illusion of technique.* New York: Doubleday, 1979.

Bednar, R. L., & Kaul, T.J. Experimental group research: Current perspectives. In Garfield, S.L., & Bergin, A. (Eds.), *Handbook of psychotherapy and behavior change.* New York: John Wiley, 1979.

Bednar, R.L., Weet, C., Evansen, P., Lanier, D., & Melnick, J. Empirical guidelines for group therapy: Pretraining, cohesion, modeling. *Journal of Applied Behavioral Science*, 1974, *10*, 149–165.

Berenda, C.W. Is clinical psychology a science? *American Psychologist*, 1957, *12*, 725–729.

Bradford, L.P., Gibb, J.R., & Benne, K.D. *Group therapy and laboratory method.* New York: John Wiley, 1964.

Conant, J.B. *Modern science and modern man.* New York: Doubleday, 1952.

Ferlinghetti, L. *Pictures of the gone world.* San Francisco: City Light Books, 1955.

Greenspoon, J. The effect of verbal and non-verbal stimuli on the frequency of number of two verbal responses. Unpublished Ph.D. dissertation, Indiana University, 1951.

Kanfer, F.H., & Phillips, J.S. *Learning foundations of behavior therapy.* New York: John Wiley, 1970.

Kaplan, A. *The conduct of inquiry.* San Francisco: Chandler, 1964.

Kintz, B.L., Delprato, D.J., Mettee, D.R., Persons, C.E., & Schappe, R.H. The experimenter effect. *Psychological Bulletin*, 1965, *63*, 223–232.

Lieberman, M.A., Yalon, I.D., & Miles, M.B. *Encounter groups: First Facts.* New York: Basic Books, 1973.

Melnick, J. Risk responsibility and structure: Necessary ingredients for the initiation of group psychotherapy. Paper read at the Annual Meeting of American Psychological Association, 1974.

Melnick, J., & Woods, M. An analysis of group composition research and theory for psychotherapeutic and growth-oriented groups. *Journal of Applied Behavioral Science*, 1976, *12*, 493–512.

Perls, F., Hefferline, R.F., & Goodman, P. *Gestalt therapy.* New York: Dell Publishing Co., 1951.

Pfeiffer, J.W., & Jones, J.B. *A handbook of structure exercises for human relations training.* Vols. I–III. Iowa City: University Associates Press, 1969.

Polster, I., & Polster, M. *Gestalt therapy integrated.* New York: Brunner/Mazel, 1973.

Rabin, H. Preparing patients for group therapy. *International Journal of Group Psychotherapy*, 1970, *20*, 135–145.

Rosenthal, D. Changes in some moral values following psychotherapy. *Journal of Consulting Psychology*, 1955, *19*, 431–436.

Smith, E.W.L. The roots of Gestalt therapy. In Smith, E.W.L. (Ed.), *The growing edge of Gestalt therapy.* New York: Brunner/Mazel, 1976.

Stevens, J.O. *Awareness.* Moab, Utah: Real People Press, 1971.

Woods, M., & Melnick, J. Patient selection in group therapy. *Small Group Behavior*, 1979, *10*, 155–175.

Zinker, J. "Gestalt therapy in permission to be creative." *Voices*, 1974, *9*, 4.

Zinker, J. *Creative process in Gestalt therapy.* New York: Brunner/Mazel, 1977.

17

A Gestalt Approach to Psychological Education

John H. Childers, Jr.
Don T. Basse

Under the umbrella of psychological education, Gestalt approaches offer methods for gaining awareness of self and of the environment and for increasing a sense of responsibility. This article presents Gestalt exercises that can be readily worked into a classroom curriculum at the elementary level. Alschuler and Ivey (1973) postulate that "Gestalt may be even more important as a teaching tool than as a therapeutic alternative" (p. 686). The exercises presented below have used the potential enrichment of Gestalt therapy in the classroom.

Gestalt Goal of Awareness

The Gestalt goal of awareness is an important affective, developmental skill for elementary school children to learn and practice.

Reprinted from *Elementary School Guidance and Counseling*, 1980, *15*, 120-121. Copyright 1980 American Association for Counseling and Development. Reprinted with permission.

Children who experience awareness training may become more aware of their environment and their internal experiences than children who are not given explicit awareness training. An awareness group can be nourishing and growth producing to all students, not just for those who have a specific concern or difficulty.

Briefly examining major tenets of Gestalt therapy may clarify what is meant by awareness. "The immediate aim of Gestalt therapy is the restoration of awareness" (Naranjo, 1971, p. 136). Perls (1969) believed that everything is grounded in awareness, which is the only basis for knowledge and communication. Awareness means being in touch with and being aware of what one is doing, planning, and feeling. Stevens (1971) described three kinds of awareness or zones of awareness:

1. Awareness of the outside world. This is actual sensory contact with objects and events in the present: What I now actually see, hear, smell, taste or touch.

2. Awareness of the inside world. This is actual sensory contact with inner events in the present: What I now actually feel from inside my skin—itches, muscular tensions and movements, physical manifestations of feelings and emotions, discomfort, well-being, and so forth.

3. Awareness of fantasy activity. This includes all mental activity beyond present awareness of ongoing experience: All explaining, imagining, interpreting, guessing, thinking, comparing, planning, remembering the past, anticipating the future, and so forth. [Pp. 5–6]

Teachers and counselors can help children discover and attain all three kinds of awareness (Naranjo, 1971; Stevens, 1971). Restoration of awareness is one of the first steps in facilitating client growth. Hamlin (1975) asserts that helping youth become aware of what they do and how they do it provides an authentic basis for choice and change.

A Gestalt Education Program

The following exercises are representative of procedures developed by the author, G.I. Brown (1971), and J. Lederman (1969) for use with elementary school students. The exercises have been organized into three separate units. These units focus on learning how to be more aware of oneself and one's environment. The goal of Unit 1 is to teach the skills necessary for increasing awareness of one's external environment or the outside world (Stevens, 1971). The goal of Unit 2 is to teach the skills necessary for increasing awareness of the inside world or one's internal experiences (Stevens, 1971). The goal of Unit 3 is to teach students how to be more aware of their own emotions and how to be more effective in expressing emotions.

The three units are developmental. That is, the exercises in Unit 1 have been sequentially arranged to build on one another to prepare a student for the exercises in Unit 2. Unit 2 exercises build on one another and lead to Unit 3 exercises. All the units have been field tested with classroom groups ranging from kindergarten through eighth grade. For each exercise, there are instructions for the counselor and outcomes for the student and teacher. Student outcomes have been written as observable behaviors that students will be able to perform as a result of each exercise. Teacher outcomes focus on ways the teacher may choose to integrate these awareness skills into the curriculum. Other teacher outcomes suggest strategies for giving the teacher the opportunity to practice and to integrate these skills into his or her classroom management style.

The remainder of this article presents one representative Gestalt awareness exercise from each of the three units. Our purpose is to offer several Gestalt exercises and to introduce a Gestalt-oriented program that can be gainfully used by practicing counselors in the elementary schools.

Unit 1: Awareness of the Outside World

Exercise 1: Awareness of sights.

1. Warm-up discussion. Have students discuss what they see by looking around and discussing what they have seen by relating it to one of the five senses.

2. Exploration. Have the students and the teacher walk around the room, exploring various objects with their eyes. After a few minutes, ask the students to choose an object that interests them (small enough to carry) and take the object back to their seat.

3. Description. Explain to the students that they are now going to look at (study with their eyes) their object and then will describe their object to their classmates. Model first by describing your object;

include the dimensions of color, size, texture, and shape. Then ask each student to describe his or her object. Ask questions about color, size, and so forth if a student has difficulty describing the object.

4. Exploration. After all students have had an opportunity to describe their object, instruct the class to let their eyes roam around the room and select an object they do not like. Ask for volunteers to describe, as before, the object they dislike. Then ask the following questions: What do you dislike most about your object? Can you find something you like about the object? Now that you have really looked at and described the object, how do you feel about it? Do you still dislike it?

Student Outcomes:

The student will be able to:

1. Name the five senses.
2. Choose an object and look at it.
3. Identify sight as one of their five senses.

Teacher Outcomes:

The teacher will:

1. Become more aware of the relationship between sight awareness and attention focusing of students.

2. Find five opportunities during the week to ask students to describe what they are seeing (e.g., during a science lesson, nature walk, messy roomtime).

Unit 2: Internal Awareness

Exercise 1: Arms, Hands, Neck, and Shoulder Awareness

1. Exploration 1—Flying. Have the students stand with their arms at shoulder level. Then ask them to move their arms up and down slowly (demonstrate). Ask them to become aware of how their arms feel. Where do they notice tightness? Then have the students put their arms to their sides and breathe in deeply as they raise their arms, exhaling as they lower their arms. Repeat this exercise until someone says, "I'm tired." Ask the class if anyone else's arms feel tired.

2. Exploration 2—Neck and Shoulders. Have the class sit in a circle and experiment with moving and being aware of their necks and shoulders. Then have them do the following exercises in unison: (a) shrug your shoulders, (b) make your shoulder muscles tight, (c) bring your shoulders forward, (d) tighten your neck, and (e) relax your shoulders and neck by moving your head around loosely.

3. Exploration 3—Arms and Hands. Have students select a partner, one person designated as participator and the other as the observer. Have the partners face each other. After each of the directions below, the observers should be instructed to make "I see you. . ." statements to their partners, pointing out what their partner's body is doing. The counselor should model this activity first with a volunteer from the class. For example, "I see you pointing your finger." After the exercises have been completed and observer feedback is given, have everyone reverse roles and repeat:

—Hug yourself.
—Wave your arms.
—Lean on your elbows.
—Push something away.
—Fold your arms over your chest.
—Point your finger and wave it in the air.
—Use your arms and hands to direct an orchestra.
—Twiddle your thumbs.
—Clench your fists.
—Fold your hands in your lap and keep them still.

4. Postdiscussion. Use all or part of the following suggestions to get the students to process the exercise experience: How do you use your hands and arms when you talk? Have a student stand up and talk to the class with his or her hands clasped behind his or her back. Ask several students to tell the class what they are doing with their neck, shoulders, arms, and hands.

Student Outcomes:

The student will be able to:

1. Make awareness statements about his or her arms, hands, neck, and shoulders.

2. Describe what his or her partner is doing with his or her arms and hands.

Teacher Outcomes:

The teacher will be able to:

1. Use the flying exercise to relax students during the next week.
2. Ask students during the week to state an awareness of what they are doing with their arms and hands. This can be particularly helpful when the students' arms and hands are distracting.
3. Point out to students what their arms, hands, shoulders, or neck are doing by stating, "I see you. . . ."
4. Experiment with various hand and arm motions while talking with individual students and rate their reactions.

Unit 3: Expressing Feelings

Exercise 1: Creative Expression: Art and Music

1. Visual awareness and feelings. Show the students pictures, such as of a cuddly kitten or of a snake displaying its fangs, that will elicit strong feelings. Then ask several students to share their feelings about the pictures. Call attention to nonverbal reactions noted in the group as a whole, such as a gasp.

2. Expressing feelings on paper. Demonstrate how a feeling can be expressed on paper using a crayon. Model first to the class the following directions: Remember a situation in which you experienced a strong feeling. Remember who you were with; what was said. Remember how you felt; were your fists clenched or were you happy? Begin making marks on your paper to express your feelings. After modeling, have the students do the exercise, repeating the directions after the paper has been distributed. Ask for volunteers to share their feelings and expressive designs with the class.

3. Hearing and feelings. Play contrasting selections of music. Elicit verbal sharing from the students by asking how they felt during the playing of the music.

4. Expressing feelings through movement. Play contrasting musical selections. Then have students express feelings by moving around the room in response to the music.

Summary

Gestalt approaches can serve as a valuable tool for psychological education. They serve to enhance self-awareness and responsibility. Gestalt approaches can enliven a curriculum and promote self-understanding.

Teachers who have no experience with Gestalt approaches can be taught how to use them in their classes. An important role of the counselor is to serve as a consultant to teachers in this process. Following the reference section, additional sources regarding Gestalt work and psychological education strategies are included for interested counselors.

The purpose of presenting these units is to provide counselors with the confidence to implement a Gestalt-oriented, psychological education program in elementary schools. And in reviewing these three units, the material will encourage counselors to develop their own units.

References

Alschuler, A.S., & Ivey, A.E. Getting into psychological education. *Personnel and Guidance Journal*, 1973, *5*, 682-691.

Brown, G.I. *Human teaching and human learning: An introduction to confluent education.* New York: Viking Press, 1971.

Hamlin, B. *Awareness experiences for school use.* Dayton, Ohio: Dimensions of Personality, 1975.

Lederman, J. *Anger and the rocking chair: Gestalt awareness with children.* New York: Viking Press, 1969.

Naranjo, C. Contributions of Gestalt therapy. In Otto, H., & Man, J. (Eds.), *Ways of growth: Approaches to examining awareness.* New York: Pocket Books, 1971.

Perls, F. *Gestalt therapy verbatim.* Lafayette, Calif.: Real People Press, 1969.

Stevens, J.O. *Awareness: Exploring, experimenting, experiencing.* Moab, Utah: Real People Press, 1971.

Additional Readings

Brown, G.I. Awareness training and creativity based on Gestalt therapy. *Journal of Contemporary Psychotherapy*, 1969, *2*, 25-32.

Canfield, J., & Wells, H.C. *100 ways to enhance self-concept in the classroom: A handbook for teachers and parents.* Englewood Cliffs, N.J.: Prentice-Hall, 1976.

Harmon, R. Goals of Gestalt therapy. *Professional Psychology*, 1974, *5*, 178-184.

Harmon, R. Techniques of Gestalt therapy. *Professional Psychology*, 1974, *5*, 257-263.

Harmon, R. A Gestalt point of view on facilitating growth in counseling. *Personnel and Guidance Journal*, 1975, *53*, 363-366.

Ivey, A.E., & Alschuler, A.S. An introduction to the field. *Personnel and Guidance Journal*, 1973, *5*, 591-597.

Ivey, A.E., & Alschuler, A.S. (Eds.). Psychological education: A prime function of the counselor. *Personnel and Guidance Journal*, 1973, *51*, 584-691.

Mosher, R.L., & Sprinthall, N. Psychological education in secondary schools: A program to promote individual and human development. *American Psychologist*, 1970, *25*, 911-924.

Palamares, U.H., & Rubini, T. Human development in the classroom. *Personnel and Guidance Journal*, 1973, *5*, 653-657.

Polster, E., & Polster, M. *Gestalt therapy integrated.* New York: Brunner/Mazel, 1973.

SECTION VI

Client-centered Counseling

For constructive personality change to occur, it is necessary that these conditions exist and continue over a period of time:

1. Two persons are in psychological contact.

2. The first, whom we shall term the client, is in a state of incongruence, being vulnerable or anxious.

3. The second person, whom we shall term the therapist, is congruent or integrated in the relationship.

4. The therapist experiences unconditional positive regard for the client.

5. The therapist experiences an empathic understanding of the client's internal frame of reference and endeavors to communicate this experience to the client.

6. The communication to the client of the therapist's empathic understanding and unconditional positive regard is to a minimal degree achieved.

No other conditions are necessary. If these six conditions exist, and continue over a period of time, this is sufficient. The process of constructive personality change will follow.

— Carl Rogers

Client-centered counseling has had a profound effect on the development of counseling and therapy for the past four decades. Many training institutions emphasize this approach in theory and practicum courses, and consequently a large proportion of practicing counselors adhere to its basic premises and techniques. It has been widely

173

used as a treatment modality with adolescent and adult populations. The child population has been less extensively, and only recently, treated with this model. As a consequence, specific adaptation of techniques to the preadolescent population has not been emphasized, and research in this area is conspicuously absent. Despite this handicap, the basic conceptual model is readily adaptable to child clientele.

Client-centered counseling is built on the foundation of phenomenological psychology. Phenomenological assumptions focus on several major concepts: the phenomenological field, the self system, and individual perception. The field is the environment in which the individual exists, and particular attention is directed to the individual's perception of environmental events. His or her unique perceptions govern the development and growth of the self system. Faulty perceptions lead to incongruence in the self system, which is the basis for inconsistent behavior and maladjustment.

Carl Rogers has been the major spokesman for the client-centered approach to counseling. Accepting the tenets of phenomenological theory, he has constructed a theory of counseling that is noticeably free of specific techniques. He prefers to focus his attention on the counselor-client relationship. For Rogers, the relationship is the major change agent in therapy. This relationship has certain characteristics that are essential to effective counseling. Among them are empathy, genuineness, warmth, and unconditional positive regard. The primary behavior of the counselor in this relationship involves listening and reflection of feeling. In general, the focus of client-centered counseling is on the affective growth of the client in the context of the helping relationship.

An article by C. H. Patterson opens this section of readings. He provides a comprehensive overview of the phenomenological school of thought. He begins by comprehensively defining phenomenology, and he compares it to the more classical systems of psychotherapy. Eight major tenets of the theory are discussed, and special emphasis is given to the development and maintenance of the self-concept in an individual.

Roy Mayer and John Cody, in the second reading, approach the client-centered model from an unusual perspective. They relate Festinger's concept of cognitive dissonance to Rogers' concept of incongruence in the self system by proposing that both concepts are similar and both produce psychological discomfort in an individual. In an atmosphere of discomfort, positive self growth is inhibited. This type of threatening environment will lead to defensive reactions on the part of the client. The concepts of cognitive dissonance and incongruence are specifically related to school counseling via the counseling relationship, and more effective counseling behaviors are suggested. Excerpts from a case transcript with a twelve-year-old client and a brief summary of a case of an eleven-year-old boy illustrate their topic. The counselor's use of reflection techniques is particularly apparent in the transcript illustration.

The concluding article in this section, by Ernst Beier, focuses specifically on the involuntary client in the school setting. His article creatively uses case examples to demonstrate a client-centered approach with a variety of different client age levels and presenting problems. The school counselor frequently encounters involuntariness and resistance, and Beier's presentation offers ways of dealing with these phenomena.

18

Phenomenological Psychology

C.H. Patterson

It is a basic tenet of so-called depth or dynamic psychology that behavior is determined by deep unconscious motives, and that in order to understand, predict, or control behavior one must understand these motives. This is not a simple matter, since one cannot easily recognize motives. The apparent or obvious motives, or the motives reported by the subject, are not the real motives. Indeed, the so-called real motives are commonly the reverse of those reported by the subject. Thus nothing can be accepted at face value. Nothing is what it appears to be. Reports of subjects are not to be trusted. The widespread acceptance of this point of view, by lay as well as professional people, attests to the influence of Freud and psychoanalysis.

There is another point of view, which has not been widely accepted, but which is increasing its influence in psychology. This approach suggests that for the purpose of understanding and predicting behavior it is profitable to make the assumption that things *are* what they appear to be, that the significant determinants of behavior are not some mysterious unconscious motives nor some so-called reality but the individual's perceptions of himself and his environ-

Reprinted from *The Personnel and Guidance Journal*, 1965, *43*(10), 997-1005. Copyright 1965 American Association for Counseling and Development. Reprinted with permission.

ment. "There is more to seeing than meets the eyeball" (Hanson, 1958). "We see things," to quote Gibson (1951, p. 98) "not as *they* are but as *we* are." Or to say it another way, it is not "seeing is believing," but "believing is seeing." In more technical terms, the response defines the stimulus, rather than the stimulus defining the response. Gombrich, in a discussion of art and illusion (1960, p. 394) notes that ". . . we can never neatly separate what we see from what we know." "The individual sees what he wants to see, not in the sense that he manufactures out of whole cloth, but in the sense that he appropriates to himself, from what is given, the pattern that he needs" (Murphy, Murphy, & Newcomb, 1937, p. 218).

This second point of view is phenomenology. It is not widely accepted. Snygg (1961), in reviewing a recent book, states: "Phenomenology is not in this country an honored, going concern with a historical past. American phenomenologies therefore emerge rather suddenly, as workers in applied fields run into problems they cannot solve by the traditional objective approach, are forced to develop conceptual models better suited to their needs, and then go on to apply them in wide fields." It is interesting to list some of the names of those who have come to entertain a phenomenological approach. They include William James, John Dewey, George H. Mead, the Allports, Wertheimer, Koffka, Koehler, Kurt Lewin, Adelbert Ames, and Carl Rogers.

Phenomenology and Introspection

A number of years ago a colleague declared that Rogers had set psychology back by fifty years. His basis for the statement was the identification of phenomenology with introspection. It is not necessarily undesirable that we go back fifty years, since it might be contended that psychology has been on the wrong track or in a blind alley during this time, and that it is necessary to go back and pick up a new fork in the road. Psychology has been dominated in the past fifty years by behaviorism and psychoanalysis. While these two approaches or systems are antithetical in many respects, they are similar in that they view the individual from an external position, as an object. Phenomenology, on the other hand, takes the internal form of reference, and in this respect is related to introspection. However, there is a difference. Introspection was concerned only with the subject's report or description of his conscious sensations and feelings.

Phenomenology is concerned with the individual's report, not only of his own sensations and feelings, but of his perceptions of the external world as well as of himself. While phenomenology is thus related to introspection, and to some extent grew out of it, phenomenology as represented by Gestalt psychology, as Boring (1953) points out, was a protest against classic introspection.

Phenomenology, using introspection in the form of verbal reports, produced extensive and significant experimental research in perception. In using verbal reports, phenomenological experiments are no different from psychophysical experiments, in which the subject reports psychical sensations or judgments. In fact, much of current experimental psychology, including behavioristic psychology, depends upon verbal reports, so that phenomenology cannot be condemned as unscientific because it also utilizes verbal report. It is true that there are problems involved in the use of self-reports, but as Bakan (1954) points out, in this respect the method is so different from any other method of science. And there is no other way in many instances to study certain significant problems, such as the self-concept, or to determine the perceptual field of the subject. Nevertheless, it must be recognized that the description of the perceptual field by a subject is not identical with the field itself.

It is interesting that stimulus-response psychology supports the phenomenological point of view. It has been noted that for phenomenology, the response defines the stimulus. Experimental psychologists have come to realize this in the recognition that the same objective or physical stimulus means different things to different subjects, and that if the stimulus situation is to be standardized, it must be in terms of the subjects' perceptions of the stimulus, not the stimulus as objectively defined, or as perceived by the experimenter. In this respect all stimuli are response-inferred (Jessor, 1956; Wylie, 1961, 13-21).

Phenomenology Defined

What is phenomenology? It is the purpose of this paper to attempt to describe briefly the phenomenological approach to behavior. English and English (1958, p. 387) define phenomenology as follows: "A theoretical point of view which advocates the study of phenomena or direct experience taken naively at face value; the view that behavior is determined by the phenomena of experience rather than by external, objective, physically described reality." Phenomenalism is defined as "a philosophical doctrine teaching that human knowledge is limited to appearances, never reaching the true nature of reality" (English & English, 1958, p. 386). Phenomenology as a distinct philosophical point of view is a development mainly of the present century, usually being associated with the philosopher Husserl whose phenomenological writings date from the early years of the century (Spiegelberg, 1960). A brief description of philosophical phenomenology is impossible, in part because of differences among its exponents; there are phenomenologies rather than a school. But they agree in that they are all concerned with experience as the basic data of knowledge. Knowledge can come only from experience, whether sensory or nonsensory, or extrasensory. Whether there is some reality that gives rise to experiences, and, if so, what is the nature of this reality, is unimportant, since it can only be known through experience. Taking this experience, phenomenology attempts to study it, through observing, describing, and analyzing it, attempting to generalize from the particular experiences, determining relationships, studying the various appearances of phenomena and the development of perceptions and conceptions in the phenomenological field.

The position that we can never know the true nature of reality is resisted, both by those who feel that common sense indicates that there is a reality, as when we stub a toe on a brick, by those whose needs or desires require the certainty of some reality, and by scientists who accept their objective measurements and operational definitions as reality. But it should be obvious, both to common sense and to objective observation and measurement, that "reality" varies with different attitudes, motives, desires, or points of view, and with different operations. Whether or not these individual realities add up to a general, absolute, natural reality is a question that has little if any practical significance, for reasons that will become apparent. Philosophically, a phenomenologist may or may not be a realist. Phenomenology represents a "neutralism with regard to reality rather than an outright commitment to realism" (Spiegelberg, 1960, p. 636).

Spiegelberg (1960), in his history of philosophical phenomenology, notes that "Phenomenology is hardly one of the leading philosophical movements in the United States." He later states that "actually in the United States phenomenology has had a much bigger impact on extraphilosophical studies such as psychology and theology, though to be sure in forms which differ considerably from those stressed by the philosophical phenomenologists" (p. 637). In psychology, he continues, "the reaction against behaviorism takes more and more the form of developing a wider phenomenological approach, which tries to give introspection as objective and critical refinement as possible" (pp. 643-644).

While, as has been indicated, the Gestaltists were essentially phenomenological, as well as a number of social psychologists identified with sociology, notably G. H. Mead, the first specific treatment of phenomenological psychology was the 1941 article by Snygg (1941). At the present time perhaps the most definitive statement of phenomenological psychology is that of Snygg and Combs, first published in 1949, and recently revised (Combs & Snygg, 1959).

A Synthesis of Phenomenological Psychology

What is phenomenological psychology? What are its distinguishing features? Phenomenology in psychology did not develop from philosophical phenomenology, but arose almost independently, although psychologists such as James, Koehler, and Lewin had some contact with the latter. There is, as yet, no formal school of phenomenological psychology. It is thus not possible to present a statement of a formal or complete system. The outline of the characteristics of a phenomenological approach to human behavior that follows is an attempt to synthesize or integrate the ideas of those who have been identified as phenomenological in their psychological approach to behavior. The attempt rests most heavily, perhaps, on Combs and Snygg (1959).

1. *The individual is a living, and therefore active, organism engaged in the attempt to organize its world.* Two characteristics of this fact are important.

a. The individual is not an empty organism, waiting to be prodded into action by external or even internal stimuli. The response seeks the stimulus, rather than waiting for the stimulus to evoke it.

b. The interaction of the organism with its environment is the basis for experience. This experience constitutes the basic data of psychology. It consists of, or underlies and gives meaning to, overt behavior. Phenomenological psychology is concerned with the study of the experiencing individual.

2. *The organization which the individual gives to the world is known as his perceptual or phenomenal field.* This is more than the area of sensory perception, including cognition, conceptions, and knowledge. The importance of phenomenology was first recognized by perceptual psychology, since the study of perception was the focus of early psychology and the lack of a constant relation of perception to the objective stimulus became apparent.

The phenomenal field is the universe, including the individual himself, as it is perceived and experienced by him. It consists not of the so-called "reality," but of the world as it appears to him, as he perceives it. He can only know the world through his perceptions, and there is no reality for the individual other than what constitutes his perceptual or phenomenal field. "To each individual, his phenomenal field *is* reality; it is the only reality he can know" (Combs & Snygg, 1959, p. 21). The perceptual field of the individual is influenced by his needs and beliefs. "What is perceived is not what exists, but what one believes exists, . . . what we have learned to perceive as a result of our past opportunities or experiences" (Combs & Snygg, 1959, pp. 84, 85).

Perceptions are often referred to as accurate, true, or veridical or as inaccurate, wrong, or distorted. It is probably better not to think of perceptions in these terms, since they involve an evaluation from an external frame of reference. All perceptions, from the point of view of the perceiver, are accurate and true, since there is no other experience, at the time of perceiving, with which they may be compared and evaluated. A perception may not agree with the perceptions of others under the same conditions, or with the perception of the same individual at another time or from another vantage point. All perceptions are thus true or accurate, as perceptions. In the case of so-called illusion, such as the Ames demonstrations, the illusion is á true perception. What is in error, what is wrong, is the inference from a perception regarding the nature of the stimulus. What is perceived, from one angle, as a chair, is found not to have the qualities of a chair from another angle and is not perceived as a chair from the changed position. Thus, inferences regarding the stimuli may be changed, or corrected, on further experience with a stimulus. The same point of view may be taken with regard to what have been called distorted perceptions resulting from the needs of the perceiver (Combs & Snygg, 1959, pp. 154-155). It is not the perceptions that are distorted—they are experienced as clear and unambiguous. It is the stimuli which are distorted.

3. *The individual can act only on the basis of his perceptions, his phenomenal field.* As Combs and Snygg state it, "All behavior, without exception, is completely determined by, and pertinent to, the perceptual field of the behaving organism" (1959, p. 20). Appearances may be deceiving, but we act on them, nevertheless. We can act on nothing else, of course. "People can behave only in terms of what seems to them to be so" (Combs & Snygg, 1959, p. 5).

Some confusion has arisen because of a lack of understanding of the nature of the phenomenal field. Two problems in particular may be mentioned.

a. Combs and Snygg state that the perceptual field is "each individual's personal and unique field of awareness" (1959, p. 20). This word *awareness* has been equated with consciousness by some, and the phenomenological approach criticized for neglecting unconscious motivation (Smith, 1950). The concept of unconscious motivation cannot be dealt with here, other than to say that both the concept of the unconscious and of motivation are so fuzzy that when combined it is doubtful that the resulting construct has any real meaning or value. But the point to be made is that awareness is a matter of degree. As Combs & Snygg point out, "Although the perceptual field includes all the universe of which we are aware, we are not aware of all parts with the same degree of clarity at any moment" (1959, p. 27). Much of the field is ground, rather than figure, in Gestalt terminology. But what is in the ground is not unconscious. The individual may not be able to label or to report all the elements of his perceptual field, but unreportability is not to be equated with the unconscious. (See Phillips, 1956, Chapter 3, for a consideration of this problem.)

b. A second problem has arisen because of the apparent ahistorical nature of phenomenology. If all behavior is determined by the perceptual field at the moment of action, then are not we leaving out of consideration the important historical determinants of behavior? The answer to this is relatively simple. Snygg and Combs (1950) reply that "certainly the events of an individual's life affect his behavior. But it is important for us to recognize that it is the perceptions of these events and not the events themselves which are the *immediate* causes of behavior." Earlier events are part of the phenomenal field; as Lewin (1943) puts it: "The behaver's field at any given instant

contains also the views of the individual about his past and future.
... The psychological past and the psychological future are simul-
taneous parts of the psychological field existing at a given time." It
must also be recognized that it is not the event as it occurred objectively, nor even the individual's perception of it as it occurred at the
time, but his present perception of it which is a determinant of behavior. This fact perhaps explains the lack of a strong relationship
between early significant or presumably traumatic events and later
behavior, and suggests a phenomenological approach to the study of
the relation of childhood events to later behavior.

4. *The phenomenal field is an inference, and thus a hypothetical
construct.* It is an inference of the subject as well as of the observer.
It is not open to direct observation. Inferences concerning the phenomenological fields of individuals may be developed in several ways.

a. The phenomenal field may be inferred from the observation of
behavior. While this is an objective method, it is limited, and inferences can be dangerous. Sufficient observation may not be possible,
the observer may project himself into the situation, and his inferences may be interpretations which force behavior to fit a preconceived theory or system of behavior analysis.

b. The individual may be asked to report on his phenomenal field.
The ability of the human subject to verbalize his perceptions offers
us an approach to his phenomenal field. However, there are limitations. First, the subject may not wish to communicate certain aspects
of his experience or perceptions. Second, he may not be able to report accurately, because of the lack of clarity and low awareness
level of much of the field. Third, the conscious concentration upon
the field changes the field. While attention to the field may crystal-
lize something for the first time, and bring into clearer focus or
awareness parts of the field that were at a lower level of awareness,
the field then changes and further report is influenced by the
changed field. Fourth, some aspects of the field may not be capable
of being expressed in words or may not be represented adequately by
verbalizations.

c. The phenomenal field may be studied by means of tests and
inventories. The usefulness of this approach is limited, however, by
the lack of data upon which to make inferences regarding the perceptual field. Tests and inventories have been studied almost entirely in
terms of empirical relationships to external behavior, or, in the case of
some projective techniques, external evidence of internal experience

or hypothesized dynamic characteristics. A technique such as the Rorschach might be useful in understanding the phenomenal fields of individuals if we knew how to assess the meanings of the stimuli to the individual or convert the responses into information relevant to the subjects' perceptual fields. It is my hypothesis that insofar as the Rorschach is useful it is a result of its use in this way, and the generally negative results of its use are related to the fact that it is not usually employed in this manner.

d. Perhaps the most useful approach to inferring the phenomenal field of another is the use of the free, unstructured interview. The free interview method is less likely to impose the investigator's structure on the subject's field. It also minimizes some of the disadvantage of the self-report, in that the subject's attention or concentration is less consciously directed at analysis of the field. In other words the report may be more clearly descriptive rather than interpretive. This approach leads us to a basic distinction between the so-called objective and the phenomenological approach to the study of behavior.

5. *Phenomenology, as should be apparent by now, takes the internal frame of reference rather than the external frame of reference in its study of behavior.* As Snygg (1941) points out, this is similar to the commonsense approach, when an observer, in attempting to understand "Why did he do that?" asks "Under what circumstances would I have done that?" This approach has been resisted, both because it is seen as subjective, and perhaps too close to common sense. The approach, however, is useful with animals as well as humans. Koehler (1931) pointed out long ago the common error of animal psychologists of structuring the test situation in terms of their own perceptual and conceptual field rather than in terms of the rat's. Tolman once said (1938), in response to a question or charge of anthropomorphism, that he would "go ahead imagining how, if I were a rat, I would behave" because it gave him insight and understanding of his results. Snygg (see references in Snygg, 1941) has demonstrated the fruitfulness of this approach in developing hypotheses, which were confirmed, regarding the perceptual behavior of rats.

In using the internal frame of reference the investigator attempts to place himself, insofar as possible, in the subject's place in order to view the world and the subject as the subject does. This is the approach to the unstructured interview suggested above for the investigation of another person's phenomenal field. The investigator avoids as much as possible the influence of his own phenomenal field on the subject's report by refraining from structuring, probing, or direct questioning or from interpreting or evaluating the productions of the subject.

6. *Since the phenomenal field of the individual determines his behavior, prediction for the individual becomes possible when one knows the behaver's phenomenal field, which is then projected into the future field.* Understanding of the inferred future field makes possible the prediction of future behavior. Such predictions for an individual should be more accurate than predictions based upon group characteristics and memberships. The process is complicated, not only by the difficulty of inferring the present field, but because some aspects of the future field, which will be affected by external conditions, cannot be known. Nevertheless, such an approach to prediction is promising. It is similar to the proposals of the Pepinskys (1954), Koester (1954), Parker (1958), McArthur (1954), and Soskin (1959) that suggest the development of a hypothetical model of an individual. The application of this method, as in the studies by McArthur and Parker, have not been successful, however. These investigators suggest that the counselors were too hasty and premature in building their models of the clients. Another more important reason for the lack of success might be the failure to build the model on the basis of the phenomenal field of the subject.

7. We finally come to the matter of the self and the self-concept. *The self is part of the individual's phenomenal field.* It includes all the perceptions and conceptions he has about himself, his attitudes and beliefs about himself. Whether there is a real self apart from the perceptual or phenomenal self is a hypothetical or philosophical question. The phenomenal self is the real self in terms of the individual's behavior. The perceptions which others have of an individual's self may influence the phenomenal self. But the perceptions of others, even though in agreement, are still phenomenal and do not necessarily constitute any "real" self.

The phenomenal self is a most significant part of the phenomenal field since it is the central or pivotal part of the field, about which perceptions are organized: it is the frame of reference for the individual. "All perceptions . . . derive their meaning from their relation to the phenomenal self" (Combs & Snygg, 1959, p. 131). "What a person thinks and how he behaves are largely determined by the concepts he holds about himself and his abilities" (Combs & Snygg,

1959, p. 122). Combs and Snygg (1959, pp. 126-127) distinguish between the phenomenal self and the self-concept, the latter being defined as "those perceptions about self which seem most vital or important to the individual himself." However, the difficulty of defining and applying criteria to make this differentiation would seem to give it little usefulness. It is no doubt true that some perceptions about the self are more central and vital than others, but it is doubtful that there is any dividing line that can be drawn between these and other less vital self-perceptions. We shall therefore make no distinction between the phenomenal self and the self-concept.

Since the self-concept is the crucial point about which the phenomenal field is organized, its importance in understanding the field and making inferences about it for predictive purposes is apparent. The centrality of the self in phenomenological psychology is indicated in the postulate that the single motive for behavior is the preservation and enhancement of the phenomenal self.

8. We have indicated that since perceptions, particularly the perceptions of the self, determine behavior, in order to change behavior we must first change perceptions. What are the conditions under which perceptions change? *Essentially, perceptions change under those conditions that have relevance to the basic need for the preservation and enhancement of the self.* Conditions that are not relevant to this need are not perceived. It appears then, that the first condition for perceptual change is an experience which is relevant to the self or self-concept. But if the experience, even though relevant, is consistent with or reinforces the self-concept, it seems clear that change is not likely to occur. To lead to change, the experience must be inconsistent with the existing self-perception, raise a question, or pose a problem. Since the existing self-concept is the object of the need for preservation, it is apparent that it is resistant to change, and that experiences that are inconsistent with the self-concept may not enter into or become the figure in the perceptual field. The so-called mechanisms of defense, the misinterpretation of stimuli or experiences, the failure to perceive, which is represented by tunnel vision, and the denial of the experience are ways in which the self resists perceiving experiences that are inconsistent with the self-concept. It would thus appear that the less important or more peripheral aspects of the self will change more readily than the central core.

This reaction of the organism to preserve its perceptual field, particularly the phenomenal self, is the characteristic reaction to threat.

It would seem to be apparent, then, that an individual under threat does not easily change his perceptions, but instead becomes resistant to change. Stimuli or experiences that are perceived as threatening tend to be relegated to the ground rather than being focused upon a figure. Now this does not mean that threat does not change behavior —it is obvious that threat results in withdrawal, resistance, aggression, or other kinds of obstructing behavior. It may also result in acquiescence, submission, and so forth. These are all the result of changes in perception of the individual, and the recognition of the threat, leading to attempts to cope with it by capitulation if this is felt to be necessary or desirable for the preservation or enhancement of the self. Thus, behavior, and perceptions, can be influenced and changed by threat, or by other forms of manipulation. The question is raised as to whether this is desirable, from an ethical and moral standpoint, and, even though the goal of the manipulator is claimed to be for the good of the person manipulated or influenced, whether the ends justify the means, or even whether the ends are acceptable under any circumstances, since they are imposed from the outside and thus deny the individual freedom of choice and independence of action. Thus, if voluntary changes of behavior are desired, behavior which is responsible and independent, it would appear that threat should be avoided. Combs and Snygg (1959, pp. 163-196) suggest that ". . . other things being equal, change in the self is most likely to occur in situations which do not force the individual to self defense."

It appears, then, that for the phenomenal field to change, there must be a clear experience that is relevant to but inconsistent with the existing field, yet not highly threatening to the self.

In Summary

This paper has attempted to present the nature of phenomenological psychology. While this approach to human behavior begins with a commonsense level, it goes beyond this to an analysis of the nature and conditions of behavior and its changes. The central nature of perception in behavior leads to the study of perception in all its aspects, including the perception of the self as the point about which the phenomenal field is organized.

There is evidence that psychology is turning to the study of experience, and to the phenomenological method. Koch, the editor of the monumental *Psychology: A Study of Science,* indicates the trend as follows: "Behavioral epistemology is under stress; behaviorism is on the defensive, while neobehaviorism enfolds itself in a womb of its own manufacture. There is a strongly increased interest in perception and central process even on the part of the S-R theorists; in fact a tendency for the central area of psychological interest to shift from learning to perception. There is a marked, if as yet unfocused, position on the part of *even* fundamental psychologists to read human phenomena and to readmit questions having experient erence" (Koch, 1961). In other words, psychology is b psychological, and is returning to a study of experience in its psy logical aspects, after a half century of wandering in search of the objectivity of physics on the one hand, and the subjectivity of depth psychology on the other. From the extremes of the empty organism of the behaviorists and the organism seething with unconscious desires and motives of the depth psychologists, we are striking the happy medium of the experiencing organism interacting with and being shaped by and shaping its environment. This approach promises to lead to a fruitful era in the understanding of human behavior.

References

Bakan, D. A reconsideration of the problem of introspection. *Psychological Bulletin*, 1954, *51*, 105-118.

Boring, E. G. A history of introspection. *Psychological Bulletin*, 1953, *50*, 169-189.

Combs, A. W., & Snygg, D. *Individual behavior*. Rev. ed. New York: Harper, 1959.

English, H. B., & English, Ava C. *A comprehensive dictionary of psychological and psychoanalytical terms*. New York: Longmans, Green, 1958.

Gibson, J. J. Theories of perception. In Dennis, W. (Ed.), *Current trends in psychological theory*. Pittsburgh: University of Pittsburg Press, 1951.

Gombrich, E. H. *Art and illusion. A study in the psychology of pictorial representation*. New York: Pantheon Books, 1960.

Hanson, N. R. *Patterns of discovery: An inquiry into the conceptual foundations of science*. New York: Cambridge University Press, 1958.

Jessor, R. Phenomenological personality theories and the data language of psychology. *Psychological Review*, 1956, *63*, 173-180. Also in Kuenzli, A. E. (Ed.), *The phenomenological problem*. New York: Harper, 1959, pp. 280-294.

Koch, S. Psychological science versus the science-humanism antinomy: Intimations of a significant science of man. *American Psychologist*, 1961, *16*, 629-639.

Koehler, W. *The mentality of apes*. London: Kegan Paul, Trench, Trubner and Co., 1931.

Koester, G. A. A study of the diagnostic process. *Educational and Psychological Measurement*, 1954, 473-486.

Lewin K. Defining the "field at a given time." *Psychological Review*, 1943, *50*, 292-310.

McArthur, C. Analyzing the clinical process. *Journal of Counseling Psychology*, 1954, *1*, 203-208.

Murphy, G., Murphy, Lois B., & Newcomb, T. M. *Experimental social psychology.* Rev. ed. New York: Harper, 1957.

Parker, C. A. As a clinician thinks ... *Journal of Counseling Psychology*, 1958, *5*, 253-261.

Patterson, C. H. The self in recent Rogerian theory. *Journal of Individual Psychology*, 1961, *17*, 5-11.

Pepinsky, H. B., & Pepinsky, Pauline. *Counseling: Theory and practice.* New York: Ronald, 1954.

Phillips, E. L. *Psychotherapy: A modern theory and practice.* Englewood Cliffs, N.J.: Prentice-Hall, 1956.

Smith, M. B. The phenomenological approach in personality theory: Some critical remarks. *Journal of Abnormal and Social Psychology*, 1950, *45*, 510-522. Also in Kuenzli, A. E. (Ed.), *The phenomenological problem.* New York: Harper, 1959. Pp. 253-267.

Snygg, D. The need for a phenomenological system of psychology. *Psychological Review*, 1941, *48*, 404-424. Also in Kuenzli, A. E. (Ed.), *The phenomenological problem.* New York: Harper, 1959. Pp. 3-30.

Snygg, D. Review of Kilpatrick, F. P. (Ed.) Explorations in transactional psychology. *Journal of Individual Psychology*, 1961, *17*, 230.

Snygg, D., & Combs, A. W. The phenomenological approach and the problem of "unconscious" behavior: A reply to Dr. Smith. *Journal of Abnormal and Social Psychology*, 1950, *45*, 523-528. Also in Kuenzli, A. E. (Ed.), *The phenomenological problem.* New York: Harper, 1959. Pp. 268-279.

Soskin, W. F. Influence of four types of data on diagnostic conceptualizations in psychological testing. *Journal of Abnormal and Social Psychology*, 1959, *38*, 69-78.

Spiegelberg, H. *The phenomenological movement: a historical introduction.* 2 vols. The Hague: Martinus Nijhoff, 1960.

Tolman, E. C. Determiners of behavior at a choice point. *Psychological Review*, 1938, *57*, 243-259.

Wylie, Ruth C. *The self concept: A critical survey of pertinent research literature.* Lincoln: Univ. of Nebraska Press, 1961.

Additional Readings

Combs, A. W. A phenomenological approach to adjustment theory. *Journal of Abnormal and Social Psychology*, 1949, *44*, 29-35.

Ittelson, W. H. *The Ames demonstrations in perception.* Princeton, N.J.: Princeton University Press, 1952.

Jessor, R. Issues in the phenomenological approach to personality. *Journal of Individual Psychology*, 1961, *17*, 28-38.

Kuenzli, A. E. (Ed.) *The phenomenological problem.* New York: Harper, 1959.

Landsman, T. Four phenomenologies. *Journal of Individual Psychology*, 1958, *14*, 29-37.

MacLeod, R. B. The phenomenological approach to social psychology. *Psychological Review*, 1947, *54*, 193-210. Also in Kuenzli, A. E. (Ed.), *The phenomenological problem.* New York: Harper, 1959. Pp. 149-181.

Patterson, C. H. *Counseling and psychotherapy: Theory and practice.* New York: Harper, 1959.

19
Festinger's Theory of Cognitive Dissonance Applied to School Counseling

G. Roy Mayer
John J. Cody

Descriptions of human behavior in the sociological and psychological literature are abounding. Festinger's (1957) theory of cognitive dissonance has received more widespread attention from personality and social psychologists in the past ten years than any other contemporary statement about human behavior (Bem, 1967). It is a theory concerned with process. Since counseling theories are process oriented also, it seems reasonable to consider possible relationships between these two areas of study. Aspects of Festinger's (1957) theory and Rogers' (1951) theoretical approach to counseling are similar and are supported by research. However, only limited attempts have been made to generalize aspects of Festinger's (1957) theory to counseling. The purpose of this presentation is (a) to describe aspects of Festinger's theory of cognitive dissonance which appear similar to Rogers' description of incongruence, and (b) to apply the apparently complementary notions of Rogers and Festinger to the *practice* of counseling for behavioral modification through "public commitment" in the school setting.

Reprinted from *The Personnel and Guidance Journal*, 1968, *47*(3), 233-239. Copyright 1968 American Association for Counseling and Guidance. Reprinted with permission.

Dissonance and Incongruence Defined

Dissonance, according to Festinger (1957), is an uncomfortable state which an individual attempts to alleviate or change by bringing his cognitions closer together. The term "cognitive" or "cognition" simply emphasizes that the theory deals with relations among items of information. The items might relate to behavior, feelings, opinions, or things in the environment. Any two items of information which psychologically do not fit together are said to be in a dissonant relation to each other. Thus, if "a person knows various things which are not psychologically consistent with one another, he will, in a variety of ways, try to make them more consistent" (Festinger, 1957).

Rogers (1951), in a similar vein, referred to a discrepancy between the self as perceived and the actual experience of the individual as a state of incongruence. He emphasized that the source of conflict is between the self-concept and organismic experiences, and that this disturbance tends to be reflected in an unrealistic self-ideal or an incongruence between self and ideal self.

Incongruence and dissonance then seem to refer essentially to an intrapersonal mediating state during which an individual experiences contradictory perceptions either about himself or his environment. Both of the terms, incongruence and dissonance, represent an uncomfortable state of affairs for the individual, or feelings of tension and conflict, which an individual attempts to reduce or alleviate. And both suggest that the individual is, as a consequence, motivated to lessen the incompatibility of the perceptions or cognitions.

Means of Reducing Psychological Discomfort

Individuals must change if they are to mature mentally, psychosocially, and physically, and dissonance or incongruence increases the likelihood of change. A variety of ways of reducing psychological discomfort (dissonance or incongruence) apparently exist. An individual may resort to denial or distortion. To deny or distort sensory or visceral experiences with a resultant nonsymbolization into the self is likely to result in psychological maladjustment, according to Rogers (1951).

Changing the physical situation is another means which an individual might use to reduce psychological discomfort. A student might request that a teacher allow him to sit among a group of boys rather than between two girls in a specific class. By changing the situation he may find greater security. However, it seems clear that in many situations manipulation of the environment is unlikely. Due to tradition and the rigid structure of some classroom situations, the likelihood of a student changing the situation seems remote. Behavioral standards, regulated social interactions, adult controls, and mass educational practices are apparently formidable obstacles to a student who seeks to modify his immediate environment.

A third means is personal change. An individual may attempt to adapt his behavior to the requirements of a particular set of circumstances. That is, rather than denying or distorting his experiences, an individual might examine his contradictory perceptions in order to symbolize and organize his experiences into some acceptable relationship with his perceptions of self. In this sense, change is not necessarily an extrinsic force molding an individual's behavior to some predetermined value structure. Rather, change may be regarded as a modification of personal perception or behavior as a result of some intrinsic motivation to alleviate personal tension. In this structure, school counselors, behavioral modifiers, and teachers might employ relatively distinct methods to enhance the possibility of a self-directed and initiated change, which at the same time permits these practitioners to preserve their unique values relative to the rights and nature of the human organism.

Present school practice suggests that the third means, personal change, is indeed important and perhaps essential to the enhancement of a student's maturational process. Educators, including school counselors, are generally most concerned with providing conditions which will facilitate "positive" personal changes in student attitudes, knowledge, and behavior. Rogers (1951, 1954, 1957, 1959, 1961, 1962, 1964) and his colleagues (Barrett-Lennard, 1962; Gendlin, 1961, 1962; Truax, 1963, 1965a, 1965b) have massed considerable evidence to support their contention that under certain conditions, primarily involving absence of threat to the self-structure, experiences which are inconsistent with the self may be perceived and examined, and the structure of the self revised to assimilate and include such experiences.

Festinger's work has led to a number of similarly related postulates. For example, research has suggested that a person who is induced under minimal pressure, threat, or reward to listen to, to say,

or to do something that is contrary to his private opinion, the greater
is the probability that he will change his opinion and bring it in line
with what he has heard, said, or done (Janis & King, 1954; Hovland,
Campbell, & Brock, 1957; Cohen, Terry, & Jones, 1959; Festinger &
Carlsmith, 1959; Brehm & Cohen, 1962; Brock, 1962; Bem, 1965,
1967; Elms & Janis, 1965). Furthermore, the probability that he will
change his opinion and bring it in line with what he has said or done
seems increased if he is informed that his parents or other significant
human figures are aware, or will be made aware, of the newly expressed attitude or behavior (Hovland, Campbell, & Brock, 1957;
Brehm, 1959; Brehm & Cohen, 1962; Bem, 1965, 1967). Brehm's
(1959) study provides an example of this latter relationship. He obtained like-dislike ratings from eighth graders for thirty-four vegetables. Each student was given a small reward if he would eat a
vegetable he heartily disliked. Some of the subjects were then casually
informed that as part of the experiment a letter was to be sent home to
the parents indicating which vegetable that person had eaten. The
subjects were then asked to rate the thirty-four vegetables again. Both
groups gave higher ratings to the test vegetables after having eaten
them. However, the subjects whose behavior was allegedly reported to
their parents changed significantly more in their ranking of the
previously disliked vegetable than those whose behavior was not
allegedly reported to their parents.

It should be noted that student performance in the postevaluation
situation described in Brehm's (1959) study was not the actual behavior of eating foods which was initially avoided. Obtaining a reported attitude change is not a direct means of evaluating behavior in
a life situation. However, it seems reasonable to assume that change
in behavior is likely when an individual is capable of verbalizing or
reporting a change in perception, attitude, or opinion.

Implications for School Counseling

Several implications for school counseling can be drawn from the
concepts and findings discussed above. Rogers' and Festinger's positions persuasively suggest that it is important for the school counselor to realize that students should feel relatively threat-free during
counseling, and should not be forced or pressured into receiving
counseling. Caution should be exercised, however, in interpreting the
term "threat-free" as synonymous with a special set of interview

techniques or a specific counseling persuasion. The present discussion is confined to a consideration of only limited aspects of the counseling process applicable to several counseling persuasions. Furthermore, this discussion does not deny that observable behavioral change can occur under conditions of threat, pressure, or punishment. It does contend, however, that an individual is less likely to change his self-perception under threatening conditions. For example, Rogers (1951) contended that the characteristic reaction to threat, punishment, or pressure is for the individual to behave in a manner which will permit him to maintain his perceptions of his environment and self. Patterson (1965), in agreement with Rogers (1951), contended that the phenomenal self, when threatened, is typically preserved through denial or distortion, or by the person becoming acquiescent, submissive, withdrawn, resistant, aggressive, or obstructing. These latter behavioral changes or capitulations are, however, not usually considered to be very positive or permanent. Moreover, Combs and Snygg (1959) corroborated this point when they stated, "Other things being equal, change in the self is most likely to occur in situations which do not force the individual to self-defense."

Another implication for counseling is that the student or counselee is likely to experience dissonance, a prerequisite to attitudinal and behavioral change, if he has seen, heard, expressed, or initiated an attitude, opinion, or behavior contrary to his deeply held opinion or previous behavior. Counselors, then, are confronted with the major responsibility of recognizing that some individuals probably need and perhaps seek assistance in developing sufficient dissonance, or an awareness of their dissonance, in order to enhance or stimulate alternative thoughts and courses of action. Some might consider this latter point as undue intervention on the part of the counselor, especially if the dissonance is initiated or increased by the counselor. However, if man is viewed in the process of "becoming" (Rogers, 1951, 1961, 1964), dissonance or incongruence seems an essential element in an individual's maturational process, perhaps sufficiently to justify its instigation by the counselor. As a scholar is seldom satisfied with his current level of knowledge, a maturing individual seems unsatisfied with his present status of psychological development.

A dissonance-creating situation, yet one that minimizes threat, can be fostered in several ways. For example, a counselor might express verbally what the counselee is "experiencing" (Gendlin, 1961), though not necessarily verbalizing, and accept this experiencing. The counselee will have heard a statement which will create dissonance providing that which was verbalized for him by the counselor was contradictory to or inconsistent with his previously held beliefs and attitudes. By *verbalizing* and *accepting* the counselee's experiencing, the counselor also has made it easier for the counselee to express verbally and clarify his *own* experiencing (Gendlin, 1961).

The counselor should also be able to provide a dissonance-creating situation in a relatively threat-free counseling relationship by permitting the client the freedom to confront himself under the safety and security of the postulated "necessary and sufficient conditions" (Rogers, 1957). When the counselor is perceived by the student as being genuinely himself—one who expressed liking with no "strings attached," and who is empathic in his total behavior—the student can voice dissonance in the form of doubts and other forms of self-exploration.

To help the student perceive the counselor as being genuinely himself, the counselor might express his own experiencing as advocated by Rogers (1961, 1962, 1964) and Gendlin (1961, 1962). An expression of the counselor's experiencing could introduce an attitude, behavior, or some other item of information inconsistent with the counselee's opinion or attitude, thus creating dissonance. For example, a student may express doubt concerning the counselor's respect for him (the counselee). The counselor would attempt to communicate his understanding of this expression of concern and also express (verbally and nonverbally) his personal experiencing of high respect for the student. Thus, a dissonance-creating situation would be enhanced. Perhaps the recognition by the student that there is incongruence between his perception and that of the counselor could be the first step toward the resolution of this difference (Rogers, 1964).

Since the counseling process is usually characterized by conditions of minimal threat, the dissonance or incongruence created within the student is likely to result in a personal change congruent with the newly stated attitude (Janis & King, 1954; Hovland, Campbell, & Brock, 1957; Festinger & Carlsmith, 1959; Brock, 1962; Elms & Janis, 1965). But what if the newly expressed or performed attitude, opinion, or behavior is socially undesirable? Will the counselee change in a "negative" direction in order to reduce his dissonance? Rogers (1951) contended that in counseling, where an atmosphere of safety and acceptance prevails, the firm and defensive boundaries of the self are relaxed, and an individual is better able to evaluate *objec-tively* his contradictory perceptions and experiences. If Rogers is cor-rect, the described counseling environment appears to encourage independence of thought and expression. In such an environment the individual would seem able to evaluate the consequences of his be-havior more rationally. Thus, he would probably select or retain behavior which would avoid negative social consequences such as punishment. It would seem then that a new, negative expression or behavior would *less* likely be retained than a positive one, since the student in counseling is better able to evaluate objectively and ration-ally his contradictory perceptions in the light of environmental real-ity and social consequences. If some form of negative behavior occurs, as determined by the school, the counselor is left with an ethical decision of whether to accept this as a natural outcome and ignore it, or refer the counselee for some other form of treatment, or select some other possible alternative.

An additional finding from certain of the previously mentioned studies (Hovland, Campbell, & Brock, 1957; Brehm, 1959; Bem, 1965, 1967) seems to have important implications related to counsel-ing. The results of the studies suggest that intrapersonal change would be facilitated if the counselee were to inform his important significant others (teachers, parents, and possibly peers) as to the outcomes or decisions he arrived at during the counseling process. This change would likely result, provided he was not forced to do so (Brehm & Cohen, 1962) and he usually tells them the truth (Bem, 1965). If he did not usually tell his significant others the truth, his statements to them concerning his decisions arrived at in the counsel-ing relationship would not likely result in an attitudinal or behavioral change (Bem, 1965). Such statements would not be meaningful or dissonance-creating (Bem, 1965, 1967). Furthermore, as indicated earlier, the counselee should not be forced or pressured into behaving in a manner against his will. Thus, he should not be pressured into informing others of his decisions. Providing, then, that the assump-tions of truthfulness and minimal pressure are met, the activity of informing significant others (teachers, parents, or peers) would seem to facilitate the counselee's self-directed change through publicly committing him to change (Hovland, Campbell, & Brock, 1957; Brehm, 1959; Bem, 1965, 1967).

Excerpts from two counseling sessions should help clarify the prac-tical application of public commitment in counseling. The first ex-

cerpt was taken from the context of the second interview with a
twelve-year-old, sixth-grade boy who achieved an IQ equivalent to
107 on the Wechsler Intelligence Scale of Children.

Student: I guess good grades are more important than I figured—before.

Counselor: You just discovered that good grades are important to you.

Student: No, I knew it all the time. I just never wanted to admit it. Because
once you admit something then you have to do it. You know if I really believe—
like religion—then you have to—like study and that stuff.

Counselor: Then doing something about getting good grades is really important to you now.

Student: I hope so, but I guess there's no way of knowing, is there? How can
you tell if I really mean it?

Counselor: Perhaps we can tell if you really mean it. Are you willing to give
yourself a test?

Student: That depends what kind of test.

Counselor: Are you willing to go either alone or with me to your teacher and
your mother and tell them that you are really going to work hard and bring your
grades up?

Student: What if I don't?

Counselor: I don't know, what do you think?

Student: OK, I'll go with you.

Counselor: You want me to go with you?

Student: You really think it will help?

Counselor: Do you really respect these people, your mom and teacher? Do
you really want to improve?

Student: I hope it does because I am kind of sick of having everyone think I'm
lazy.

Sometimes the student needs assistance in publicly committing
himself. In the above situation, the student and the counselor went
together to respected adults. In the example that follows, the student
(an eleven-year-old) went by himself to inform significant others of
tended action.

Student: Yeah, I gotta be a winner. I shouldn't. I gotta lose sometime. It ain't
that bad. Maybe I can live it a little. A little at first maybe and then a lot more.
Yeah, that's the way to do it. Just a little then some more.

Counselor: You don't sound sold on it.

Student: Yes I am. (Pause) I need a helper. Somebody should say stop—don't
get mad, laugh. (Pause) Uh huh, a helper, a dwarf.

Counselor: Maybe your best friend could be that dwarf.

Student: Oh Zippie ain't much, he's the same. He might help. You talk to
him, too? I can help him. He can help me. That's the way. You go get Zip.

Counselor: Zip is my friend?

Student: I don't know, he's mine.

Counselor: Maybe we . . .

Student: Yeah, I'll get him to do it. I'll tell him my idea.

Counselor: You're sure it'll help you?

Student: Huh. (Nods yes.)

Counselor: Maybe you could tell the whole group you reformed. Then you would have a lot of helpers.

Student: No, they're not—yeah—no way to do it.

Counselor: Why not kid them, you know, say in a kind of teasing way.

Student: Like—I reformed—my counselor says I got to—OK you can help that way.

Counselor: It might be worth a trial.

Student: Maybe—OK, I'll try.

This eleven-year-old managed to tell his classmates using the counselor as the "goat." He managed it, however. It seems that under some circumstances public commitment flows naturally out of the situation.

As a result of being publicly committed to change, significant others now *expect*, and are likely to reinforce, the new attitude or behavior, particularly if they perceive the new attitude or behavior as positive. Furthermore, since the client knows that important others have been told of his change, he is likely to perceive others as seeing him in this new light. If we tend to perceive ourselves and behave as we believe others perceive us, as Cooley (1902) indicated, notifying significant others of a change would seem to increase the chances of the change lasting through changing the "looking glass self" (Cooley, 1902). Bem (1967) has presented considerable evidence indicating that self-perception explains the cognitive dissonance phenomena. Perhaps, then, this explains why several of the previously mentioned studies have indicated that intrapersonal change is more likely to persist if a child's important others (teachers, peers, or parents) are told that a change in attitudes or behavior, which is contrary to the child's previous attitudes or behavior, has taken place.

Conclusion

Counseling students within the school seems to offer an excellent environment in which the complementary notions of "dissonance" and "incongruence" and the concept of "public commitment" might be employed with little difficulty. The reader should be cautioned, however, that the counselor activity of publicly committing students must be viewed as suggestive. Its particular value or the particular circumstances under which it may be of value (i.e., when and when not to employ it) has not, as yet, been experimentally demonstrated in the school setting. For this reason, some of the conclusions reached must be viewed (a) as tentative and suggestive of the kinds of school counselor activities which may increase the counselor's effectiveness in facilitating change, but (b) in need of systematic and detailed research.

References

Barrett-Lennard, G. T. Dimensions of therapist response as causal factors in therapeutic change. *Psychological Monographs*, 1962, 76, Whole No. 562.

Bem, D. J. An experimental analysis of self-persuasion. *Journal of Experimental Social Psychology*, 1965, 1, 199-218.

Bem, D. J. Self-perception: An alternative interpretation of cognitive dissonance phenomena. *Psychological Review*, 1967, 74, 183-200.

Brehm, J. W. Increasing cognitive dissonance by a *fait accompli*. *Journal of Abnormal Social Psychology*, 1959, 58, 379-382.

Brehm, J. W., & Cohen, A. R. *Explorations in cognitive dissonance*. New York: John Wiley, 1962.

Brock, T. C., & Blackwood, J. E. Dissonance reduction, social comparison and modification of others' opinions. *Journal of Abnormal Social Psychology*, 1962, 65, 319-324.

Cohen, A. R., Terry, H. I., & Jones, C. B. Attitudinal effects of choice in exposure to counterpropaganda. *Journal of Abnormal Social Psychology*, 1959, 58, 388-391.

Combs, A. W., & Snygg, D. *Individual behavior: A perceptual approach to behavior*. (Rev. ed.) New York: Harper, 1959.

Cooley, C. H. *Human nature and the social order*. New York: Scribner, 1902.

Elms, A. C., & Janis, I. L. Counternorm attitudes induced by consonant versus dissonant role playing. *Journal of Experimental Research on Personality*, 1965, 1, 50-60.

Festinger, L. A. *A theory of cognitive dissonance*. Evanston, Ill.: Row, Peterson, 1957.

Festinger, L., & Carlsmith, J. M. Cognitive consequences of forced compliance. *Journal of Abnormal Social Psychology*, 1959, 58, 203-210.

Gendlin, E. T. Experiencing: a variable in the process of therapeutic change. *American Journal of Psychotherapy*, 1961, 15, 233-245.

Gendlin, E. T. Experiencing: A variable in the process of therapeutic change. *American Journal of Psychotherapy*, 1961, 15, 233-245.

Hovland, C. I., Campbell, E. H., & Brock, T. The effects of "commitment" on opinion change following communications. In Hovland, C. I. et al. (Eds.), *The order of presentation in persuasion*. New Haven, Conn.: Yale University Press, 1957.

Janis, I. L., & King, B. T. The influence of role-playing on opinion-change. *Journal of Abnormal Social Psychology*, 1954, 49, 211-218.

Patterson, C. H. Phenomenological psychology. *Personnel and Guidance Journal*, 1965, 43, 997-1005.

Rogers, C. R. *Client-centered therapy.* Boston: Houghton Mifflin, 1951.

Rogers, C. R., & Dymond, R. F. (Eds.) *Psychotherapy and personality change.* Chicago: University of Chicago Press, 1954.

Rogers, C. R. The necessary and sufficient conditions of therapeutic personality change. *Journal of Consulting Psychology,* 1957, *21,* 95-103.

Rogers, C. R. A theory of therapy, personality and interpersonal relationships as developed in the client-centered framework. In Koch, S. (Ed.), *Psychology: A study of a science,* Vol. 3. New York: McGraw-Hill, 1959. Pp. 184-256.

Rogers, C. R. *On becoming a person.* Boston: Houghton Mifflin, 1961.

Rogers, C. R. The interpersonal relationships: The core of guidance. *Harvard Educational Review,* 1962, *32,* 416-429.

Rogers, C. R. Client-centered therapy. In Arieti, S. (Ed.), *American handbook of psychiatry.* New York: Basic Books, 1964.

Truax, C. B. Effective ingredients in psychotherapy: An approach to unraveling the patient-therapist interaction. *Journal of Counseling Psychology,* 1963 *10,* 256-263.

Truax, C. B., & Carkhuff, R. R. Client and therapist transparency in the psychotherapeutic encounter. *Journal of Counseling Psychology,* 1965, *12,* 3-9 (*a*).

Truax, C. B., & Carkhuff, R. R. Experimental manipulation of therapeutic conditions. *Journal of Consulting Psychology,* 1965(*b*), *29,* 119-124.

20

Client-centered Therapy and the Involuntary Client

Ernst G. Beier

It is generally recognized that the most favorable condition for successful psychotherapy exists when the client himself feels ready to seek help for his problems. Rogers (1942) lists the client's wish for help as one of the "most significant steps in therapy." Fenichel (1945) states "the method of psychoanalysis is based on the cooperation of a reasonable ego." Freud's "basic rule" certainly can be followed only by an analysand who desires to be helped by analysis.

However, there is increasing evidence that therapists of all orientations have been called upon to make their services available to clients who do not seek their assistance. We need only to think of the efforts of some workers to give psychotherapeutic treatment to juvenile delinquents (Gerstenlauer, 1950), to prisoners (Powelson & Bendix, 1951), to court referrals (Guttmacher, 1950), to employees (Cantow et. al., 1951), to students referred by deans' offices, and last but not least, to children who, after all, rarely come to the clinic of their own free will.

It is the intent of this paper to discuss methods available to the therapist to assist the "involuntary" client—the client who does not make the decision for therapeutic help himself—to make appropriate

Reprinted from *Journal of Consulting Psychology*, 1952, *16*, pp. 332-337. Copyright 1952 by the American Psychological Association.

use of the therapeutic hour. It should be understood from the outset that assisting an involuntary client toward "therapy-readiness" can never mean that the therapist is attempting to make a client out of a nonclient. Rather, the therapist can hope to work with an "unready client" only if he deals with a *client* in the first place, that is, an individual who engages in maladaptive behavior and who has some wish to free himself of such behavior. An involuntary client, then, would be an individual in whom resistance toward giving up symptoms and substitute gratifications is greater than his desire for help. With an involuntary client, the therapist must still attempt to support the client's own motivation for treatment.

The phase of the psychological contact which deals with supporting the client's own readiness for therapeutic help shall be called here the "pretherapeutic phase." In clinical experience, various types of pretherapeutic phases seem to be recognized. As yet, no information is available to indicate that one approach is more successful than another. It is likely that none of the approaches practiced can be "successful" per se, but that each approach can achieve its maximum gain in dealing with specific syndrome-constellations. Accordingly, in the following presentation, we are not aiming at finding a panacea. All we wish is to present a few incidents with involuntary clients, follow them through to success or failure (does the client become ready to seek help on his own?), and discuss their implications, perhaps with a hint here and there concerning how this problem can be investigated more properly (Grant & Grant, 1950). We will, however, present the incidents in some order, being guided in this respect by our recognition of some types of "pretherapeutic" approaches which can easily be distinguished.

In our experience, counselors who are confronted with the involuntary client generally deal with him in one of the following ways:

A. They do not accept him, but "wait him out," until he is ready to seek help on his own.[1]

B. They accept him and actively engage in resistance reflections.

C. They accept him and discuss with him in an "above-board" fashion the fact that he is considered a client and the ways he can go about helping himself (anxiety-arousal).

Below we will present incidents and discussions relative to each of these major approaches for dealing with the involuntary client.

A. *The counselor does not accept the involuntary client but decides to "wait him out" until he is ready to seek help on his own*

Incidents:

1. Billy, aged seven, was referred to the clinic because of aggressive behavior. His parents brought Billy to the clinic against his will and he refused to follow the play therapist to the playroom. The worker accepted Billy's refusal and permitted him to stay downstairs in the waiting room. The parents, themselves engaged in a counseling hour, were given to understand that it was felt desirable for Billy to make his own decision and they accepted this. For the second session, Billy stayed for only ten minutes and left again. In the third session, Billy stated that he really liked to come, and stayed for the whole hour. At this time the parents reported that even after so few contacts Billy's behavior had changed markedly. To what extent this change was due to parent counseling was not clear but the worker felt that Billy's early freedom of choice had much to do with it.

2. Johnny, a withdrawn child, aged seven, did not want to enter the playroom. He was given free choice to leave. The mother, in a counseling session, was informed as to the purpose of the free choice for Johnny. After three meetings, during which Johnny never entered the playroom, the mother decided to leave. She stated that Johnny was too immature to make such a decision. The workers felt that the mother would have given the clinic more time if Johnny had been *taken* to the playroom. She felt that by offering Johnny a free choice, he was presented with an unnecessary, and at this time insurmountable, problem.

3. Brown, a student, referred by the dean's office because he "literally fell asleep in class," protested during the first hour that he had no problems and did not wish to come to the clinic. The therapist structured to him that he did not have to come, even though the dean's office had sent him. Brown, first making certain that he had understood correctly, almost instantaneously began to make use of the hour.

4. Smith, a young woman, was referred to the clinic by the dean's office for "emotional rehabilitation." Smith felt that she did not want to come to a psychological clinic. She was given free choice in the matter of entering into a counseling relationship and decided to leave. After two months the report came to the clinic that Smith had had a nervous breakdown and had left school.

5. An athletic team was requested by the administration to report to the psychologist for the purpose of helping with the team's *esprit de corps*. The members of the team, deeply resentful of their coaches, transferred this resentment toward the psychologist and made an agreement that none of them would talk. The psychologist structured to them at their first session that they *did* have to be present but *did not* have to talk. As was hoped, a long discussion ensued which was directed toward their relationship with their coaches. The very permission "not to talk" had effected in the team a feeling that the psychologist was on their side.

6. A student had to enter a counseling relationship by court order. He sat through twelve silent hours with the therapist. The therapist had structured to

him that he did not have to talk and the client accepted this at face value. Reflections of silence were recognized by the client but not utilized. From the diagnostic record, severe emotional disturbances were indicated, and the worker felt by the end of the time that no gains had been made, that the silence had been a sign of defiance. Follow-up information supported this diagnosis and the worker's opinion.

Discussion. In all these incidents, the therapist's intent was to assist the involuntary client in his motivation toward therapy and growth. Following the thinking of client-centered theory, the therapist communicates to the client from the start that he respects the integrity of his client, that he does not identify with the referral agency, and that he has faith and confidence in the client's ability to be a person and to make his own decisions. The quickly achieved "therapy-readiness" in Cases 1, 3, and 5 supports the therapist's decision to offer free choice to the involuntary client from the start. The clients clearly benefited from this acceptance and seemed to utilize it well.

An analysis of Cases 2, 4, and 6, however, indicates that the same approach—with different clients—may fail. Here, too, the therapist tried to communicate his acceptance, but the clients, particularly 2 and 4, were not ready to sense permissiveness or acceptance. Throughout their life experience they had possibly never been asked to make a major decision by themselves, and now they were suddenly presented with this opportunity. They were not ready, not free enough emotionally, to make this decision objectively. Perhaps these two clients may even have been burdened by this choice. They were confronted with an additional difficult problem. The therapist's communication, "you alone can decide whether or not you need me," might have been easily misunderstood by them as another rejection. They had never had the opportunity to get to know the therapist and might have misinterpreted his statement as one of indifference. Case 6, the "forced" involuntary client, illustrates very neatly how the client persisted in thinking of the therapist in defiance. The therapist had accepted the court referral because of pressure ("you take him, or off he goes"), but he had given the boy free choice to use the hour as he wished. Apparently, the boy was so preoccupied with the idea that he was forced into this situation that he never could sense the therapist's acceptance. There were indications that he perceived permissiveness as hypocrisy.

Misunderstanding, misinterpretation, and the possible lack of readiness to admit and sense permissiveness are hindrances in making this pretherapeutic phase effective with some involuntary clients. It seems to be effective with clients of a certain maturity, but fails to work where emotional factors are in the way. The obvious questions that one would have to investigate more closely would be: What are these emotional factors that prevent some clients from being effectively reached? What are the behavioral correlates? Which cues can the therapist take into account to determine whether or not he should give free choice to a client without taking the risk of losing him altogether (Case 4)? Are other, more adequate methods available?

It should be carefully noted that we are speaking of approaches to therapy and not of the basic attitudes of the counselor. The respect for the integrity of the client and the acceptance of the client are not intended to be placed in doubt as basic requirements. When we speak of various approaches to helping motivate the involuntary client, we mean ways of responding to very real needs of the client.

B. *The counselor accepts the involuntary client and engages in resistance reflections*

Incidents:

1. The mother of a young child, who, at an earlier contact, had refused to enter into a counseling relationship, was asked to "give it a chance." The staff had decided, in this case, not to take the child (aged three) unless the mother would also accept counseling for herself. The mother reluctantly agreed. She stated in her first session that she really had no problem and that she did not know what she could discuss. The therapist reflected her anger about being pushed into the counseling situation. He also commented during the hour on other manifestations of resistance, her embarrassment (perpetual laughing), her ambivalence (twice leaving the room), her difficulty in starting (silences, laughing, stating that she was talking in circles), and finally her very real wish to obtain help herself (although not based on *expressed* communication). What seems here to have been a merciless onslaught on the part of the therapist was understood by the client as very deep concern for her, as supported by the client's own "testimonial" after the pretherapeutic phase had long since passed into a therapeutic one: "For the first time in my life (during the first hour), I felt that somebody was concerned with *my* troubles." The therapist felt that without his very real effort to communicate understanding to the client, the client would have maintained her feeling that nobody could be interested in her feelings and would have stayed out of the relationship. It should be noted that considerable dependency had been established between the therapist and the client which had to be worked through in later contacts.

2. Another involuntary client, a young woman, came to the clinic and told the therapist that her husband had sent her because she was "upset too easily." She

expressed some resentment toward her husband's behavior, particularly that he had not come with her. She stated that she did not know what to talk about and thought that her husband certainly would not want her "to give away secrets." She was seen for six one-hour sessions, in which she either kept silent or discussed her bus trip to the clinic. In staff discussion, she was seen as an involuntary client who was badly in need of help and who was unable to break through her feelings of resistance. In the seventh hour, the therapist, in order to help her to feel more deeply understood and to establish a more therapeutic relationship, reflected to her a feeling that was implicit in many of her previous statements. She had never directly expressed the feeling, of which she was either unaware or could not yet bring herself to communicate, namely, hostility toward her husband. She felt her husband seemed to hold her responsible for all difficulties in the family. A statement to that effect, however, although cautiously worded, did not at all assist her towards a deeper relationship, but increased her resistance to the point where she had good reason to break the contact.

3. Another involuntary client, a delinquent boy of fifteen, had been accepted for therapy by court order. He had decided that he did not need us as he was not "nuts" and for two hours the boy maintained silence, a remarkable feat for a fifteen year-old. We were convinced that the boy had severe emotional problems (he had been caught prowling in a number of buildings, stealing women's dresses), and decided in staff conference to consider reflection of resistance. The therapist reflected the boy's unexpressed feeling of bewilderment in this situation, his unexpressed fear that this might not be confidential, his fear of being called "nuts," his resentment and helplessness (biting of fingernails), and the stress under which the silence placed him. Rapport was established when the therapist used four-letter words to reflect the boy's feeling of anguish. He began to feel more at ease and work proceeded on more therapeutic lines.The therapist had established himself as a person who did not identify himself with authority, and in effect the boy could feel that he was being understood.

4. A girl was sent over by the dean's office because she was unable to do her schoolwork efficiently. She claimed that she was blind in one eye, although medical examination revealed no defect. The student stated that she had no problems and accepted her blindness without any signs of anxiety. She stayed with the therapist for a number of hours which seemed most unproductive. She would say that she knew that she had to come to the clinic but that there was nothing wrong with her. After twelve contacts, a more active pretherapeutic phase was recommended by the staff. During the next few hours, the therapist reflected her unexpressed ambivalence about coming to the clinic (there was no pressure from the dean's office), her unexpressed worry about the effects of her symptom (fear of getting behind in her classes), her feeling about the therapist (fear of dependency), and her anger about the university (the dean had discussed with her suspicions of sexual promiscuity). The therapist felt that the effect of his closer participation and his communication of concern helped the girl to become more thoroughly motivated toward the counseling relationship. The student brought more intimate material for discussion and the contact lasted for some thirty-five hours. The girl left school and recent reports state that she is free from her symptoms.

5. Another involuntary client, a student who had been referred to the clinic by the student court, had four contacts during which he was clearly evasive. He would pointedly talk about the weather and related subjects. From the record, it was evident that the student was under great tension; he was also known to engage in homosexual behavior. After the fourth hour, the therapist began to participate more readily, reflecting on the meaning of the evasive comments, reflecting unexpressed feelings such as resentment over being sent in and the fear that he might reveal unpleasant material during the hour. No change in behavior on the part of the client was noted, and he came for the remaining eight hours with the very same attitude we had witnessed in the beginning. (The student court was requested not to use the clinic in this manner in the future.)

Discussion. We assume that the therapist can only help an "involuntary" client to become a motivated client if the "involuntary" client is an individual with crippling problems, and who is either unaware of them or does not wish to communicate a need for assistance. The approach utilized in the above incidents is one in which the therapist tries to assist the client toward accepting therapeutic help by reflecting unexpressed and unrecognized needs (resistance reflections) in order to communicate to the client his deep concern for him (Beier, 1951). The therapist's attempt to understand the client better than he understands himself is meant to be supportive in nature, a support needed to work through feelings of resistance.

While advantages and disadvantages of approach A are closely related to the maturity of the client (will he sense the acceptant atmosphere?), the present approach is more directly involving the activity of the counselor. The maturity of his judgment would be an important variable. The bias of the free-choice approach (A) is: "I behave toward the involuntary client as if he can help himself (and I take the risk that he can*not*)." This stands in contrast to the bias of the second approach (B): "I behave toward the involuntary client as if he needs my support (Cases 1, 3, and 4); and I take the risk that my specific support is unacceptable to him (Cases 2 and 5)." The therapist not only has decided to give support but has to decide throughout the contact where to give support. Such an attitude on the part of the therapist seems to contradict orthodox client-centered counseling, and yet the contradiction is only superficial. In the cases cited, the therapist's basic attitude has been to base the counseling on the second tenet of client-centered counseling: to present a non-threatening situation. Support was given not to establish the authority of the counselor, but to help the client to perceive the deep concern of the counselor for him and his unexpressed needs.

It seems clear to us that, with support, some clients will be reached who otherwise would leave the situation. The obvious questions which arise with such an approach would be the following: Who are the clients who would profit by such support? What sort of behavior will we have to differentiate to make a decision with confidence? At which state of his own development as a therapist is the worker ready to make "adequate" judgments with respect to the client? Answers to such questions will help us to evaluate the effectiveness of various types of pretherapeutic approaches.

C. *The counselor discusses in an "above-board" fashion the fact that the involuntary client is really a client (anxiety-arousal)*

Incidents:

1. A group of parents had been asked to participate in counseling sessions along with play therapy for their children. For seven hours these parents discussed their children's problems almost exclusively. The therapist felt that the parents were operating according to a preconceived set and that there was some need for reorientation. At the eighth hour, he started the session by considering with the parents the need for discussing one's own problems in order to understand other people's problems a little better. He put it squarely up to them to see themselves as clients.

The parents reacted in an expected way with some confusion and some silence. This phase of the contact was understood by the therapist as a time of reorientation in which the older defenses (talking about children only) no longer worked. The therapist reflected the silence and the aroused anxieties of the parents. Our records indicate that during this hour, as well as the following hours, the parents discussed their own relationships and problems to a much larger extent and the counselor felt that he had a closer relationship with the parents.

2. An involuntary client, a school teacher who had been sent to the clinic by her supervisor, discussed some personal problems of her supervisor and the effects of these problems on the faculty. Afterwards she inquired of the worker what she was to do in this hour, and the worker structured the hour to her as an opportunity during which she would be able to talk about anything she wished. He also stated something to the effect that sometimes people can be helped to become happier when they have an opportunity to talk about themselves and their problems. This statement was apparently very threatening to the teacher. She said to the counselor: "I only talk to God about my problems," and left the contact.

3. A student was referred to the clinic (and to the infirmary) by the dean's office. The student suffered from paranoid delusions and insisted that other students stuck pins into his legs. He rationalized his being sent to see a psychologist with a very neat delusionary system. He demanded that the psychologist attend to his mother who, in his own words, was "the queerest woman you have ever seen." He described certain behaviors of his mother which were clearly delusionary (sleeping with his uncle the very day that he, the student, had poisoned his

father). The student stated that he did not wish to come back until the psychologist had evaluated his mother's state of mind. The therapist, in order to motivate the student toward working through his own problems, discussed with him for some four continuous hours various aspects of the situation as the student saw them. During this phase, the therapist accepted the student's delusions but also participated with such observations as the fact that the student would be in a much more favorable position if he himself would be less tense. Although certain anxieties were aroused by the therapist, it appeared that these anxieties, when recognized, deepened the rapport. The student saw the therapist daily during the following week at the end of which he was referred to a therapist near his home (as he had to leave school), now more highly motivated toward seeking help on his own.

Discussion. The "above-board" method, telling the involuntary client that he is a client and should behave as one, is a crude method at best. It can be understood as an attempt by the therapist to support the involuntary client's own motivation toward help by arousing motivating anxiety. Such a method would seem clearly to contradict the basic tenets of client-centered therapy. And yet, in a search for appropriate ways of dealing with various clients, the therapist's active participation, his attempt to arouse motivating anxiety which will help the involuntary client to become more ready to accept therapy, may very easily have a place in special cases. Case 1, perhaps, is not a good case in question. It can be argued that the therapist had a preconceived notion as to what parents should talk about and his relationship developed more readily when the parents acquiesced. Case 3, on the other hand, seems to be more specifically suited to this approach, and therapists who have worked with schizophrenic patients may have had occasion to wonder about this problem. It is here, with special clients, that client-centered therapy will have to expand its views. Again some obvious questions come to mind: Which are the best methods to arouse just enough anxiety so that it is motivating and yet does not serve to terminate the contact (Case 2)? When is anxiety arousal the most adequate pretherapeutic procedure? How, precisely, is the therapist's challenge perceived by the client? If we have even tentative answers to some of these questions, the therapist may be in a position to differentiate his clients' needs more clearly.

Concluding Statement

It is probably true that we will never have a science of psychotherapy which takes all variables into account. Each client, and each therapist, is an individual in his own right, and not too consistent an individual at that. What we can hope for, at best, is a more thorough understanding of the therapeutic process and this by way of gathering many observations. Such observations may indicate general trends which hold true for many clients and many therapists. With regard to an evaluation of a pretherapeutic procedure designed to assist the involuntary client in becoming a motivated client, we face the very same difficulties. We will never know if a given approach was just the right one with a given client, or if another approach would have worked as well or even more effectively. We can, however, make it our practice to observe closely, to report and evaluate our observations, and, last but not least, become psychologists who ask the right questions.

Note

1. Category A actually deals with "involuntary clients" who *can* absent themselves and those who *cannot* absent themselves from the therapeutic hour. The latter, who cannot absent themselves from the hour (court referral), present an extra problem.

References

Beier, E. G. The problem of anxiety in client-centered therapy. *Journal of Consulting Psychology*, 1951, *15*, 359-362.

Cantow, L. A., Brickman, H., Edgecomb, W., & Kallen, A. A psychiatric approach to the problem of human relations in industry. *Personnel*, 1951, *27*, 431-439.

Fenichel, O. *The psychoanalytic theory of neurosis*. New York: Norton, 1945.

Gerstenlauer, C. Group therapy with institutionalized male juvenile delinquents. *American Psychologist*, 1950, *5*, 325. (Abstract)

Grant, J. D., & Grant, Marguerite Q. "Therapy readiness" as a research variable. *Journal of Consulting Psychology*, 1950, *14*, 156-157.

Guttmacher, M. S. Adult court psychiatric clinic. *American Journal of Psychiatry*, 1950, *106*, 881-888.

Powelson, H., & Bendix, R. Psychiatry in prison. *Psychiatry*, 1951, *14*, 73-86.

Rogers, C. R. *Counseling and psychotherapy*. Boston: Houghton Mifflin, 1942.

SECTION VII

Existential Counseling

Counseling is essentially a process of making-free, a humanizing of the person who has lost his freedom in sectors of his existence where he can no longer transcend his life situation by freely giving meaning to it. He behaves there more or less as a lower form of being, as a dehumanized, determined existence. It is the aim of counseling to assist the person in regaining his freedom in these areas by creating insight into the meanings he attributes to these situations, by starting the extinction of the responses which the counselee—after gaining insight—no longer likes to retain, and by the conditioning of other responses corresponding to his new free evaluation of reality.

— Adrian van Kaam

Existentialism, as a psychological school of thought, has been slow in gaining acceptance among practicing counselors and therapists. It remains today in the minds of many a mood, an attitude, a philosophy of life, rather than a systematic therapeutic procedure. It has been overlooked particularly by those professionals specializing in child and adolescent counseling. They feel it is too philosophical, too intellectual, too abstract for an immature clientele. However, this does not have to remain the case in the future. A theory of personality and theory of counseling are beginning to emerge from the philosophical predisposition of existential thought, and they can be applied to preadolescents and adolescents. Because the articles in this section

213

present a thorough exposition of existential counseling theory, only several brief points will be highlighted in this introduction.

An existential theory of personality does not consist of specifically stated assumptions about human behavior. Instead, it relies upon generally conceived notions of the nature of man and his existence. Human freedom is a central concept; however, responsibility and accountability are inherent in this notion. If people are to be free and live in a democratic community, they must be responsible and accountable for their behavior. Versatility is characteristic of existential counseling techniques. The recommended techniques vary from analytically oriented to behaviorally oriented, and the selection of specific techniques depends on the client and his or her life experiences. However, most existential therapists concur regarding the importance of the counseling relationship; this I-Thou relationship is the basis for all human understanding and growth.

Leif J. Braaten, in the first article, presents the major philosophical assumptions of existential thought. His specific insights into the implications of each assumption are particularly relevant for the practitioner.

Vontress, in the second article, states that "humans are fundamentally more alike than they are different." The practitioner will appreciate his existential perceptions of the implications of working with culturally different clients. The third reading, by Gerald Pine, relates existential theory specifically to school counseling. He discusses the role of the counselor and focuses on effective counseling attitudes and behaviors. This chapter is more concretely related to the day-to-day functioning of the counselor than are the previous two readings. Existential counseling procedures with adolescent clients are creatively demonstrated in the final article by Marilyn Bates and Clarence Johnson. They isolate six major concepts of existential thought and discuss the implications of each for the counseling process. Client and counselor verbalizations are presented to contrast possible nondirective counselor statements with appropriate existential counselor statements.

21
The Main Theories of "Existentialism" from the Viewpoint of the Psychotherapist

Leif J. Braaten

The philosophical movement loosely designated as "existentialism" has recently been received with renewed interest by serious thinkers in psychology, psychiatry, and theology. Schaffner (1959) describes this trend as follows:

... the existentialists performed a valuable service in starting to free contemporary thinkers from the shackles of philosophic, ethical, and religious systems that were keeping scientists and laymen alike from seeing man more clearly and more realistically.

Another sign of such an interest is that the American Psychological Association incorporated a symposium entitled "Existential Psychology and Psychotherapy" into its 1959 annual conference.

The writer has read a great number of published books and articles on this subject. The interested reader is referred to some of the more significant contributions(Barrett, 1958; Buber, 1955; Collins, 1952; Herberg, 1958; Kaufmann, 1956; May, Angel, & Ellenberger, 1958; Rogers, 1958; Sartre, 1957; Tillich, 1952). Nowhere, however, was there available a systematic survey of the main themes of "existentialism." The present paper is an attempt to provide such a survey and relate the themes to the clinical experience of a psychotherapist.

Reprinted from *Mental Hygiene*, 1961, *45*, pp. 10-17. Reprinted by permission.

Although the writer is fully responsible for this paper, he wishes to acknowledge the value of his dialogical encounters with Drs. Eugene Gendlin, Carl R. Rogers, John M. Shlien, and Mrs. Hellene Sarett.

Several attempts were made to abstract these main themes. The list which is presented here is the last one, and it is open for further revision. Each theme is stated in terms of a brief, freshly formulated message. Then the theme is paraphrased and related to "existentialist" writing. This section is followed by some selected comments and reactions from the viewpoint of psychotherapy.

The Main Themes of "Existentialism" and Psychotherapy

Man, You are Free; Define Yourself

Nobody has perhaps been a more vigorous advocate for the roads of freedom than Sartre (1957). He is constantly puncturing all alibis of unfreedom which man has invented, such as heredity, environment, upbringing, and the current culture. He claims that you are only what you make of yourself. In other words, man has to invent man. This is man's greatest achievement in life. Just as there are endless vistas ahead in space, there are many unexplored ways of becoming more genuinely "human." Within the psychological profession, Gardner Murphy has recently explored "human potentialities."

The experience of feeling free necessarily involves some anxiety or trembling, but this is a driving force in seeking out the new possibilities. Every new venture of the human spirit implies a certain loneliness in the process of exploring and groping into the unknown.

From the external frame of reference, the scientist believes that under certain conditions, such as the therapist's congruence in the relationship, his empathic understanding, and his unconditional positive regard, the client will display movement along particular dimensions of personality change (Rogers, 1957). On the other hand, it seems that psychotherapy would be inconceivable without some subjective experience of freedom to choose on the part of the client.

The essence of therapy is the client's movement from feeling unfree and controlled by others toward the frightening but rewarding sense of freedom to map out and choose his new personality. When he, for once, has realized that it is possible to break away from old patterns, his appetite for creative newness increases progressively. It is a challenge to the therapist to become especially sensitive to the client's struggle for a more satisfying self-definition. In so doing, the therapist must alert himself to the client's readiness for freedom which varies considerably along the therapeutic process for each client, as well as between clients.

Cultivate Your Own Individuality

Several "existentialists" have been strong individualists. Nietzsche once made this famous statement: "Be a man and do not follow me—but yourself." One is advised to develop whatever is unique and special about oneself. Only in this way can mankind show progress. Every human being is challenged to cultivate what is *special* about himself, whether this involves becoming creative with ideas or objects. We all have to find out what is particularly satisfying for ourselves.

One of the greatest individualists of all times was Kierkegaard. He wanted the following inscription on his gravestone: "That Individual." Among psychologists, Jung (1957) is convinced that the client would like to be understood in all his separateness, rather than as the average person. An experienced therapist knows that many clients are quite obsessed with a need to be understood accurately. Nothing but a full understanding will suffice.

The writer has some research evidence to the effect that an increased emphasis upon this private, inner self is positively and significantly correlated with one dimension of "success" in psychotherapy: namely, the mental health rating by the TAT-diagnostician. Heidegger calls this inner self *Eigenwelt*. According to Rollo May, et al. (1956), Freud taught us much about the average, dynamic human being; Fromm, Horney, and Sullivan enlightened us on the interpersonal aspects of the person; yet there is still much to learn about how to facilitate man's relations with his own unique self.

Live in Dialogue with Your Fellow Man

The "existentialists" believe that there are some qualities of being which can only be distinctly developed in relation to another person. In other words, you are dependent upon your fellow man for certain exceptional experiences. Buber (1955) has devoted a lifetime to spell out the characteristics of a genuine meeting of two human beings, in which each person brings about significant change in the field of the other. The proper focus to discover what is particularly human is, according to him, *between* man and man.

Such a life in dialogue requires an open awareness, and occasionally a human encounter will shake one's foundations as a person. But the recommendation is rather to make a difference in the field of your fellow man than to be ignored, even if the meeting may temporarily be disturbing for both. During a recent convocation address at the University of Chicago, Dr. Joshua Taylor made this recommendation to a new group of academicians. We were urged to take a stand in society, to participate in the community, and to let our knowledge make a real difference in our dealings with other individuals.

The psychotherapist is more challenged than many other professionals to live in dialogue with his fellow man. The very essence of therapy is a person-to-person meeting. Once the therapist has learned to appreciate the anxieties and the rewards of helping the client to develop a truer self, he is missing the experience of such a relationship when he periodically is not active in the performance of therapy. Part of this feeling is that his need to be helpful toward others is frustrated, but, more importantly, the therapist is deprived of enjoying a certain quality of emotional coexistence. He cannot *be* some important mode of himself outside a deep relationship to another human being.

This mutual dependency is even more significant from the client's point of view. The client can only develop certain human qualities, such as trust and understanding, to the extent that the therapist is able to demonstrate these qualities in action. Therefore the ambitious therapist is constantly trying to push the limits of freedom and safety within the relationship. Thus he becomes less and less limited by his own attitudes in his desire to help others.

If you are going to live successfully in dialogue with your fellow man, it is essential that you learn to recognize the true "boundaries" between yourself and the other person. We are not surprised that children often operate as if other persons—the parents, siblings, and so on—form a part of their extended self. But it is shocking to realize how difficult it is even for adults to act as if both they and others are free centers of subjectivity rather than ego-extensions to manipulate.

Through the help of therapy, the client ceases to expect specific reactions to stimuli he emits toward others. Instead, he learns to accept the more modest goal of just making some difference to his fellow men in a broader sense. The client realizes that he can only take responsibility for his part of a relationship. What the other person does with it, he can only decide. Similarly, the therapist should be judged by how well he can provide optimal growth conditions for the client. Ultimately, it is up to the client to decide whether he wants to make use of the therapeutic relationship. One implication of this principle is that the therapist should not always be held responsible if significant personality change does not take place.

Your Own Experiencing Is the Highest Authority

The "existentialists" urge you to live your own life, to become sensitive to important happenings in your own existence, particularly choices at significant crossroads. Your own experiencing is your best guide. This greatly limits what you can learn from others because they have to interpret their experience. Therefore, you cannot trust, fully, even the wisest men; they can only provide you with stimulation. You can receive their impact, but you should never forget that your own uniqueness necessarily will color your interpretations. Binswanger has much to say about the importance of discovering one's *Eigenwelt*. If this development does not take place, a person will never achieve a real sense of his own existence; he will not develop toward an authentic human being.

Within the client-centered group, nobody has been a more vigorous advocate for the "function of experiencing" than Gendlin. His thesis is that therapy is "successful" to the extent that the client is helped to become open and sensitive to his ever ongoing stream of experiencing. If a person is completely aware of his experience, he will tend to make the most intelligent and satisfying choices in life.

Rogers has also emphasized experiencing as the ultimate guide for human existence. He says: "No one else's ideas, and none of my own ideas, are as authoritative as my experience. It is to experience that I must return again and again, to discover a closer approximation to truth as it is in the process of becoming, in me." A declaration of a similar nature, which is even more meaningful to me, runs as follows: "Neither the Christian church nor the priests—neither Freud nor Rogers—neither the revelations of others nor research—can take precedence over my own direct experience."

Such an approach toward life will necessarily involve some conflict with other people. But if a person is fully open to his experience, he will consider all the relevant factors and decide when it is appropriate to yield or take a fight. One such factor will be the other person's right to be guided by *his* experience.

Be Fully Present in the Immediacy of the Moment

"Existentialism" is focused upon the individual's existence from moment to moment. The past is not so important; it is what you are *right now*. Jaspers once exclaimed: "What we are missing of full human presence!" Rollo May has pointed out that in therapy and life in general there are so-called "pregnant moments," occasions when a radical change can take place in a person's existence. Many "existentialists" show an awesome respect for the significance of certain emerging developments. Tillich (1952) has coined the word *kairos* for the moment when "eternity touches time," when some critical fulfillment can occur.

The writer found in his doctoral research that the more "successful" the client was, seen by both the therapist and the TAT-diagnostician, the more likely it was that he showed a movement toward greater emphasis upon an immediate, emotional experiencing of the self. In other words, "successful" clients tend to become more truly open to their existence *right there and then* within the therapeutic relationship. Rogers believes that the essence of therapy is that the client is experiencing such deep moments of integration of the self. These moments he considers the real "molecules of therapy."

There are critical points during the treatment process when the therapist's wisdom and skills are particularly called for, when what he *is* as a total person determines whether the client is given a chance for a spurt of growth or quits, when therapy is immensely speeded up or temporarily upset. Sometimes the client may go through such critical moments more quietly. At other times he may experience fully for the first time certain denied aspects of himself dramatically. This intensive experiencing may give the client what the psychoanalysts call "abreaction" which implies that the denied material will never any more have the same threatening character.

There Is No Truth Except in Action

The "existentialist" is disgusted with thinking which is not reflected in action. He feels that a small action is often more significant than a thousand words. Sartre argues that "existentialism" implies that you are willing to accept the full consequences of your viewpoints. There must be congruence between belief and action. There is an emphasis upon commitment: that is, to be an aware participant in society rather than merely an observer. Accordingly we find that several "existentialists" have been very concerned about the predicament of man. They have been uncompromising in their criticism of depersonalization in our mass culture.

The relevance of this message for psychotherapy is that the therapist must not only experience the proper conditions for constructive personality change within himself; he must actively communicate these attitudes to the client so that they make some perceived difference in his field. Frieda Fromm-Reichmann has eloquently stated this rule in psychotherapy: "What the patient needs is an experience, not an explanation!" It is more important what the therapist is able to *be* and *do* than what he just says. One implication of this principle is that the therapist must not try to be somebody he is not. Pretense is detrimental to good therapy. The client often senses, at some level within himself, to what extent the therapist strikes him as an authentic person. A basic requirement for progress in treatment is that the therapist is able to transparently be himself, that there is congruence between his inner awareness and his actions.

You Can Transcend Yourself in Spurts

Although modern "existentialists" acknowledge some historical roots, they believe that it is possible, even characteristic, for the authentic man to throw off the burden of the past and transcend his old self. According to their position, a person's development cannot always be accounted for by a gradual, stepwise evolution. In Sartre's "existential psychoanalysis" the therapist tries to help the client perform significant choices which will make him rise above old, unsatisfying patterns of behavior.

The transcending of oneself is naturally more characteristic late in "successful" therapy than earlier in the treatment. During the beginning of therapy, the client feels very much chained to his past; he moves around, psychologically speaking, only with the greatest efforts. But as treatment progresses, the client becomes quite excited by planning a truer, more satisfying self. He feels dissatisfied by merely repeating old "personal constructs."

The client feels less compelled to appear consistent over time. There is a keen enjoyment in experimenting with oneself. A high value is placed upon surprising oneself as well as others. It even happens that a client feels free to throw overboard a whole old set of rules and assumptions and replace them with something radically new and different.

Live Your Potentialities Creatively

When Nietzsche wrote about *Übermensch,* he had in mind a person who is creatively actualizing himself, an individual who refuses to be bound by his past, somebody who, rather, is in a continuous process of becoming. With the expression "will to power" Nietzsche was referring to the individual's power of self-fulfillment, not to his desire to dominate his fellow man. He wanted everybody to push toward his own unique potentials.

This creative approach toward oneself and different subject matters implies a certain distrust of the past as the source of understanding and inspiration for future development. For the creative person, the past holds only a small part of his attention. He is rather preoccupied with the present and the future and assumes that there are infinite areas of human endeavor yet to be explored. He takes it for granted that he can change and develop.

Toward the end of "successful" therapy the client does not feel fixated by his past conditioning, abilities, and interests. He knows that the challenge is to grow beyond himself. Areas where his potentials are best tend to be selected for further improvement. A playful spontaneity is characteristic of his behavior. He is toying with ideas and materials. New combinations are tried out. As therapy progresses, the client is groping for fresh expressions which more accurately reflect significant experiencing. He is becoming fond of his *Eigenwelt* regardless of recognition from others. He is joyfully pushing toward the frontiers of his own talents for living and self-expression.

In Choosing Yourself You Choose Man

Existentialism has often been accused of leading to moral nihilism. Such critics argue that there would be no two sets of values which would be similar in important respects when everybody is challenged to define himself. According to Sartre, this line of reasoning is unjustified because in choosing for yourself you are also choosing for mankind. When you are planning some course of action, you would always have to ask yourself: "What would our society be like if everybody did like me?" In other words, the existentialists strongly emphasize man's responsibility toward his fellow man. One of the heroes of Camus is going through agonies because he was not given a second chance to save a woman whom he saw commit suicide. An implicit assumption in this theme is a belief in the basic unity of man, a feeling that we are all faced with the same task of having to learn to live constructively with ourselves and other people.

In theories of therapy and personality, some lean toward a conception of man as basically evil, destructive, and sinful, while others think they have observed that man is rather good, sociable, and forward-moving. Freud and many of his followers seem to belong to the first group, and so do many theological thinkers on pastoral counseling. Mowrer seems to fall into the second group, emphasizing what he has called the "pleasure of consciousness," that man often finds pleasure in doing what would be constructive for all men. Rogers (1956) is certainly closer to Mowrer than Freud; he has observed that human nature is basically self-actualizing and good. As I understand him, this does not mean that Rogers denies man's freedom to choose between good and evil; rather it means that when man becomes more "fully functioning," he tends to make socially constructive choices because this tendency is part of his basic nature.

You Must Learn to Accept Certain Limits in Life

Earlier in this paper much was said about man's capacity to transcend himself creatively. This does not mean that there are no limits to self-actualization. The "existentialists" feel that contemporary man has to be reminded that he shows a little more imagination in the way he defines himself. On the other hand, the "existentialists" are certainly also very concerned about limits in our existence, especially the ultimate limit—death. In European "existentialism" the concern with death is central.

It has often been said that being in the world can only be fully grasped in relation to not being. Since the opportunity to commit suicide exists for every human being, great importance is attached to an active confirmation of living. In other words, you have to be "born again" to become an authentic person. An individual who has worked through his feelings in relation to death often achieves a new quality to his living. He becomes very concerned about making the most of his existence right here and now.

It can be argued that since death is the ultimate limit, death is the prototype of all limits. In psychotherapy very significant events are connected with limits of one kind or other. Rogers early recognized that the setting of limits for himself and the client was an integral part of constructive treatment. From the therapist's point of view there is a certain limit to how much responsibility he is willing to assume, how much time he can offer his client, and how much affection and aggression he can tolerate. It is important for the therapist to be aware of his limits at all times and behave accordingly. He must also strive to push his own limits farther.

From the client's viewpoint it is often one of his most significant achievements that he learns gracefully to accept certain limits of reality both within and outside the therapeutic relationship. Sometimes his whole emphasis, then, changes toward becoming more concerned about what he can do *within* the limits of the therapy hour, his level of intelligence, his present marriage situation, etc.

Summary and Perspectives

In this paper the writer has endeavored to discuss the main themes of "existentialism" from the viewpoint of a psychotherapist. Since no systematic survey of "existentialism" seemed feasible for our topic, an attempt was made to arrive at a fresh list of the most important "existentialist" themes. Each theme was then presented and discussed in relation to selected issues of psychotherapy.

Our tentative list of the main "existentialist" themes includes: (1) Man, you are free, define yourself; (2) Cultivate your own individuality; (3) Live in dialogue with your fellow man; (4) Your own experiencing is the highest authority; (5) Be fully present in the immediacy of the moment; (6) There is no truth except in action; (7) You can transcend yourself in spurts; (8) Live your potentialities creatively; (9) In choosing yourself, you choose man, and (10) You must learn to accept certain limits in life.

It is the conviction of the writer that the "existentialists" have an important message to communicate to modern man in general and the psychotherapist in particular. The stimulation from this movement may also open up new, fresh perspectives for the scientific investigation of psychotherapy and personality change.

References

Barrett, W. *Irrational man: A study in existential philosophy*. New York: Doubleday, 1958.

Buber, Martin. *Between man and man*. Trans. by R. G. Smith. Boston: Beacon Press, 1955.

Collins, J. *The existentialists: A critical study*. Chicago: Henry Regnery, 1952.

Herberg, Will (Ed.) *Four existentialist theologians: A reader from the works of Jacques Maritain, Nicolas Berdyaev, Martin Buber and Paul Tillich*. New York: Doubleday, 1958.

Jung, Carl G. *The undiscovered self*. Trans. by R.F.C. Hull. Boston: Little, Brown and Co., 1957.

Kaufman, W. (Ed.) *Existentialism from Dostoevsky to Sartre*. New York: Meridian Press, 1956.

May, R., Angel, E., & Ellenberger, H.F. (Eds.) *Existence: A new dimension in psychiatry and psychology*. New York: Basic Books, 1958.

Rogers, Carl R. What it means to become a person. In Moustakas, C. E. (Ed.), *The self: Explorations in personal growth*. New York: Harper and Brothers, 1956. Pp. 195-211.

Rogers, Carl R. The necessary and sufficient conditions of therapeutic personality change. *Journal of Consulting Psychology*, April 1957, *21*, 95-103.

Rogers, Carl R. A process conception of psychotherapy. *American Psychologist*, April 1958, *13*, 142-149.

Sartre, Jean Paul. *Existentialism and human emotions*. New York: The Wisdom Library, 1957.

Schaffner, B. Thoughts about therapy today. *Mental Hygiene*, July 1959, *43*, 339-350.

Tillich, Paul, *The courage to be*. New Haven, Conn.: Yale University Press, 1952.

22

Cross-cultural Counseling: An Existential Approach

Clemmont E. Vontress

During the past three decades, considerable attention has focused on problems inherent in cross-cultural counseling. In spite of numerous essays and much empirical research, counseling ethnic minorities and international sojourners remains problematic for professionals in the United States. Counselors manifest frustration by suggesting that only minorities counsel minorities, that counselors who are of the ethnically dominant group receive intensive courses in how to counsel the culturally different, that behavioral approaches be used with minorities, and other proposals. Needed urgently is a philosophical orientation that enables counselors to transcend culture.

This article proposes existentialism as a philosophy that makes it possible for counselors to bridge cultural differences. Admittedly, existentialism is a view that eludes precise definition because major contributors have been a diverse lot with widely differing perceptions of existence. Among them are Albert Camus and Ernest Hemingway,

Reprinted from *Personnel and Guidance Journal*, 1979, *58*(2), 117–121. Copyright 1979 American Association for Counseling and Development. Reprinted with permission.

often labeled nihilists; Martin Heidegger, a short-term Nazi; Paul
Tillich, Rudolf Bultmann, and Nicholai Berdyaev, theologians; Karl
Marx, political economist; Viktor Frankl, psychiatrist and father of
logotherapy; and Rollo May and Carl Rogers, American psychologists. A tenable conclusion is that an existentialist is anyone who
philosophizes, theorizes, or speculates about human existence.

I make no attempt to interpret an existentialism as posited by
various writers or to advance a set of techniques to guide counselors.
Rather, I describe a philosophical vantage point constructed to help
counselors bridge cultural differences. Binswanger's (1962, 1963)
concepts, Umwelt, Mitwelt, and Eigenwelt, are the framework for
developing the argument that helping professionals should discon-
tinue their preoccupation with analyzing cultural differences and
concentrate instead on the commonality of people. Individuals, regardless of their race, ethnic background, or culture, are more alike
than they are dissimilar; therefore, professionals espousing an approach based on Binswanger's triadic view of existence can be effective cross-cultural counselors.

Umwelt

Prerequisite to effective cross-cultural counseling is the recognition
that the human species, as all living organisms, exists in the Umwelt,
a concept that frustrates exact translation. English-language writers
have rendered the German word with expressions such as surrounding world, natural environment, or simply environment. It is the
support system for all life, the medium in which everything that is a
part of nature exists in symbiosis (Burton, 1974; Midgley, 1978).

Cross-cultural counselors should take a telescopic view of human
beings in the Umwelt. It is one in which they, from a mental,
miniaturizing distance, see people, in spite of their differing external
appearances, as members of the same species, living and moving
among a staggering organic diversity (Wilson, 1978). Individuals,
regardless of their genetic makeup, ethnic heritage, or geographical
location on earth, are in the same predicament: They confront the
same basic survival problems. Housed in a frail, soft, naked body,
humans exist in arid, frozen, rocky, fertile, and tropical environments
cluttered with a multiplicity of potentially destructive forces (Silvano,
1972). An avalanche, a drop of water, the bite of a snake; a flame of

fire, a morsel of poisoned berry—these and many other things in the environment can terminate life immediately (Midgley, 1978).

Although the Umwelt is, as Wilson (1978) indicates, home for more than a million species of animals (of which humans are but one), it is a temporary place of existence, which can be viewed as a great natural terminal, where humans are constantly arriving, interacting in the interest of survival, and departing unwillingly in different ways at different times for a common destination. Death is, in fact, the end of the world for all individuals (Macquarrie, 1972). Recognition of this fact creates existential anxiety—the apprehension that comes from the knowledge that all living things in the Umwelt die and that all humans, themselves, have appointments with death.

This view of the Umwelt is a first step in freeing counselors of an overemphasis on human differences. Members of Homo sapiens have the same biological traits (La Barre, 1972). This means that human-kind's representatives, no matter what their skin color, stature, hair texture, or native language, can interbreed: They comprise one species. They have no choice but to live in the same "house"—in Umwelt—and share the same life-support system and destiny.

Mitwelt

Counselors wishing to transcend cultural differences also need to understand Binswanger's (1962, 1963) Mitwelt, which often is translated with expressions such as the interpersonal world, the being-with world, and the world of interpersonal relations. Although the meaning of Mitwelt is difficult to impart, it suggests that individually humans are incomplete (Macquarrie, 1972). Humans are social animals. They reach out perforce to others of their species—to be with them in the world, to communicate with them, and to know them sexually; by so doing, they not only perpetuate their species, but, equally important, they validate their own existence (Buber, 1970; Frankl, 1975). Although people crave human company, they experience simultaneously a great deal of interpersonal tension as they interact to survive with the greatest pleasure and the least pain in the Umwelt (Harris, 1977; Frankl, 1967; Morris, 1969). (The concept of interpersonal tension subsumes such emotions as fear, anger, rage, hatred, guilt, pride, despair, suspicion, envy, jealousy, lust, grief, disappointment, and aggression, which Martin Gross [1978] considers common to all humans. Whether acting singly or interactively, they contribute to the general state of psychological disequilibrium characteristic of most human groups.)

The compelling need of humans to be with conspecifics is simultaneously a boon and a bane, when considering the resultant global intergroup harmony (or lack of same). It was and remains an advantage for people to live together in social units: families, clans, tribes, and nations. In so doing, they attend to survival more efficiently and economically. Hunting for and cultivating food, protecting members from outsiders, supervising and socializing the young, caring for invalids and elders, and other functions that the social group has performed are, with increasing cultural complexity and division of labor, now given over to specialists (Midgley, 1978).

Tribes and supertribes (nations) develop a variety of linguistic communities, religious beliefs, governmental systems, and other cultural components (Wright, 1969). The membership in, and allegiance to, specific groups often becomes so strong and value laden that nonmembers are perceived as ipso facto inferior. The more different the out-group is in appearance, behavior, and belief, the more inferior (physically, mentally, and morally) it is considered.

As in earlier times, groups use various symbols to voluntarily identify their members. These include, among other things, coats of arms, badges, permanent (scars and tattoos) and painted marks on the body, intentional mutilation, headgear, uniforms, flags, handshakes, and anthems. But some human beings are born with physical attributes that can be used by those not possessing them as involuntary identifying badges, as Morris (1969) indicates. A good example is black people who cannot conceal their "differentness" from other groups who equate external uniqueness with inferiority.

According to Jordan (1968), the African's badge of color made him fair game for whites who took the out-group characteristics (color, hair, non-Christianity, and strange customs) as justification for abduction, enslavement, and exploitation. Even though racism is as irrational and scientifically unfounded today as it was centuries ago, ostensibly reasonable people continue to act on the belief that those who differ from them are, in fact, innately inferior in their thought processes, in their ability to acquire skills, and, even, genetically.

In the United States today, blacks constitute a cast (Montagu, 1974). Regardless of their station in life, they cannot elude their blackness. This visible badge automatically denies them general opportunities that most whites take for granted. Indeed, racism is endemic to the society. Therefore, it infects all of society's institutions, including those of the family, the church, the school, and business.

The Family

Generally, a cast group is denied intimate equal contact with other groups (Montagu, 1974). Because the family, by virtue of its involvement in the most private and inviolate aspects of human existence—sex, nurturing, socialization, sickness, and death—is the most intimate unit in society, it is understandable that a politically and ethnically dominant group would sanction in law barriers to intercast marriage (Jordan, 1968). Public policy and attitudes concerning intimacy between blacks and whites have not relaxed much since the earliest presence of people of black African descent in America. In fact, state laws prohibiting interracial marriages were not declared unconstitutional until 1967 (Bruce & Rodman, 1973).

Although antimiscegenation statues are null and void, the caste status of blacks remains evident in the few interracial marriages (less than one-third of one percent of black marriages) in the United States (Murstein, 1973; Heer, 1974). It is also apparent in the fact that the offspring of such unions are almost always socialized as black, regardless of the Negro parent's degree of white ancestry (TenHouten, 1970). Usually the white parent in the marriage expresses concern about her (the feminine pronoun is used here, because approximately 90 percent of black-white marriages in the United States are between black males and white females) children growing up proud of their race—the black race—a fact that indicates that she is more allegiant to the prevailing racial sentiment than to genetic reality (Black, 1973). It is no surprise that children in such families often are confused about their racial identity. Socialized in contradistinction to their appearance and that of one parent, many are hostile toward one or both racial groups that their parents represent (Adams, 1973).

The Church

The Christian church falls a close second to the family as the most segregated institution in the United States. Undoubtedly, the dominant group's fear of a close contact with members of the stigmatized group—blacks—explains why only about 3 percent of Negro church-goers belong to predominantly white churches. In the main, the integrated churches are Roman Catholic and Episcopalian, ones that are highly ritualistic and formal compared to the generally informal fellowship-oriented Protestant churches (Roy, 1964).

Fellowship, a concept basic to Christianity, suggests friendly associ-ation with people of similar interests and background—a company of equals. It also suggests the brotherhood of all people, black and white, an idea debated heatedly in state and federal legislative bodies during the days of slavery (Jordan, 1968). That whites did not believe in the equality of blacks explains the existence of segregated churches in this country in the first place. That the house of God remains almost totally segregated confirms that whites still perceive blacks as their inferiors. This helps to account for Sunday morning being the most segregated part of the week, a time when blacks and whites pass each other en route to worship presumably the same God in different churches.

The School

The institution in society that has evoked the in-group's display of overt aversion to association with blacks the most has been and remains the public school. In objecting to the integration of public education, whites have articulated numerous concerns. One which is seldom expressed but always tacitly understood and feared is the socialization of young blacks and whites as equals, a situation that could result in members of the stigmatized group marrying into the dominant group (St. John, 1964).

De jure and de facto segregation has been the most offensive assault on the human dignity of blacks in this country: They are equal taxpayers, although they have hardly ever received equitable treat-ment in the schools their taxes support. After the Civil War "separate but equal" schools were established. When these were declared unconstitutional in 1954, de facto segregation rapidly replaced de jure separation of students (Low, 1962). Today, the majority of black children, even those enrolled in integrated schools, continue to receive an inferior education compared to that obtained by their white counterparts (King, Mayer, & Borders-Patterson, 1973).

One reason for their academic disadvantage is that they are made to feel like outsiders in their own schools. After twenty-five years of school integration in this country, teachers, counselors, and administrators continue to attend classes, workshops, and seminars to learn how to teach, counsel, and cope with the "culturally different," as though to suggest that blacks are so unlike whites that special expertise is required to educate them (Stein, 1971).

Employment

The cast status of Afro-Americans has been and remains evident in the employment sector. During slavery, the plantation economy of the southern United States supported two main racial groups (Franklin, 1965). One was the whites, many of whom owned blacks. The other was the African slaves, considered intellectually inferior to all whites. It is easy to understand how work came to be divided into two categories: white work, considered to demand a level of intelligence possessed only by Caucasians, and black work, which required the brute strength of slaves, who were perceived by whites as devoid of significant intellectual ability (de Saint-Mery, 1913). In general, whites found it dissonant with their self-avowed superiority to see blacks engaging in work that suggested mental, hence racial, equality (Rainwater, 1970).

After the Emancipation, work remained dichotomized by race. Although blacks worked in the same settings as whites and sometimes held the same job titles, their work was more menial, laborious, and lower paid than that of their white co-workers. Moreover, it was understood that they would not be assigned positions in which they would supervise whites.

Today, blacks have advanced little, relatively speaking, in terms of equal employment opportunities. Their unemployment rate is about twice that of whites (U.S. Department of Commerce, 1973, 1975). They earn on the whole about 60 percent of what whites earn. The dirtiest and least numerative work is still reserved for them (Pifer, 1977). For example, in the federal government, most black employees work in GS 1–9 grades, on a scale that reaches 18. Throughout society, few blacks are working in high-level supervisory positions. In integrated work settings requiring high academic training, black employees seldom achieve what Gross (1958) refers to as occupational colleagueship. That is, they remain, in effect, social isolates. White colleagues exchange informal after-work calls and visits and engage in significant job-related discussions among themselves. Black colleagues are seldom included.

Blacks have been singled out for discussion because they, the most visibly different group in American society, represent clearly an out-group that has been ostracized consistently. Although they have been in the country longer than any other racial or ethnic group, other than Native Americans, they continue to be pushed to the end of the opportunity line with the arrival of each new group, the most recent being the Vietnamese.

Indeed, Afro-Americans are a caste, as has been demonstrated in this examination of their status vis-à-vis the family, church, school, and employment sectors. In general, whites continue to hold an attitude of superiority, disdain, and prejudice toward them. It seems clear that the sentiment is still based on the belief that people of African descent are innately inferior.

Counselor in the Mitwelt

As indicated already, individuals wishing to be effective cross-cultural counselors should visualize themselves from a distance as members of the universally undifferentiated human species in the Umwelt, subject to the laws of nature and destined, therefore, to ultimate nonexistence. This Weltanschauung provides philosophical strength and courage, a prerequisite to assisting others in the same existential situation.

In addition to their recognizing that they are inhabitants of the Umwelt, counselors should be cognizant that they perforce exist and interact with fellow human beings in the Mitwelt. Their professional title, counselor, suggests that they, especially, are committed to helping equally, without reservation or discrimination, all individuals with whom they have an existential encounter. If they wish to be with others in-the-world in what Buber (1970) calls an I-Thou relationship, they must purge themselves of their in-group allegiances. This implies that they become fully self-actualized men and women who are able to transcend to a large extent the values and attitudes of their native culture. They are not so much Americans as they are world citizens, who first and foremost are members of the human species (Maslow, 1971).

Professionals unable or unwilling, for whatever reason, to view and accept all clients as equal and worthy members of the human group can anticipate a series of almost insolvable relationship, diagnostic, prognostic, and intervention problems in cross-cultural counseling.

Eigenwelt

Counselors desiring to bridge cultural and racial barriers successfully also need to understand Binswanger's (1962, 1963) Eigenwelt, which is generally translated as personal or private world. According to Burton (1974), it is that part of self that is difficult to share, because it is housed in the human body, a unified, but relatively closed psychosomatic system. This intricate network of nerves, bones, muscles, blood, and tissue provides the only mode of contact with the world.[1] With it, human beings are able to experience the reality of their existence (Lowen, 1969). The external environment acts on them, affecting their senses; they, in turn, respond to this stimulation by acting on the environment. This reciprocal process operates simultaneously in the Umwelt, the Mitwelt, and the Eigenwelt, itself. Human beings have private experiences, but these experiences are with something or somebody. An understanding of the triadic and experiencing phenomenon of the individual human being should help counselors understand themselves and their clients at the same time, because every person is everybody.

Experiencing the Client's Private Umwelt

Cross-cultural counselors can experience the client's private encounters with the Umwelt by reflecting on their own cognitive and affective interations with it. Because humans are biologically alike, they experience the natural environment with the same sensory systems (Montagu, 1974). Except for some variations as a result of

---

1. Intellectually curious and innovative, even prehistoric Homo sapiens created a variety of tools or extensions of their bodies to assist them in experiencing the world more fully, as Macquarrie (1972) points out.

genetic combinations and handicaps, they see the same objects, hear the same sounds, and smell the same aromas (La Barre, 1972). Throughout the world, they recognize different objects in their environment and assign them distinct names.

The Umwelt is basic to existence (Dewey, 1959). Humans breathe air from an apparent emptiness, eat food grown from the ground, and drink water from rivers (Aristotle, 1943). Not only is the natural environment supportive of life, but it contributes to psychological homeostasis. The sights, sounds, and odors of the Umwelt, in conjunction with requisite nutriments, constitute nature's own preventive and remediative therapy (Emerson, 1941).

In general, people are fascinated and pleased by the natural environment. They enjoy the food, delight in witnessing sunsets, are excited by the cry of newborns, are drawn to animals, and respond generally to the beauty and mystery of their natural surroundings (Mullahy, 1970). Individuals are so enthralled by the Umwelt that the depiction of real life in art forms creates in them responses that are almost as stimulating and enjoyable as is reality. And, because each person is a human template, counselors need only to generalize their experiencing of the Umwelt to their clients. In this way, they know and feel, in large measure, the private Umwelt of their clients, regardless of their cultural or racial background.

Gaining Access to the Client's Inner Mitwelt

Being with others in-the-world is vital to human life (Macquarrie, 1972). People are dependent on others for personal and collective identities, for survival, for general and sexual fulfillment, and for continuity of the human species (Dewey, 1959; Santayana, 1936). Perforce, cross-cultural counselors are interested in gaining access to the private interpersonal world of their clients. However, they often doubt their ability to tap inner feelings about their Mitwelt simply because the clients are "culturally different."

The key to counselors' understanding the private interpersonal world of clients is the understanding of their own (Johnson, 1971). It is important to recognize that humans want to be with others, to merge with them, and to hold on to them in the unstableness of childhood; in the love, tenderness, and passion of sexual embrace; in the lassitude of sickness; and in the approach of the Grim Reaper

(Frankl, 1975). Holding on to others makes life and death easier to manage.

To be alive is to be in-the-world; to be in-the-world is to have feelings, good and bad, about others (Lowen, 1969). Often, feelings are so intense that they cannot be personally recognized and expressed. Sometimes they must be camouflaged to oneself and to others, to blunt or deflect their emotional impact. Indeed, all clients, as all counselors, have private interpersonal experiences. Counselors who are able to empathize with clients on the human, rather than cultural, level will be able to identify and share these experiences, in spite of differences in cultural or racial background (Maslow, 1968, 1971).

Experiencing the Client's Inner Eigenwelt

To experience the client's most private feelings about self is to understand the unified psychophysiological sensations of another human being. Physical and psychological components of human organisms are complementary (Lowen, 1969). Humans "feel" their bodies when they eat, drink, urinate, defecate, have sex, give birth, are in pain, are fatigued, are sick, or are wrestling with death. These bodily feelings affect them psychologically. People also experience themselves strongly when they are in psychological states. Inner sensations—such as anger, happiness, envy, sexual arousal, boredom, and other such emotional conditions—are universal. They also influence significantly physical well-being (Jourard, 1964).

Cross-cultural counselors who acknowledge the sameness of humanity should be able to identify with the physical sensations and psychological states of their clients by considering their own bodily sensations and emotional states (de Montaigne, 1970). They can explore the client's Eigenwelt by simply using basic probing techniques, if beforehand they focus on human psychophysiological similarities instead of cultural differences.

Conclusions

Existentialism as discussed in this article offers great promise to counselors interested in bridging cultural, racial, and ethnic differences.

It is needed especially in countries segmented by numerous in-group allegiances based on irrational and unscientific ideologies. American counselors, as products of such a culture, are often carriers of attitudes and values that impede their ability to help international sojourners and members of racial and ethnic groups other than their own.

Needed is an effort designed to instruct professionals in the essence of existentialism as a philosophy that ought to be basic to counseling. Although existentialism tends to deglamorize human existence, it is not sentimental, lachrymose, or exclusively feeling-oriented. Instead, it generally is undergirded by some brand of rationalism, as MacIntyre (1972) points out. In fact, significant contributors to the loosely unified school referred to as existentialism have included not only theologians and phenomenologists but rationalists, pragmatists, atheists, naturalists, and nihilists as well.

Counselor educators should be the first to be instructed in the philosophy because they are responsible for educating the counselors who, in turn, provide philosophical counseling for clients in search of direction and reason for being in life. Culturally provincial educators encumbered with various xenophobic reflexes are in no position as human beings to impart a panspecific view of humanity.

Counseling organizations and associations should devote time and resources to helping counselors understand and accept the fact that all humans are basically alike. Suggesting that people are different and therefore should be treated uniquely plays right into the hands of in-group bigots who maintain that the out-groups are not only different but inferior.

References

Adams, P.L. Counseling with interracial couples and their children in the south. In Stuart, I.R., & Abt, L.E. (Eds.), *Interracial Marriage: Expectations and realities.* New York: Grossman, 1973. Pp. 62-79.

Aristotle. Parts of animals. In Loomis, L.R. (Ed.), *Aristotle on man in the universe.* New York: Walter J. Black, 1943. Pp. 41-82.

Binswanger, L. *Existential analysis and psychotherapy.* New York: Dutton, 1962.

Binswanger, L. *Being-in-the-world: Selected papers.* New York: Basic Books, 1963.

Black, A.D. Expectations and realities of interracial marriage. In Stuart, I.R., & Abt, L.E. (Eds.), *Interracial marriage: Expectations and realities.* New York: Grossman, 1973. Pp. 7-16.

Bruce, J.D., & Rodman, H. Black-white marriages in the United States: A review of the empirical literature. In Stuart, I.R., & Abt, L.E. (Eds.), *Interracial marriage: Expectations and realities.* New York: Grossman, 1973. Pp. 147-159.

Buber, M. (I and thou) (W. Kaufmann, trans., with a prologue "I and you"). New York: Charles Scribner's Sons, 1970.

Burton, A. Existential and humanistic theories: Ludwig Binswanger and Ronald D. Laing. In Burton, A. (Ed.), *Operational theories of personality.* New York: Brunner/Mazel, 1974. Pp. 161-210.

de Montaigne, M. Of experience. In Frame, D.M., (Trans.), *Michel de Montaigne: Selected essays.* Roslyn, N.Y.: Walter J. Black, 1970. Pp. 291-364.

de Saint-Mery, M. *Voyage aux Etats-unis de L'Amerique, 1793-1798.* New Haven, Conn.: Yale University Press, 1913.

Dewey, J. The unity of the human being. In Peterson, H. (Ed.), *Essays in philosophy.* New York: Pocket Books, 1959. Pp. 381-400.

Emerson, R.W. Nature. In Haight, G.S. (Ed.), *The Best of Ralph Waldo Emerson: Essays, poems, addresses.* Roslyn, N.Y.: Walter J. Black, 1941. Pp. 73-116.

Frankl, V.E. *Psychotherapy and existentialism: Selected papers on logotherapy.* New York: Simon and Schuster, 1967.

Frankl, V.E. *The unconscious god.* New York: Simon and Schuster, 1975.

Franklin, J.H. The two worlds of race: A historical view. *Daedalus,* 1965, *94,* 899-920.

Gross, E. *Work and Society.* New York: Crowell, 1958.

Gross, M. *The psychological society.* New York: Random House, 1978.

Harris, M. *Cannibals and kings: The origins of cultures.* New York: Random House, 1977.

Heer, D.M. The prevalence of black-white marriage in the United States, 1960-1970. *Journal of Marriage and the Family,* 1974, *36,* 246-258.

Johnson, R.E. *Existential man: The challenge of psychotherapy.* New York: Pergamon Press, 1971.

Jordan, W.D. *White over black: American attitudes toward the Negro, 1550-1812.* Baltimore: Penguin, 1968.

Jourard, S.M. *The transparent self.* Princeton, N.J.: Van Nostrand, 1964.

King, C.E.; Mayer, R.R.; & Borders-Patterson, A. Differential responses to black and white males by female teachers in a southern city. *Sociology and Social Research,* 1973, *57,* 482-494.

LaBarre, W. *The human animal.* Chicago: University of Chicago Press, 1972.

Low, W.A. The education of Negroes viewed historically. In Clift, V.A.; Anderson, A.W.; & Hullfish, H.G. (Eds.), *Negro education in America.* New York: Harper and Brothers, 1962. Pp. 27-59.

Lowen, A. *The betrayal of the body.* Toronto: Macmillan, 1969.

MacIntyre, A. Existentialism. In Edwards, P. (Ed.), *Encyclopedia of philosophy* (Vols. 3 & 4). New York: Macmillan, 1972.

Macquarrie, J. *Existentialism.* New York: Penguin, 1972.

Maslow, A.H. *Toward a psychology of being.* (2d ed.) New York: Van Nostrand, 1968.

Maslow, A.H. *The farther reaches of human nature.* New York: Viking, 1971.

Midgley, M. *Beast and man: The roots of human nature.* Ithaca, N.Y.: Cornell University Press, 1978.

Montagu, A. *Man's most dangerous myth: The fallacy of race*. 5th ed. New York: Oxford University Press, 1974.

Morris, D. *The human zoo*. New York: McGraw-Hill, 1969.

Mullahy, P. *Psychoanalysis and interpersonal psychiatry: The contributions of Harry Stack Sullivan*. New York: Science House, 1970.

Murstein, B.I. A theory of marital choice applied to interracial marriage. In Stuart, I.R., & Abt, L.W. (Eds.), *Interracial marriage: Expectations and realities*. New York: Grossman, 1973. Pp. 17-35.

Pifer, A. Black progress: Achievement, failure, and an uncertain future. In *Annual Report 1977: Carnegie Corporation of New York*. New York: Carnegie Corporation of New York, 1977. Pp. 3-14.

Rainwater, L. *Behind ghetto walls: Black family life in a federal slum*. Chicago: Aldine, 1970.

Roy, R.L. Roman catholicism, protestantism, and the Negro. *Religion in life*, 1964, *33*, 577-591.

Santayana, G. The life of reason. In Edman, I. (Ed.), *The philosophy of Santayana*. New York: Modern Library, 1936. Pp. 42-333.

Silvano, A. *The will to be human*. New York: Quadrangle, 1972.

Stein, A. Strategies for failure. *Harvard Educational Review*, 1971, *41*, 158-204.

St. John, N.H. De facto segregation and interracial association in high school. *Sociology of Education*, 1964, *37*, 326-344.

TenHouten, W.D. The black family: Myth and reality. *Psychiatry*, 1970, *33*, 145-173.

U.S. Department of Commerce. *We the black Americans*. Washington, D.C.: U.S. Government Printing Office, 1973.

U.S. Department of Commerce. *The social and economics status of the black population in the United States 1974*. Washington, D.C.: U.S. Government Printing Office, 1975.

Wilson, E.O. *On human nature*. Cambridge, Mass.: Harvard University Press, 1978.

Wright, Q. Nationalism and internationalism. In *Encyclopedia Americana* (Vol. 19). International ed. New York: Americana Corporation, 1969.

23

The Existential School Counselor

Gerald J. Pine

Introduction

Today's students are deeply concerned with questions regarding the meaning of human existence. These questions are expressed in such terms as Who am I? Where am I going? What is the meaning of life? What is the meaning of *my* life? What is the purpose of learning? How relevant is education to life? The search for the answers to these queries is a significant element in the existential counseling relationship.

Because existentialism emphasizes freedom with accountability and focuses on man as the creator of his culture and the master of his destiny, it has become an attractive and dynamic philosophical force in counseling. Its potential for school counseling is now being fully explored and translated into the reality of schools.

Common Existential Principles

A great deal of diversity may be found among such existential writers as Sartre, Heidegger, Kierkegaard, Marcel, Jaspers, and Buber. As a philosophical movement existentialism embraces a variety of

Reprinted from *Clearing House*, 1969, *43*, pp. 351-354. Reprinted by permission of The Clearing House.

viewpoints. However, running through these various existential view-points are several common denominators which can be identified and which have special relevance for those who hope to arrive at a more effective counseling approach through the medium of existentialism.

(1) The basic philosophical principle of existentialism is that *existence precedes essence*. Man chooses his essence; he exists first and then defines himself through the choices he makes plus the actions he takes. Thought without action is meaningless. Man is what he does.

(2) At every moment man is free. He is free of external forces. He is free of himself—of what he has been. An individual's past life is history, it no longer exists *now* in the present. An individual is influenced by external agents or by his past life only when he chooses to be influenced by these forces.

(3) Accompanying man's freedom is the awesome burden of responsibility. Each man is responsible for what he is. In choosing and acting for himself each man chooses and acts for all mankind. Man cannot avoid the weight of his freedom. He cannot give away his freedom and responsibility to the state, to his parents, to his teachers, to his weaknesses, to his past, to environmental conditions.

(4) Every truth and every action implies a human setting and a human subjectivity. There is a world of reality but it cannot be reality apart from the people who are the basic part of it. Reality lies in each man's experience and perception of the event rather than in the isolated event; for example, two men may hear the same speech, the same words, the same voice. One man's reality may be that the speaker is a political demagogue; for the other man the reality is that the speaker is an awaited political savior.

(5) Man must rely upon himself and upon his fellow creatures to live out his life span in an adamant universe. Man's relationship to others must be that of self-realization for all and creature comfort (empathic love).

(6) Man is not an object; he is a subject. Each man is unique and idiosyncratic. To view man scientifically is to view man as an object. Science fails to find the "I" in each man.

Existential Counseling Principles

Flowing from these common and vital existential principles a special helping and facilitative human relationship between student and counselor has evolved. The existential school counselor has translated existentialism into a counseling approach designed to increase freedom within the pupil, to assist the pupil in discovering meaning for his existence, and to improve his encounter with others.

The existential school counselor sees counseling as more an attitude than a technique. It reflects the self of the counselor and represents a sharing of the counselor's self in a personal and human relationship with a fellow human being.

School counseling is viewed primarily as an encounter which implies a special kind of relationship requiring the counselor to be totally present to the student, to participate in the student's existence, to be fully with him. The counselor strives to know the student by entering the student's reality and seeing as the student sees. He empathizes with the counselee.

The counselee is not reduced to an object to be analyzed according to theoretical constructs. He is not diagnosed and evaluated by the counselor because diagnosis and evaluating are conducted in terms of externally established norms and standards.

The counselor who depends on cumulative records and test data to work with the student locks himself outside the student's internal world. Entrance into that world is gained by an emotional commitment in which the counselor risks himself as a person.

Knowing the student as a person becomes more important than *knowing about* him. This demands counselor movement away from the traditional diagnostic approaches which mirror an external objective perspective to an internal, subjective, and personal experience with the counselee.

The existential school counselor operates on the immediate view of human experience. Counselor behavior is a function of the immediate view of the student. There is no reliance on historical or external determinism.

The immediate view stresses that it is the way the student sees his situation today, at this instant, which produces his behavior at this instant. The student behaves at this time on the basis of his ways of seeing, choosing, and acting at this moment in time. What the counselor is and what he does in his relationships with students is the key to developing facilitating and enabling relationships among counselees.

This implies that the counselor and the student can effect change together without the counselor knowing the case history of the student; it suggests that change can evolve in students without necessarily effecting change in parent behavior or in the neighborhood environment.

The existential school counselor knows that no matter what the student has endured elsewhere, a positive facilitating *present* experience is enabling and growth producing. Providing positive present experiences does not depend on knowing what a person's past experiences have been.

"Student Responsibility and Role"

Directing, guiding, and advising students are not part of the existential approach to counseling. Choices must be made by the counselee. *The student assumes full responsibility for choice and action.*

Whenever the counselor structures the counseling situation toward a counselor choice he infringes upon the freedom and the commitment of the student. The student increases his freedom and his sense of personal responsibility only when he experiences freedom and responsibility.

Counseling provides him with such experiences when it is built upon an authentic belief in the potentiality of the student and his capacity for choosing. The more the counselor acts on that belief the more he discovers the student's potentiality and capacity for choosing and acting in self-actualizing ways. This demands enormous faith and consistency on the part of the counselor.

The counselor conveys his faith in the student through his attitudes which indicate to the student, "You can become more independent and self-sustaining" and "The direction for your life ultimately must come from you." Through his attitudes the counselor communicates the feeling that the student *can be* more than he is rather than the feeling he *must be* more than he is.

The existential heart of counseling is the recognition of the student's right to make his own choices and his own "mistakes." Counseling is an encounter in which the counselee is free to become more free. The student who feels trusted to make his own choices begins to trust in himself more and becomes aware that the meanings of his experiences, the meaning for his existence, emerge from within himself.

The ideas of freedom and accountability indicate that *the student must be free to choose whether he wishes to participate in the counseling process.* Counseling should not be imposed nor bureaucratized.

As one student put it, "Counseling is one of the very few things that students feel they have freedom in. I think it is their choice alone whether they would like to use the program. I think we are adult enough to decide for ourselves whether we need or want counseling."

Unfortunately, in all too many school systems, the practice is to require every student to see the school counselor a given number of times during the year. Such practice is perceived by students as a routine mechanical assembly-line process of interviewing. To some counselors allowing the student to decide whether or not he will make use of the counseling service poses a real threat because it puts their counseling program "on the line."

The existential school counselor would not hesitate to allow students the right to choose whether or not they would make use of counseling since he would feel that (1) a counseling relationship that has been initiated by the student is built on a firmer footing than one into which he has been forced; (2) a counseling program will attract voluntary self-referrals in proportion to the quality of the counseling; and (3) required and routine counseling negates what existentialism stands for—it infringes on freedom.

For the existential school counselor the central role in the relationship must be left to the student. Counseling exists primarily for the student and must be used by the student on his terms. The more the counselor focuses on the needs, problems, and feelings of the student, the more he emphasizes the existential character of counseling.

Focusing on the student and his frame of reference enables the student to become more aware of his internal resources and facilitates in the student an understanding of the reality of his being in the school, in the home, in the world. In this kind of atmosphere the student learns that it is *he* who is important; it is *his* experience which counts and not someone else's; it is *his* being that is significant; it is *his* internal advice that is relevant.

"Tuning In"

Nonevaluative listening is a particularly important dimension in existential school counseling. This doesn't refer to a polite or social listening in which the counselor tolerates the student's verbalizations or waits for the student to finish talking and then jumps in to get a point across. Listening, in an existential sense, means tuning into the experiential wavelength of the counselee, being in complete emotional and cognitive contact with him.

While the counselor listens he does not analyze, evaluate, or judge what is being communicated. He immerses himself completely in the counselee's perceptions and experiences so that he is sensitive to all levels of communication—the verbal and the nonverbal—the affective and the cognitive.

It is essential that the existential school counselor know himself. He can only like students as much as he likes himself; he can accept students to the degree that he accepts himself; he can understand students in so far as he can understand himself. When he knows his own values he can become more sensitive to the dangers of imposing those values on others.

By looking at himself as he is and is becoming the counselor becomes more aware of the influencing dimensions of his behavior and how they affect his counseling function. He develops a deeper sensitivity and richer appreciation of the unique potentialities in those counselees who differ from him in behavior and values.

24

The Existentialist Counselor at Work

Marilyn Bates
Clarence D. Johnson

When Beck (1963) integrated philosophical foundations of guidance with psychological models of man, counseling completed its rites of passage from childhood to maturity. In the childhood of counseling, the various models of personality served as useful conceptual tools that allowed counselors to function from a scientific base, but counseling could not come of age until larger ontological questions at least were raised. Asking questions, however, remains an academic exercise until philosophical and theoretical answers are translated into operational procedures in the counseling office.

The purpose of this paper is to translate one philosophy—existentialism—into behavior for the counselor at work. This paper attempts to spell out the nitty-gritty of what the givens of existentialist philosophy might mean to counselors working in public school settings. Relevant existential postulates are identified and briefly elaborated. Main emphasis is placed on implications of the concepts for a counselor as he works in his office. The reader is referred to other sources for more thorough presentation of existentialist philosophy (see References).

Reprinted from *The School Counselor*, 1969, *16*(4), 245-250. Copyright 1969 American Association for Counseling and Development. Reprinted with permission.

Since a source of confusion among various theoretical counseling positions seems to lie between existentialist and self-theory practices, each existentialist postulate is translated into dialogue that contrasts a representative nondirective response with a representative existentialist response.

Concept: Existence Precedes Essence

Man is flung into the world from an unknown and doomed to struggle toward an unknown—death. His only known is that he is. His existentialist task in life is to define himself through his being in the world. Throughout life man is in process of becoming.

Implications for Counseling

If man's task in life is to define himself through the process of becoming, it follows that the counseling function of midwifing the self-actualizing process ought to be available throughout an individual's life. The existentialist concept of life as a continuous process of definition implies that counseling services ought logically to begin with preschool play therapy and to end in a geriatric setting. In public schools the existentialist counselor, who is developmentally oriented rather than crisis-centered, would most certainly begin his activities in elementary school and ideally would work with families before children reached school age. Follow-up counseling to the existentialist would be routine rather than exceptional.

Another implication of the concept that living is a process of self-definition lies in the area of record keeping. To the existentialist, collection of data concerning a counselee is fairly futile until these data enter the awareness of the counselee. "Pure" practice consonant with existentialist theory would suggest that the counselor develop jointly with each client a developmental folder for relevant data (test scores, physical development charts, records of interest patterns, autobiographies written at various grade levels, cumulative transcripts, teacher's anecdotes, etc.) gathered in the process of the counselee's education. The isolation of collected materials beyond immediate reach of the counselee is inconsistent with the school counselor's existentialist concept of defining essence.

The following dialogue illustrates the translation of concepts into operational terms—verbal behavior.

Client: I don't really know who I am or where I'm going, or how I'm going to get there.

Nondirective: You're pretty confused right now about what life is all about.

Existentialist: Before you can make choices about what you want to do, first of all you somehow have to find out the sort of person you are.

Concept: Man Is Condemned to Freedom

Existentialist man is free. No matter how he tries to escape this awesome, terrible freedom, he cannot. Man must choose for himself and accept full responsibility for the consequences of those choices. There are no responsibility-free wombs into which existentialist man can retreat. His life sentence is a freedom which carries no possibility of reprieve or commutation.

Implications for Counseling

Since man must choose, his best chance of being human is to make as many choices as possible *in awareness.* If man bungles through his life a puppet on a string, strung out by chance and only activated by deus ex machina choices, his life-style will be at best a series of blunders and at worst a meaningless tragedy. Only when man uses his sentence of freedom to make conscious choices is he really alive. The existentialist counselor who conceptualizes man in this fashion will see as one of his counseling functions the clarification of alternatives open to the client. In the counseling relationship counselor and client examine realistic courses of action open to the client and their probable consequences. The client, condemned as he is to freedom, then chooses his actions with awareness, and in his consciously made choices finds that he is human. Clarification of alternatives might involve course selection, college choice, job opportunities, changes of program, dropping out of school, and so forth. The constant need for decision making in the school setting, whether changing a program or selecting a job field, offers an opportunity for counselor and client to experience an encounter. Functions which other theoretical orientations may label *routine* and *clerical* can be used by the existentialist counselor to assist clients to make conscious choices with awareness of responsibility for consequences. Every client contact, brief or extensive, is seen by the practicing existentialist as a potential encounter.

Verbal behavior illustrative of applied theory might be:

Client: I'm not sure whether I should drop chemistry or not. I know I need it for college, but I'm not doing well in it.

Nondirective: You know you need chemistry for college, but you are not quite sure whether you can make it or not.

Existentialist: It seems to me that we should explore together whether or not to drop chemistry. I'm willing to help you in any way I can, but it will be your choice and your decision.

Concept: When Man Chooses, He Chooses for All Men

Condemned man makes free choices as he must, but existentialist man is aware that every choice he makes carries in it the implication that it is the best choice for *all* men since each man, in his lonely freedom, is the only representative of mankind he will ever know.

Implications for Counseling

The term *responsibility* is not an unctuous, moralistic pronouncement to the existentialist, but an inescapable fact of being in the world. As a counselee constructs his alternatives and clarifies possible consequences of his choices he must be helped to realize that *he* is the only representative of mankind he has. Thus inherent in each choice he makes is the implication that this is best for *every* man. The counselee who chooses to cheat is by his behavior stating that this is best for all of us. He cannot place responsibility for his choices on an unhappy childhood or on a poor teacher. Neither can he excuse himself by saying, "I didn't mean to do it." Rationalizations may be interesting but, in the existentialist's counseling office, irrelevant. The client, with the help of his counselor, becomes aware of the responsibility inherent in his every choice, and comes to understand that he *is* man, whether he likes it or not. He is condemned to choose for himself, but he is also condemned to choose for all mankind.

The contrasting responses of nondirectivists and existentialists to one client's verbalizations might be:

Client: I know I should have done my homework, but the teacher just didn't make it interesting, and I was bored, so I didn't get it done.

Nondirective: You know better, but somehow you just couldn't seem to work up enough interest to get at your homework.

Existentialist: You chose not to do your homework last night and would like to shift blame to your teacher. This sounds like a cop-out to me.

Concept: Man Defines Himself Only Through His Actions

Good intentions, to the existentialist, are not paving on the road to hell. They are simply irrelevant. Man is defined exclusively through what he _does_, not what he _says_ he is going to do or what he intended to do. The only final relevancy is action.

Implications for Counseling

As the existentialist counselor works with his client, the client will constantly be confronted with his visible behavior—what he actually did, not just what he felt. Intending to do homework is meaningless and of no concern. Did he do it? Feelings are relevant and worth exploration only in understanding the barriers to action. Counseling will tend to emphasize actions and feelings in the here and now, rather than to dwell on historically remote causes of behavior or to focus mainly on feelings alone. Confrontation, then—with relevant "what's" rather than irrelevant "why's" or futile "wish I had's"—is the major emphasis.

The implications for research on the effectiveness of counseling are apparent in this concept. If the only relevant end product of counseling is what the client _did,_ measuring the results of counseling can be done in operational terms, just as research can focus on observable behavior rather than on elusive attitudes.

The concept of man defining himself through his actions also has major implications for vocational counseling, since in Western culture modern man defines himself particularly through his occupational choice. What man does with his productive time is one of his major ways of stating who he is. Thus the existentialist counselor sees occupational choice as a means of self-definition and gives serious attention to vocational exploration. He will use all occupational media—interest tests, career materials, individual counseling, group counseling, group guidance, career days, and units—as useful tools in helping each client, boy or girl, seek out his statement of occupational choice.

Nondirectivists have traditionally been little interested in occupational exploration except as it involved self-concept, while the existentialist counselor addresses himself to vocational counseling with serious intent:

Client: I'm not sure what I want to be. Sometimes I think nursing, then again, no. I think I would like to be a secretary. I'm just not sure at all.

Nondirective: The whole picture of choosing a job seems pretty dim to you right now. right now.

Existentialist: Right now you seem to have at least two choices in mind. Could we think out loud what's in each job for you?

Concept: The Encounter—The "I-Thou" Relationship Defines Counseling Process and Content

The existentialist concept of encounter emphasizes that, while man essentially is alone, the bridge from "I" to "Thou" is the basis of the counseling relationship. Risk and pain for both counselor and counselee are ever present, especially in the necessary process of confrontation.

Implications for Counseling

Each encounter between counselor and counselee is a unique event and does not necessarily imply a long-term relationship. The three-minute interview concerning a program change may be an "I-Thou" encounter. Every contact the counselor has with his counselee has potential for encounter, whether the purpose is college choice exploration, personal problems, or corrections of unsatisfactory behavior referrals. The therapy requirement of many interviews over a long period of time is not essential for a public school existentialist counselor to consider himself "really counseling." The realities of time limitations can be met with a minimum of frustrations when each encounter, no matter how brief, is considered important. The quality of the relationship is far more important to the existentialist than is the quantity of time allotted to it.

The "I-Thou" relationship implies a deep commitment by the counselor to his counselee, a commitment that involves concern for *all* his behavior. The encounter must include dealing with mistakes a counselee makes in behavior, even if the mistakes involve discipline. The existentialist counselor is committed to the counselee, and remains "I-Thou" involved, whether the counselee is behaving appropriately or inappropriately. The counselor-administrator team and the counselor-teacher team working *with* a counselee would be routine for the existentialist.

This existentialist posture of dealing with all a counselee's behavior demands that the counselor be very aware of his own limitations and responses. For example, if he is not able to separate his perceptions of a counselee's behavior from perceptions of the counselee as a person of value, the counselor may then be entangled in his own hang-ups. If the counselor is operating from "I-Thou" he must be authentic, and this involves committing himself to the risk and pain of a counseling encounter that may include self-confrontation. Awareness of this risk should be made a part of professional training that includes provisions for self-exploration.

Dialogue between a faculty member and a representative nondirective and existentialist counselor might go something like this:

Faculty Member: That hood, Jim J., has been acting up in my class again. I wish you would do something about his behavior.

Nondirective: It seems to me that this is a problem better handled by the vice-principal.

Existentialist: I'll be glad to talk with Jim. Send him in fourth period: but would you take a little time right now to tell me how he's bugging *you*?

Concept: Two Worlds Exist—The World of Objective Reality and the World of Subjective Reality

A world of objective reality, governed by more or less known scientific laws, exists and is knowable by man. Another world of subjective reality governed by more or less unknown psychological laws exists and is only tentatively knowable by man.

Implications for Counseling

The concept of two different worlds operating from two different sets of laws is particularly useful for the existentialist school counselor. It allows him to use tools indigenous to *trait* and *factor* counseling governed by a set of statistical laws, presumably knowable. It also allows him to explore with the counselee the phenomenological world of the latter, while realizing that the life-space of a counselee is never fully knowable. Objective measuring instruments can be used on an "as if" basis, but are subject to alignment with the interface of the counselee's subjective world and the realities of the objective world. Because of the concept of two worlds, the existentialist counselor is highly sensitive to dangers involved in using normative data to draw ipsative conclusions.

Within the framework of the concept of two worlds the existentialist counselor is responsible for the acculturation process as well as the individualization process. One of the tools he uses to facilitate both processes simultaneously is group counseling. The safe cocoon of individual counseling is a necessary but not always sufficient condition for helping a counselee cope with his two worlds with their often contradictory dimensions, and thus the existentialist counselor often finds himself group counselor.

A final example of verbalizations of a nondirective counselor-at-work and an existentialist counselor-at-work concerns a reconciliation of these two worlds:

Client: I don't see the way clear at all after graduation. There has to be something, but I sure don't know what.

Nondirective: You're feeling pretty much up in the air about everything right now. now.

Existentialist: You know there is a world out there, some place to go, but at this point you don't see how you fit into all of it. Let's talk about it.

Summary

Fitting the concepts of existentialist philosophy into the work of the counselor has been the purpose of this paper, in which various existentialist postulates have been enumerated. An attempt was made to tease out the implications of the philosophical concepts for the work of the counselor as he operates within the framework of the school setting.

References

Arbuckle, D. S., Landsman, T., Tiedeman, D., & Vaughan, R. P. A symposium on existentialism in counseling. *Personnel and Guidance Journal*, 1965, *43*, 551-573.

Beck, C. E. *Philosophical foundations of guidance.* Englewood Cliffs, N.J.: Prentice-Hall, 1963.

Bugental, J. F. T. *The search for authenticity.* New York: Holt, Rinehart and Winston, 1965.

Dreyfus, E. A. The counselor and existentialism. *Personnel and Guidance Journal*, 1964, *43*, 114-117.

Johnson, E. L. Existentialism, self-theory and the existential self. *Personnel and Guidance Journal*, 1967, *46*, 53-58.

Van Kaam, A. *The art of existentialist counseling.* Wilkes-Barre, Penn.: Dimension Books, 1966.

Wahl, J. *A short history of existentialism.* New York: Philosophical Library, 1949.

SECTION VIII

Play Therapy

The younger elementary school child is only beginning to emerge from the stage wherein all objects are toys, all the time is for play, and work is a construct developed through role playing. While he is being indoctrinated successfully into the concept that his work is school work, he remains a creature who, largely through play, develops his social roles and concepts, and works through his frustrations and concerns. In contrast with his older sibling who can and does verbalize frustrations, love, anger, and acceptance, the younger child acts these feelings.

— *Richard C. Nelson*

In counseling, even with children, professionals have a tendency to emphasize verbal interaction at the expense of nonverbal communication. As professionals, we ask our clients to relate to us in the mode that we are most familiar with, namely spoken language. However, language is a fairly sophisticated process, requiring the manipulation of symbols and dependent on prior verbal experience. Children, particularly younger children, have not mastered completely the maze of symbolization inherent in verbal communication, and frequently they are deficient experientially in the use of language. Therefore, we may be asking children to relate in a mode that is difficult for them if not foreign in some respects. How then can we communicate with children who are verbally immature? One method is through the medium of play therapy. Play is the child's natural mode of communication. It provides him or her with a symbolic way of expressing

253

internal thoughts and feelings. Children learn, rehearse, and reality test different behaviors by playing. They are continually communicating with their environment in nonverbal, play-oriented ways. Boys and girls play with dolls, cars, soldiers, and animals. They draw, mold clay, shape sand castles, and make mud pies. They play house, play doctor, and play at occupational roles. They do all these activities in an attempt to explore their world, to gain expertise of their environment, and to communicate with each other and with adults. Play, then, can be an effective way to enter the life-space of the child.

Play therapy can be a highly structured diagnostic tool, or it can remain relatively unstructured. It can be counselor directed or client directed. It can be conducted in an expensively equipped clinic or in the corner of a classroom. Sophisticated play things and expensively outfitted offices are not necessary for working with children in play therapy. In fact, they may at times be inhibiting factors. Basic raw materials are all that is required in most situations. Recommended materials would include paper, pencils, crayons, hand puppets, small dolls, small animals, clay, games, and a mirror. Imaginative counselors can build their own play therapy kits from materials purchased at their local department stores.

This section will explore some of the various uses of play therapy, utilizing the unstructured, nondirective model. In the first reading, George Murphy outlines a brief history of the development of play therapy. He discusses the setting for therapy and some of the tools a counselor can use in the process. His comparison of structured and unstructured models is particularly informative. Murphy concludes his article by presenting general guidelines for the counselor to consider when using play therapy.

Jean Waterland, in the second selection, discusses play therapy from a nondirective point of view. She uses the concepts developed by Virginia Axline, which are based on the client-centered philosophy of Carl Rogers. She particularly focuses on the relevant counselor behaviors that are important for effective nondirective play therapy. A case study is presented using the nondirective play model. Nystul, in the third article, also uses the work of Axline, and he proposes additional strategies from Adlerian psychology and art therapy. The core of this article is the presentation of seven assumptions that constitute a blended play therapy model.

The final selection by James and Eileen Widerman is a departure from the traditional concept of play therapy with young children. The authors demonstrate how play methods can be used effectively with older children and adolescents to facilitate the development of a counseling relationship and to stimulate the client to communicate by speaking. The case of a resistant, nonverbal, adolescent client is used to illustrate the process.

25

Play as a Counselor's Tool

George W. Murphy

The intent of this article is to summarize psychological literature in an attempt to determine the value of play as a technique for understanding the child, and as a tool for the elementary and junior high school counselor.

The study of play as a means of understanding the child is a comparatively new approach in the field of psychology. It is a technique whereby the child can express his feelings and emotions with something he is familiar.

Rousseau was the first to advocate that the child be educated through play. He offered the suggestion that the teacher himself enter into the play activity (Lebo, 1955). Although Freud used play as a means of therapy, he only touched the surface of its possibilities. Only in the last thirty years have people become interested in play as a technique for better understanding the emotions of a child.

Prior to 1919 little work was done with children, because of the difficulty of utilizing free association as is achieved in adults. Prior to this time no work was done with children under six years of age (Klein, 1955). After 1919, Melanie Klein and Anna Freud began to

Reprinted from *The School Counselor*, 1960, *8*(1), 53-58. Copyright 1960 American Association for Counseling and Development. Reprinted with permission.

employ the technique of play as a means of analyzing children. Melanie Klein feels that the super-ego is highly developed in the child under six years of age, and Anna Freud feels that the child at this age has not developed a complete super-ego (Lebo, 1955).

Since the first use of play as a technique in understanding the child, much has been written about the use of toys, the type of toys, and the techniques that should be used. The tools employed have broadened to include all types of toys, psychodrama, drawings, finger-paintings, clay, music, and almost everything that is known to the young child.

Before one can fully understand the use of play as a technique, it is important to understand the development of play in the child. Play involves all types of activity, beginning in the very young child. He passes through sequential developmental stages including motor activities of grabbing, picking up objects, and placing special meanings to things. As the child progresses in age, so do his play activities. He begins to incorporate what he has learned in the past to carry out present activities. As he matures, his realm widens; first it includes friends in the neighborhood and then those at school. With each new group of friends his scope of play activities increases.

Many types of play rooms have been described in the literature. In the beginning, Melanie Klein used play in the home of the child as a technique. She felt that the child would relate better in an environment with which he was most familiar. After experimentation she found that the child would relate much better outside the home in a setting which was geared for play. By this means the child was removed from the many threats the home offered to his security (Klein, 1955).

The play room should be kept as simple as possible. With the exception of the basic furniture, the only things which should be there are toys. There should be a sink, and the floor should be washable. The toys should be the type that would instill the child to use his imagination as much as possible to reveal his emotional needs.

It should be emphasized that the type of toy used in therapy is not really important. It is far more important that it be something that will motivate the child to structure as well as endow the materials with conceptional and functional content (Woltman, 1955). Toys used should be inexpensive, for during acts of aggression it is not uncommon for the child to break the toy. It has been suggested that the child's toys be kept locked, allowing only the same child to use the toys each time. This offers the child a sense of security, feeling they are his own and no one else's (Klein, 1955). Another suggestion is that the child be allowed relative freedom in selecting the toys with which he desires to play.

Studies have been made of the type of toys which are available for the use as tools in therapy with the child. The supply of such toys is practically unlimited, and new ones are coming on the market each day. The following toys are examples of those used to demonstrate motor activity, pattern activity, mechanical activity, and unstructured activity: guns, soldiers, farm animals, baby dolls, telephone, doll family, furniture, trucks, planes, balls, nok-out bench, goose, clay, scissors, paste, pencils, crayons, and paper. The child was then observed to see which toys he picked to best express his needs. It was found that the doll family was chosen most by the child. The conclusion was that he seemed to be able to best express his feelings through this medium (Beiser, 1955).

There are two schools of thought with regard to the manner in which play therapy should be carried out. The first is unstructured play. The child is given complete freedom in his choice of toys and in setting his own stage for play. In this approach, the therapist becomes an observer, watching what the child does. He may enter into the play on the request of the child, taking whatever part the child desires. The second is the structured plan. The therapist sets the stage for play, gives the child the toys, and asks him to act out what would happen. The main advantage of this plan is that it enables the patient and the therapist to get to the root of the problem more quickly. It also enables the therapist and child to join forces in order to reach a common goal (Hambridge, 1955).

There are certain facts to be kept in mind in dealing with play as therapy. The person should have a genuine respect for the child as a person. At all times he should display patience and understanding. As in any work with a child, the therapist should first understand and accept himself. The therapist should allow himself sufficient objectivity and intellectual freedom in understanding the things the child is attempting to tell him. Sensitivity, empathy, and a good sense of humor are essential qualities demanded of the personality of the therapist (Axline, 1955).

The child should be helped to understand that he can do anything he likes in the room—that this is his play room. He should also understand that the therapist will not tolerate any physical violence to either himself or the child. Under no circumstances should the adult display any emotion when the child shows aggression and destroys a toy. At the same time, the therapist should not try to force the child to play with a certain toy. He will return to it when he is ready.

In periods of aggression, the child will often destroy the toy with which he is playing. The child will completely ignore the toy for a while, but eventually come back to play with it. Once the child has expressed his aggression and again plays with the toy, he shows the therapist that he has mastered the cause of the aggression and is accepting it in a new light. The child will often discuss how he feels using the doll family to show his emotions (Soloman, 1955).

Often in play therapy the child takes the part of the adult and asks the therapist to take the part of the child. Transference takes place between the child and the therapist. Through his role playing as a child, the therapist can feel with the child in his dealings with the world of adults. Through this medium the child is given an opportunity to learn about himself in relationship to the therapist (Axline, 1955).

The statement made by Lawrence K. Frank in his article *Play in Personality Development* sums up the theory behind this technique: "This approach to personality development emphasizes the process whereby the individual organism becomes a human being, learning to live in a social order and in a symbolic cultural world. Thereby we may observe the child from birth on, growing, developing child play as a means to exploring the world around himself" (Frank, 1955).

One of the basic factors reported in the literature was that the toys used with each child should be within his realm of play. A child should not be exposed to toys that are too old for him because he would not be able to express his true emotions through them. By using toys he is used to playing with, the child will feel freer to play and enter into the world of make-believe. The adult observing him will also obtain a truer picture of what the child is experiencing.

In order to do any work with children it is necessary for the person (psychologist, analyst, or school counselor) to understand children and have a desire to work with them. The qualities of acceptance and empathy are the most important qualities. It is essential that the person working with the child accept him as he finds him—advancing the child forward from that point toward mutual understanding of the problem. It is also necessary that the adult understand, as well as feel, what the child is experiencing if he is to be enabled to help the child.

In general all the authors were in agreement concerning the type of toys that can be used. The writer found two main differences of thought expressed in the literature. First, there is disagreement regarding the importance of the strength of the super-ego in the young child. Second, authors do not agree on the merits of using the structured techniques or the unstructured. In the case of the first, this writer feels, the therapist will be guided by his own psychoanalytical theories. This should not produce a disagreement. Basically it is a difference in ideals and training. The second difference involves the technique employed, and this will be determined by the amount of training of the therapist as well as by his ability to understand what the child is trying to say through play.

It was a general fact that the doll family was considered the best means of getting the child to express his true feelings about the home situation. When this device is used, it is important to keep the doll family limited to the size of the child's family. Quite often the child will destroy the person within the family that is causing the problem. This may be done by either breaking the doll, completely ignoring it, or stating that he is going to send him away. It is not uncommon for feelings of guilt to follow the removing of the threat to his security. Eventually, the child will again include the doll that had been out of the play. When this happens the therapist knows that the child is showing acceptance of the problem and is ready through the world of make-believe to attempt to cope with his personality conflicts.

Everyone agrees that it is extremely important for the person in therapy to be nonemotional. He should not show any display of emotion if a toy is destroyed. By keeping control, the therapist helps the child feel that the room is a place where he can do as he pleases. Usually the first time the child destroys an object, he will look at the adult for rejection. When this is not forthcoming, it will give the patient the security of acceptance. This is one of the basic factors in the use of play therapy. It helps the child understand his personality and its relation to himself as well as to the world around him.

Play therapy is a comparatively new and underdeveloped field. Its scope is wide—ranging from toys to art and music. This paper has dealt only with the use of toys employed to help the therapist better understand the child.

The three objectives of the study were to determine: (1) the value of play in understanding the child, (2) the possible use of play by the school counselor, (3) the extent to which it could be applied to the junior high school.

Due to the child's lack of ability to understand himself and the world around him, play therapy is an invaluable tool. It allows a trained person to observe the child in a certain setting. In adults this is done through talking and reasoning, using past experiences. Due to his limited experience, the child is not capable of doing this. Through the use of play, he can accomplish what the adult does by talking.

The use of this technique in our schools can be very helpful to the counselor in his efforts to aid the child to understand himself. However, it is important that the counselor always keep in mind that he is not a trained psychologist, or therapist. It should never be used to analyze a child, for that is not the counselor's job. With training, this technique could become a valuable tool to the school counselor as he endeavors to help the child achieve maturity and self-realization.

The use of toys in the junior high school guidance program is not advisable. The main objection is that chronologically the majority of junior high school pupils have little interest in toys. At this age, the child has the power to reason. Play can be used in the junior high school through such techniques as music, draw a person, draw a house—a tree—a person, finger painting, scatter drawing, and psychodrama.

References

Axline, Virginia M. Play therapy procedures and results. *American Journal of Orthopsychiatry*, 1955, *25*, 618-627.

Beiser, Helen R. Play equipment for diagnosis. *American Journal of Orthopsychiatry*, 1955, *25*, 761-771.

Hambridge, G. Structured play therapy. *American Journal of Orthopsychiatry*, 1955, *25*, 601-618.

Klein, Melanie. The psychoanalytic play technique. *American Journal of Orthopsychiatry*, 1955, *25*, 223-283.

Lebo, D. The development of play as a form of therapy. *American Journal of Psychiatry*, 1955, *12*, 418-442.

Soloman, J.C. Play technique and integrative process. *American Journal of Orthopsychiatry*, 1955, *25*, 591-601.

Woltman, A.G. Concepts of play therapy techniques. *American Journal of Orthopsychiatry*, 1955, *25*, 771-784.

Additional Reading

Conn, J.H. Play interview therapy of castration fears. *American Journal of Orthopsychiatry*, 1955, *25*, 747-755.

Frank, L.K. Play in personality development. *American Journal of Orthopsychiatry*, 1955, *25*, 576-591.

Frank, L.K., Goldenson, R.M., & Hartley, Ruth. *Understanding children's play.* New York: Columbia University Press, 1952.

Gessell, A., & Ilg, F. *The child from five to ten.* New York: Harper Brothers, 1946. Pp. 359-174.

Graham, T.F. Doll play phantasies of negro and white primary school children. *Journal of Clinical Psychology*, 1955, *11*, 11-25.

Moustakas, C.E., & Schalock. H.D. An analysis of therapist-child interaction in play therapy. *Child Development*, 1955, *26*, 143-157.

Piaget, Jean. *Play, dreams and imitation in childhood.* New York: W.W. Norton, 1951. Pp. 147-168.

26

Actions Instead of Words: Play Therapy for the Young Child

Jean C. Waterland

Play therapy may be used to modify behavior by allowing the young child to express his thoughts and feelings partly or entirely through acting them out rather than by talking them out. The counselor tries to convey to the child that he has the right to feel and act as he does. By creating an acceptant atmosphere, the child can be free without worrying about how his behavior affects the counselor's opinion of him. The counselor acts as a selective mirror, reflecting for the child his emotionalized perceptions and attitudes so that the child can become aware of them and in time change them. The decision to change or not to change his behavior always remains with the child, because the counselor cannot take the initiative in this respect without destroying the atmosphere of total acceptance of the child as he is.

Theoretical Position

Within the framework of *relationship theory*, the counselor's ability to communicate with the child in play therapy is stressed so that

Reprinted from *Elementary School Guidance and Counseling*, 1970, 4(3), 180-187. Copyright 1970 American Association for Counseling and Development. Reprinted with permission.

the counselor does not direct the child's actions or verbalizations. The counselor helps the child understand his thoughts and feelings through the cautious use of reflective phrases rather than interpretive statements which are usually analytical in nature. Nelson (1966) states that ". . . the objective of counseling should be to create conditions for expression and communication, and to avoid, generally, viewing play from an analytical frame of reference." Muro (1968) recently discussed a child's progress during play therapy where the counselor's behavior was guided by the philosophical tenets of relationship theory derived in part from the earlier work of Axline (1947) and Moustakas (1953).

Axline advocates nondirective play therapy and bases her ideas on Rogers' work. In her opinion, play represents a more natural medium of self-expression for children than does mere verbalization. Axline not only emphasizes play therapy with individual children, but also stresses its use in groups and its application to education. Proponents of relationship theory stress that the counselor develop a warm relationship with the child, establishing good rapport. The counselor must respect the child's ability to solve his own problems and should not direct the child's actions or conversations. The counselor endeavors to accept the child as he is, to recognize his feelings, and to allow him to express them. The counselor tries not to rush the play therapy process and only sets those limits needed to keep the child's therapy within the realm of reality. A central feature of Axline's philosophy is the belief that warmth, respect, and acceptance must be integral parts of the counselor's personality.

Moustakas' approach to play therapy, based largely on Axline's ideas, emphasizes attitudes. He believes that the feelings of the counselor are of major importance. The counselor should communicate three basic attitudes to the child: (a) faith, expressed as a belief in the child's ability to work out his own problems; (b) acceptance, shown through encouraging the child to express his feelings freely; and (c) respect, conveying to the child that he is regarded as worthwhile and important. The goal of Moustakas' approach is that children achieve feelings of security, worthiness, and adequacy through emotional insight. According to Moustakas, the therapeutic process begins with the child expressing negative attitudes culminating in anger and hostility. Eventually these feelings become mixed with positive feelings, and finally the attitudes become separated and consistent with reality.

The Need for Play

The play therapy approach is vital to the counselor as he works with children who have difficulty communicating with adults (Nelson, 1966). The counselor, however, must know when and how to use play. This does not imply that the counselor needs to use play therapy with all children. Only the counselor's sensitivity to the child and his situation will determine when play materials should be used. If the counselor has confidence in himself and in the child, he does not need to be concerned with how the play materials will be used; the child will start to play when he is ready.

Three Components

Play therapy has three components—the setting, the child, and the counselor.

The Setting: Playroom and Play Materials

In an ideal situation, the setting consists of a playroom and play materials. The room should be large enough to accommodate group play sessions. The room should be soundproof, have a sink with hot and cold running water, and have protected windows. If the room is to be used for teaching, it should include a one-way mirror and be wired for audio and visual tape equipment.

The toys should be arranged in an unstructured fashion so that the child feels at liberty to do what he wants (Axline, 1947). Suggested play materials include water, a sandbox, clay, paint, dolls, shovels, telephones, blocks, balloons, nursing bottles, and so forth. Dolls are important when working with family relations. Toys for working through aggressions include trucks, mallets, and soldiers. Play materials that do not inhibit the child's activities are preferable.

If a playroom and play materials are not available, some ingenuity on the part of the counselor can do much toward turning an ordinary room into a playroom.

The Child: Feelings and Actions

Most children the counselor sees in play therapy have failed to develop individual identities: development of the real self has been inhibited because of inadequate personal relationships. These children probably have been rejected by others, and subsequently have learned to reject themselves; they are struggling to establish themselves in what they perceive as a frightening environment. In their own eyes, adjusting to the environment by either withdrawing or showing aggressive tendencies gives them needed status. The children's real difficulties might be disguised by academic or health problems.

These children have behavior problems they do not know how to solve. Their maladjustments may be caused by misdirected energy, which must be channeled into constructive areas.

The Counselor: Techniques, an Implementation of One's Personality

The role of the counselor is to convey to the child, sincerely and consistently, attitudes such as permissiveness, acceptance, and respect. To transmit these relationship characteristics to the child, the counselor must possess the personal qualities of an effective counselor. Since the child is quick to sense insecurity and insincerity, the counselor cannot just play a role. In addition to these personal qualities, the counselor needs to be adept at using a variety of counseling techniques. Some of the basic counseling techniques as applied to play therapy follow.

Reflection. Reflection is one technique used by the counselor to develop the child's self-understanding. The counselor listens carefully to what the child says and how he says it. In reflecting the child's feelings, he is cautious not to add or subtract from the original meaning. For example, when the child buries the baby doll in the sand and says, "She hates the baby," the counselor reflects, "She hates the baby." The counselor is in error if he reflects, "Mother hates the baby," because the child has not named the person involved. The object of the child's feelings must be stated by the child before being reflected by the counselor (Ginott, 1961).

The counselor must be sensitive to the child's reactions to the reflection. Some children accept reflections from the counselor which may be simply restatements of what the child has said. For example, the child says as she plays with the doll, "She makes me mad." The counselor responds, "She makes you mad." Other children will be saying, "I just said that," or "Aren't you listening to me?" When the child responds this way the counselor needs to begin rephrasing, in his own words, what the child has said. For example, if the child says, "I hate the teacher because he tells me what to do," the counselor could respond, "Being told what to do makes you angry." The counselor, however, should refrain from using indiscriminate reflective phrases because such phrases are meaningless. When the child makes an offensive statement the counselor reflects using his own words (Ginott, 1961). For example, the child expressing feelings about his mother by saying, "She is a dirty rat," could be reflected by the counselor's responding, "Oh, your mother seems to be pretty bad."

Interpretation. Interpretation should be used cautiously to avoid expressing something to the child before he is ready to accept it. The child's nonverbal behavior represents how he thinks and feels. Whenever the counselor tries to translate nonverbal behavior into words he is interpreting—stating what he thinks the child's behavior means (Axline, 1942). Actually, what the counselor thinks and feels the child's behavior means is not important. How the *child* thinks and feels about his own behavior is important to the counselor. "Susie, you're crying because you want your mother," is an example of an interpretation; "because you want your mother" is only an educated guess on the counselor's part. Susie might be crying because no one is telling her what to do or because she does *not* want her mother. The counselor must examine carefully the meaning of a child's verbalizations and actions before making rapid and perhaps erroneous interpretations.

Silence. Correct handling of silences in the playroom is very important. The counselor should not push the child into conversation or play. Silence must be accepted and then gradually interpreted to the child by the counselor. Possible interpretations of silence include, "You are at a loss to know what to do," or "You don't know what to do first." These interpretations leave with the child the responsibility for initiating activity and/or a conversation. The counselor is helping the child to become independent by allowing him to assume the responsibility for making decisions and choices.

The counselor is in error if he says to a silent child, "Why don't you start playing in the sand box," or "Tell me something about your family." In these examples, the counselor has told the child what to do or what to talk about. An unlimited number of sessions may pass before the child becomes active. The child's reaction to the counselor and to the playroom is probably an indication of his past relationship patterns and the sensitive counselor can learn a great deal about the child this way. The child should make the decision to play or not to play, to talk or not to talk. The counselor must not push or hurry him.

Structure. Because structure helps create a framework for the relationship between counselor and child, the counselor must structure the play therapy sessions. Doing so also facilitates the child's keeping the relationship reality oriented. Structuring is an ongoing process and should be used as the need arises. The following are examples of the kinds of structure the counselor provides and how he can verbalize these limits to the child.

The counselor sets the departure time: "We leave the playroom at four o'clock."
The child makes the decisions: "You may play with these toys any way you want."
The child is responsible for his safety: "This is not safe for jumping."
Certain toys are built to take aggression: "Why not beat up the clown?"
The child cannot attack the counselor: "Instead of painting me why don't you use the easel?"
Play material is for use only during the session: "The car must stay in the playroom."

Once a limit is set by the counselor it should be followed consistently to provide a feeling of security for the child. When the limit is broken by the child, the counselor must follow up the infringement by reflecting the child's feelings. For example, "You are angry with me for not letting you do that." The counselor should handle the incident in an accepting manner so as not to make the child feel guilty.

The three components of play therapy—the setting, the child, and the counselor's personal qualities—are illustrated in the following case study.

Julie

Julie appeared to be a well-adjusted six year old. Her academic work was average and her social relationships were satisfactory. Last December, however, the teacher reported that Julie was acting babyish, sucking her thumb, and crying. Upon inquiry the teacher discovered that there was a new baby in the family. The teacher and counselor hypothesized that Julie was having difficulty accepting her

new role in the family structure. The school counselor felt that play
therapy might help Julie clarify this unfamiliar role. A brief conference was held with Julie's mother to explain the purpose of play
therapy.

During the first session, the counselor introduced Julie to the playroom. Although the counselor felt she had established good rapport,
Julie remained guarded in her activities. Julie was sometimes very
verbal and other times not. She seemed to be struggling with herself
in order to stay within socially acceptable limits. She explored the
room commenting on the various play things. Her comments included: "We have puzzles like this in our classroom." "Would you
like me to do a puzzle for you?" "Can I use the crayons to make a
Christmas picture?" Julie was trying to seek permission from the
counselor in order to feel free to pursue a chosen activity. The counselor would have been in error if she had responded by saying, "Yes,
Julie, why don't you do a puzzle for me," because the counselor
would have assumed the responsibility for Julie's activities. Instead,
the counselor reflected by saying, "Only if you want to," which gave
Julie the responsibility for making the final decision. Soon Julie
started to paint a picture and to splash the paint around. The counselor observed Julie's nonverbal behavior and concluded that she
enjoyed splashing paint, and accepted Julie's behavior by responding,
"You are enjoying this." An erroneous response would have been to
ask Julie to stop splashing the paint; this would have imposed an
unjustified limit on Julie. Later Julie explored the doll corner and
commented offhandedly that their family had a new baby. Julie did
not express any particular attitude about the new baby nor did she
pursue the topic. The counselor let Julie's comment pass because she
felt Julie was not interested in pursuing the statement any further at
that time. The counselor structured the end of the session for Julie
by saying that just a few minutes were left. Julie touched on her
problem only briefly, but it was apparent that she sensed the counselor's attitude of acceptance.

The beginning of the second session was similar. Julie casually
reexplored the room and the play materials, and then sat silently by
the doll corner. Cautiously she began to assume the part of a mother
taking care of her baby. Once in a while she looked quickly at the
counselor and then returned her attention to the doll. Julie made no
attempt to involve the counselor in her play activity. She quickly
stopped playing the role of the mother and assumed the role of a

small child drinking from the baby bottle, sucking her thumb, and talking in a babyish manner. After awhile Julie directed her attention to one of the grown-up dolls. She began telling the counselor about the doll. "She's a bad mother," she said. "She just feeds the little baby. She makes the little girl eat by herself." The counselor listened carefully and reflected some of Julie's important comments: "You feel she is bad," and "The little girl needs help when eating." Julie continued with a flood of negative comments about the bad mother until the end of the session.

Shortly after the beginning of the next session, Julie again became involved with the dolls. Julie acted out and expressed very negative feelings toward the mother and baby dolls. The counselor used silence, acceptance, reflection, and interpretation to help Julie express her deeper feelings. Before the end of the hour, Julie very casually began expressing some positive feelings toward the grown-up doll. She mumbled, "Mother likes to hear me read." The counselor responded by making a casually stated tentative interpretation to Julie about her verbal and nonverbal behavior: "You feel that perhaps Mother has time for both you and the new baby." The counselor felt she could make this interpretation because Julie had started to talk about "me" and not the little girl doll. This interpretation was accepted by Julie and helped her explore more positive feelings regarding her mother and the new baby.

The counselor would have been in error if she had started to ask Julie questions about what she was saying and doing. In this session Julie began to minimize the negative attitudes toward her mother (the grown-up doll).

Julie began the next session by pretending the grown-up doll was her mother, the little girl doll represented herself, and another doll was the baby. Julie appeared to be equally attentive to the grown-up doll and baby doll. This time, however, Julie started to make such statements as, "Mommy has to help the baby 'cause she's so little," and "She and I can eat together." Julie began to express the feeling of accepting her role in the new family situation. Because Julie was ordinarily a very stable child and because the counselor had accepted both her negative and positive feelings, Julie could resolve her problem.

This gradual behavioral change in Julie was substantiated by a classroom episode. Julie said, "Oh, Mrs. Jones, the baby cried all night. My mother had to get up and take care of her." Her tone of voice and the sympathy she expressed for her mother displayed an understanding of the family situation. Julie was beginning to understand that the extra care needed by the baby was a necessity. It did not mean that her mother loved the baby more than she did Julie. This episode plus Julie's mother's comment on her improved behavior indicated that Julie was beginning to overcome the momentary but important conflict over the new baby.

References

Axline, V. M. *Play therapy.* Chicago: Houghton Mifflin, 1947.

Ginott, H. G. *Group psychotherapy with children.* New York: McGraw-Hill, 1961.

Moustakas, C. E. *Children in play therapy.* New York: McGraw-Hill, 1953.

Moustakas, C. E. *Psychotherapy with children.* New York: Harpers, 1969.

Muro, J. J. Play media in counseling: A brief report of experience and some opinions. *Elementary School Guidance and Counseling,* 1968, *2,* 104-110.

Nelson, R. C. Elementary school counseling with unstructured play media. *Personnel and Guidance Journal,* 1966, *1,* 24-27.

27

Nystulian Play Therapy: Applications of Adlerian Psychology

Michael S. Nystul

This article describes Nystulian Play Therapy as an approach that grew out of early experimentation with Axline's (1947) model of play therapy. As an elementary school counselor for the Bureau of Indian Affairs for two years, I conducted daily play therapy sessions for students in grades one through three. Then, for the first four months, the groups were structured after Axline's model of play therapy. Axline described her approach as being based on the following eight assumptions, which were summarized by Keat (1972) as being:

1) The deliberate establishment of a positive relationship; 2) acceptance of the child as he is; 3) permissiveness to allow the child the freedom to explore his feelings; 4) recognition and reflection of the child's feelings by the therapist; 5) responsibility

---

Reprinted from *Elementary School Guidance and Counseling*, 1980, 15, 22-30. Copyright 1980 American Association for Supervision and Development. Reprinted with permission.

of the child for his own choices and problem-solving behavior; 6) allowing the child
to lead the way; 7) the process is gradual; 8) certain limits are necessary to anchor
therapy to the world of reality and to make the child aware of his responsibility in the
relationship. [P. 455]

In general, there were two positive outcomes of Axline's model.
First, the children seemed to project their inner thoughts and feelings
through play. Thus, their paintings and other creative offerings
became diagnostic tools to understand the child's world.

Second, when children came to play therapy sessions full of wrath
and hostility, they left more relaxed and tranquil. Typically, these
children spent ten to fifteen minutes punching the inflatable Bozo
clown, acted out aggressive episodes with puppet families, and so
forth. The play seemed to provide socially acceptable ways for the
children to displace their hostile feelings. After engaging in the play
therapy, the children had less need to display explosive behavior
outside the group.

As the children directed fewer emotional outbursts at peers, teachers, and parents, they avoided further interpersonal friction. In a
sense, play therapy seemed to provide a support service or Band-Aid
that could protect the child's emotional wounds from infection.

In some cases, the Band-Aid services allowed the emotional sore to
heal. Unfortunately, things would often happen in the child's home or
classroom that would reopen the wound. Thus, unless I could direct
some counseling effort to the source of the child's problem, long-term
outcomes would be minimal. The search for a more comprehensive
model led to the development of several additional strategies, which
were based on Adlerian psychology and the integration of Creative
Arts Therapy (Nystul, 1978).

Nystulian Play Therapy

Nystulian Play Therapy (NPT) is based on the following seven
assumptions:

Assumption 1: The counselor attempts to establish a feeling of mu-
                tual respect with the child.

The mutual respect concept and several other key concepts in NPT
were developed by Dreikurs and his associates (e.g., Dreikurs &
Soltz, 1964). Dreikurs (1971) believed that mutual respect could lead

to a feeling of equality and shared responsibility. Such a process can help establish rapport in the counseling relationship, thereby reducing the child's reluctance and resistance. Creative Arts Therapy (Nystul, 1978) is one strategy (discussed later on) that encourages rapport.

Assumption 2: The counselor believes that there are no maladjusted children, just discouraged ones. Encouragement is, therefore, the main tool of NPT.

Dinkmeyer and Dreikurs (1963) believed that children become discouraged because they haven't received adequate opportunities for cooperative involvement within the family. Dreikurs and Soltz (1964) noted that children initially want to help and achieve recognition in socially useful ways (e.g., try to dress themselves). When parents are too busy to train their children in socially useful tasks (e.g., getting dressed on their own), the children may demand recognition by moving toward one of four goals—attention, power, revenge, or assumed disability. Children that demand recognition through one of these four goals need to be reoriented toward cooperative social involvement through encouragement.

NPT gives the child the opportunity to participate in cooperative social involvement (e.g., sharing a creative expression). The counselor can teach the child that focusing on the process rather than on the product leads to self-encouragement by making comments on the child's assets while the child is working. The counselor should avoid excessive praise of the finished product. As children learn to build on strengths, they will develop a mechanism for self-encouragement (Dinkmeyer & McKay, 1976).

Assumption 3: The counselor allows the child to feel understood by identifying the hidden reasons for his or her behavior.

To identify the child's hidden reasons, the counselor must first realize that there is a reason behind the child's behavior (Dreikurs & Mosak, 1973). Children's private logic (primarily unconscious) contends that their behavior helps move them from a sensed minus to a sensed plus position (Dinkmeyer & Dreikurs, 1963). Therefore, the counselor should avoid lecturing or moralizing to children on how they are going to ruin their lives if they continue to act as they are. A more realistic approach might be to attempt to understand the child from the child's perspective. Such an understanding can be accomplished in several ways. For example, Nystul's (1978) Creative Arts

Therapy can be used within NPT to develop a phenomenological understanding of the child. Regardless of the strategy selected, the counselor should watch the child's recognition reflexes (Dreikurs & Mosak, 1973) to determine if the child is being understood.

Assumption 4: The counselor modifies the child's motivation for change by redirecting his or her teleological movement.

Once the hidden reason for the child's behavior has been understood, short- and long-term goals can be identified. Short-term goals are associated with the payoff or use of his or her current behavior. For example, if children constantly fight with people, they will receive the payoff (short-term goal) of recognition through power. After several weeks of NPT, children develop long-term goals, such as having "real" friends and doing well in school and at home. This is because of NPT's inherent social-interest value and altruistically oriented self-concept program.

Children need to be made aware of the incongruity of their short- and long-term goals. They also need to understand the cost of maintaining their short-term goals. The counselor can help children appreciate this cost by asking them what their life would be like if they never achieved their long-term goals (e.g., having a "real" friend). Children should be asked to concentrate on whatever response they make (e.g., I would be lonely), so they can experience the cost of maintaining their short-term goals. The resulting existential tension modifies the child's motivation for developing new short-term goals congruent with long-term goals.

Dinkmeyer's Developing and Understanding of Self and Others DUSO) D1 (1970) and D2 (1973) programs can be used as a motivation modification agent for several reasons. First, DUSO helps children understand that demanding recognition will not lead to real friends (understanding the incongruence of short- and long-term goals). Second, children begin to appreciate that having no friends can lead to a very lonely life (experience the cost of inappropriate short-term goals.) Third, DUSO identifies how (short-term goals) make real friends, such as by helping others. DUSO not only modifies the child's motivation for change but also provides information and learning experiences (e.g., role playing and puppeteering) to implement practical short-term goals.

Assumption 5: A NPT session starts with fifteen to thirty minutes of

the DUSO program and ends with fifteen to thirty
minutes of Creative Arts Therapy (depending on
how much time is available).

DUSO holds numerous possibilities for the growth and development of children. There are several features that make DUSO particularly attractive for use in NPT. First, it is a multimedia program that
includes colorful stories, songs, and so forth. Children of various
cultures and socioeconomic groups readily relate to DUSO. Second,
the DUSO units are sequenced in an integrative/developmental
fashion. Simple concepts become themes that are developed over
time.

After fifteen to thirty minutes with the structured DUSO program,
children tend to have a need to freely express their new insights. The
last fifteen to thirty minutes of NPT allow for this through Creative
Arts Therapy (CAT). Nystul (1978) identified four phases of CAT. A
case previously reported (Nystul, 1978) will be used to illustrate how
CAT is implemented in NPT.

Phase 1: Set the stage. The counselor should have a variety of creative
material available for the children, such as molding clay, paints,
puppets, miniature figures of families, and Bozo punching clowns.
The counselor should also be sensitive to any special creative outlet
(e.g., needlework) that the child may have.

Ron, age six, was referred to the counselor by his classroom teacher
and dormitory counselor for help in social and academic areas. Ron
was attending a Bureau of Indian Affairs boarding school. His mother
was a native American, and his father was black. The counselor was
able to work with Ron and several other primary-grade students
several times a week. They were placed in a NPT group. For the first
half hour, the children participated in a DUSO lesson related to
expression of feelings. During the last half hour, the children were
encouraged to express themselves through the play material.

Phase 2: Set an example. If a child is reluctant or resistant to participate in the creative expression lesson, the counselor can encourage
involvement through social modeling. For example, if the counselor
wants the child to try a musical expression, the counselor may need to
play or sing a song first.

Because the children seemed a bit reluctant to begin, the counselor
grabbed a guitar and proceeded to strike up a tune. One of the
children suggested that the counselor play the Johnny Cash song

heard on television the night before. The counselor suggested that instead of playing someone else's song, why not make up a song on how you feel. As is typical in NPT, the counselor was attempting to get the children to relate to what they learned in the DUSO lesson.

Phase 3: Set yourself at ease. The counselor should try to be nonevaluative when the child is involved in a creative expression. If the counselor makes a judgment about a child's creative abilities (e.g., he or she is a good or bad singer), the child may hold back for fear of not meeting the counselor's standards. If the counselor attempts to find psychological significance in the creative expression while it is in progress, the child may create a good picture, thereby avoiding authenticity.

There are several therapeutic outcomes associated with transcendental relationships. First, the children's social interests can increase as they feel the intimacy of being with the counselor. Second, children may begin to develop a more positive self-image as they see themselves through the positive energies of the counselor [as in Cooley's Looking Glass Self-Concept (Collins & Makowsky, 1972)].

As the children took turns making up songs, the counselor attempted to avoid evaluating the children (e.g., if a child was a good or bad singer or if there was psychological significance to a song.). As the counselor set himself at ease, he appeared to set Ron at ease. When Ron's turn came, Ron really let himself go. While Ron sang, the counselor simply allowed himself to get caught up in Ron's emerging rhythm. To avoid analyzing the experience, the counselor found it helpful to close his eyes and sway with Ron's music.

After Ron finished singing, there was a brief hush in the air. The group knew that Ron had finally let himself go and had allowed others a chance to share knowing him intimately. The group felt especially close to Ron at that moment. After that experience, Ron began to have more confidence in himself and more interest and trust in the counselor and other members of the group.

Phase 4: Obtain a phenomenological understanding of the client. Once the counselor and child have finished their creative expressions and the related transcendental experiences, they can use the creative expression (e.g., painting) to develop an understanding of the child from the child's perspective. Such a phenomenological perspective can be gained by asking children if they can describe themselves in terms of their music or words by saying, "What does that song say about you?"

The counselor and Ron met for an individual counseling session later that day to find out what the words to Ron's song meant. Because the counselor wanted to understand Ron from Ron's perspective, he did not try to interpret the song for Ron. Instead he asked Ron, "What do these words say about you?" and "Can you describe yourself in terms of the song?"

With the aid of the tape recording of the NPT session, Ron first determined what the words to the song were.

My mom comes home and daddy stays home
Momma goes home, daddy stays
Momma stays in the city when she wants to
Momma stays in the city when she wants to

Momma daddy, Momma daddy
I just can't seem to go

Daddy keep care of the baby
Daddy keep care of the baby
Daddy keep care of the baby
Daddy keep care of the baby

Please help me

I want to
I need help!
I need help!

I can't seem to stop
Daddy keep care of the baby
Good-bye, good-bye

Ron went on to say that his mother had a habit of drinking and leaving him for several days at a time when he lived with her on the reservation. Ron believed that because his mother went on drinking sprees, she didn't love him. Ron also mentioned that when he was born, his mother gave him up because of the racial tension associated with his father being black. Ron, therefore, spent his first few years living in a hospital before his mother reclaimed him.

As Ron talked about the song, a picture of how he viewed life began to emerge. First, he believed that because his mom did not always do what she said she would do, she didn't love him. Second, Ron believed that being black was bad; and because he was part black, he was bad.

Thus, the counselor was able to identify two mistaken ideas that were contributing to Ron's unhappiness. Several sessions were then spent reorientating Ron, replacing mistaken ideas with new ideas (see Nystul, 1978).

Assumption 6: The counselor uses logical and natural consequences to establish the limits necessary to anchor therapy to the world of reality.

Dreikurs and Soltz (1964) suggested logical and natural consequences as a democratic means of maintaining order with children. Logical consequences require the counselor to take an active role. First, the counselor needs to establish limits for NPT with the child. Typically, they are (a) limiting amount of time (i.e., one hour), (b) providing material to be used for creative expression and not to be destroyed, and (c) prohibiting the children from fighting or hurting one another.

Once the limits of NPT are established, the counselor has a responsibility to help enforce them. Again, the counselor should solicit help from the children to determine appropriate, logical consequences if the limits (rules) are broken. For example, the counselor and child could agree that if creative material is abused, the child will not be able to play with it for a while. In NPT, logical consequences are different from punishment in that the consequences are directly related to the child's acts, as are the laws of society. For example, taking away a child's allowance has nothing to do with the child's failure to clean his or her room.

If a child chooses to break the limits established for NPT, the counselor must follow through with an appropriate consequence. When the counselor does this, the counselor could restate the limit (e.g., clay is for molding and not for throwing). Avoid restating limits each week or the child will become "deaf." The counselor should use a neutral but firm voice. A harsh voice may be perceived by the child as verbal punishment. Finally, the counselor should give the child a choice (e.g., Do you want me to put your clay away, or would you like to?). Giving children an opportunity to maintain some control of their behavior can reduce resistance.

Order in NPT can also be maintained by using natural consequences. Natural consequences allow the child to learn from the natural order of life. For example, in NPT, if children wait until the last minute to do what they really want to do, time will run out. The child will learn that time doesn't stand still, and there is a limited amount of time in NPT to do activities. If the counselor wants to have children learn from natural consequences, they need to do nothing. The child will learn from the experience of natural consequences.

Assumption 7: The counselor recognizes that parent and teacher education are important adjuncts to NPT. Together they promote long-term, positive outcomes for children.

In a sense, NPT gets things started for a child. It (a) gives the child a mechanism for releasing negative energy (e.g., punching the Bozo clown), thereby reducing future interpersonal conflicts; (b) helps children feel understood by identifying the hidden reasons for their behavior; (c) modifies the child's motivation for change, thereby reducing reluctance and resistance to therapy; (d) encourages the child to seek recognition from others in socially useful ways (via cooperation); (e) provides learning experiences that contribute towards a positive self-concept and ability to interact effectively with others; (f) increases the child's social interest; and (g) allows the child to learn from the consequences of his or her actions.

The children will usually spend only between thirty minutes to an hour a week with NPT. Therefore, the children will need support outside of therapy for them to firmly internalize the learning. Parents and teachers should try to offer children an environment that is consistent with their new ideas and experiences.

Parent education programs, such as Dinkmeyer and McKay's (1976) *Systematic Training for Effective Parenting,* or the parent study-group courses based on *Children: The Challenge* (Dreikurs & Soltz, 1964) or *HELPING Your Child* (Keat & Guerney, 1980) provide training for parents who want to enhance the outcomes of NPT.

Summary

This article has provided an overview of a play-therapy program based on Adlerian strategies. NPT was described as a comprehensive approach that may affect positive change within the child. Parent and teacher education was suggested as an adjunct to NPT to ensure long-term change.

References

Axline, V.M. *Play therapy*. New York: Houghton Mifflin, 1947.

Collins, R., & Makowsky, M. *The discovery of society*. New York: Random House, 1972.

Dinkmeyer, D.C. *Developing understanding of self and others (DUSO)* (D-1 Kit). Circle Pines, Minn.: American Guidance Service, 1970.

Dinkmeyer, D.C. *Developing understanding of self and others (DUSO)* (D-2 Kit). Circle Pines, Minn.: American Guidance Service, 1973.

Dinkmeyer, D.C., & Dreikurs, R. *Encouraging children to learn*. Englewood Cliffs, N.J.: Prentice-Hall, 1963.

Dinkmeyer, D.C., & McKay, G. D. *Systematic training for effective parenting (STEP)*. Circle Pines, Minn.: American Guidance Service 1976.

Dreikurs, R. *Social equality: The challenge of today*. Chicago: Henry Regnery Co., 1971.

Dreikurs, R., & Mosak, H. (Eds.) *Alfred Adler: His influence on psychology today*. Park Ridge, N.J.: Noges Press, 1973.

Dreikurs, R., & Soltz, V. *Children: The challenge*. New York: Meredith Press, 1964.

Keat, D.B. Broad-spectrum behavior therapy with children: A case presentation. *Behavior Therapy*, 1972, *3*, 454-459.

Keat, D.B., & Guerney, L. *HELPING your child*. Falls Church, Va: American Personnel and Guidance Association, 1980.

Nystul, M.S. The use of creative arts therapy within Adlerian psychotherapy. *The Individual Psychologist*, 1978, *15*, 11-18.

28

Counseling Nonverbal Students

James L. Widerman
Eileen L. Widerman

Counseling, as taught by most graduate programs and practiced by the majority of those in the field, is primarily a verbal activity, a transaction and exchange between an identified client and a counselor. The various schools of counseling differ in their stress on verbal interchange, but all to some extent include in their model a client with a problem and an empathic counselor who listens and responds helpfully.

When the counselee, for whatever reason, is nonverbal, the counseling process breaks down. Since counselors' primary tool is talking, they become uncomfortable when confronted by a client who cannot or will not talk. One setting in which this breakdown often occurs is the school.

Most students who voluntarily approach a counselor are nervous, unsure of the counselor's role. Whether or not they ordinarily are verbal, students respond to the counseling situation, which is strange to them, with feelings of discomfort or uncertainty. It is alien to the adolescent's life-style to immediately open up and trust an adult. Even under the most conducive of circumstances, the school counselor is too often associated with authority.

Reprinted from *The Personnel and Guidance Journal*, 1974, *52*(10), 688-693. Copyright 1974 American Association for Counseling and Development. Reprinted with permission.

Many students do not come willingly for counseling; they are referred by teachers, parents, or administrators. This referral usually implies a problem; the student is a "discipline problem," a "slow learner," a "truant," and so forth, whether or not the adolescent sees himself or herself in that way.

The difficulties of dealing with an unwilling or uncooperative client are well documented in the literature. The factor that comprises a significant portion of this difficulty is the unwilling client's tendency not to talk or open up. This article offers a framework in which to view a technique for effectively counseling the nonverbal adolescent, providing a case example. While this technique does not have blanket effectiveness, we have found it useful in dealing with a significant portion of school counseling.

The Problem

Typical counseling interviews with nonverbal students are characterized as follows. The students are sent to the counselor. The counselor responds to their presence with comments or questions designed to put them at ease and to elicit from them their view of why they have been referred. Typical questions are "What can I do for you?" and "Who sent you to see me?" and they are frequently preceded by such small talk questions as "How do you like school?" and "What grade are you in?" Students generally field such questions with nods, grunts, shrugs of shoulders, and other such noncommittal expressions. They rarely maintain eye contact with the counselor, instead staring at the floor or out the window. When asked an open-ended question, they give a monosyllabic answer or say "I don't know."

Students' inability or unwillingness to interact verbally often provokes anxiety in counselors—particularly new counselors. They may respond by increasing their own verbal output—either to speak for the student, to give the student a "multiple choice," or to fill what seems like an endless silence. "I know it isn't always easy to talk." "Did you come because you are in trouble?" "You seem nervous." In this kind of situation, neither counselors nor students have their needs met; the counselors feel that they have not helped and the students feel that they are not yet on the way to a solution of their difficulties. No one has the feeling that a relationship has been established. Too often such an interchange discourages students from seeking further help; this can influence not only their present but also their future adjustment, negatively affecting their propensity to seek help from others as adults. Counselors, then, frustrated by such unrewarding interviews—and desiring to maintain their self-images as professionals operating out of a firm knowledge base—too often label nonverbal adolescents as "not amenable to counseling," a label that can hold numerous undesirable implications for others dealing with them.

A Behavioral Hierarchy

In our work with nonverbal students, we have identified a hierarchy of behaviors leading from nonverbal to verbal through which students pass if counseling is successful. The hierarchy is described and operationally expanded in four steps.

Step 1: Students Attend in the Presence of the Counselor

Rather than maintain eye contact with the counselor, students will explore their environment, although this exploration may be initially covert. To avoid relating personally, students may ask such questions as: "Is that a picture of your wife on your desk?" "What time is this period over?" An office stocked with paintings, clay, plants, cards, simple games, a typewriter, felt-tip pens, a drawing pad, a candy dish, magazines, and comics will invite uncomfortable, hesitant, nonverbal students to explore. As they become involved in an exploratory activity, students attend; and this attending becomes an important prerequisite to the attending of protracted conversation. As they become absorbed in activities of high appeal, students become more comfortable.

This transition from an uncomfortable, nonverbal client to a more relaxed one may take more than one session in the counselor's office. The length of the initial sessions can be dictated by the interest and the attention span of the student, some students taking only a part of one session and others taking several complete sessions.

Occasionally an acting-out or a more disturbed adolescent will use this Step 1 activity as an opportunity to test the counselor, the testing usually taking the form of taxing the counselor's permissiveness. The student may pound on the typewriter, handle a toy roughly, try to steal a small item, and so on. The counselor must not reject the student, but the counselor should set limits and in so doing define his or her own role. What is facilitative in this situation is not a direct reaction to this behavior but an attempt to deflect the student's attention by focusing and role definition.

The counselor's main role during Step 1, then, is to invite the student's exploration of the office, to make the student as comfortable as possible, and to encourage the student's return to the office.

Step 2: Students Comment as They Attend

Initially students come to the office and sit in silence. They steal a glance at the distractors, at first perhaps as an aside but gradually more as the central activity. They become more trusting and relaxed as they perform such activities with the counselor present. An important stage has been realized when a student follows a game or activity to completion rather than merely moving from object to object. Often the student will ask the counselor if a particular activity is acceptable and will invite a mutual definition of roles. Regardless, once the student engages in an activity the counselor can encourage comments with such questions as: "What are you drawing?" "What do you think of that puzzle?" Nonverbal students find it easier to talk while they perform than talk while they are not engaged in doing anything.

It is important to keep in mind that the nonverbal student often cannot converse at all without concomitant activity. At this second step, any discussion is encouraged. No discrimination of content is made. Counselors should gauge their own verbal output by carefully and continually assessing the student and the situation. Any conversation should encourage continued activity and should be kept nonthreatening.

Those counselors who lean toward the use of play and/or art as diagnostic tools might wish to integrate them into this step. Care must be taken, however, to allow the student to set the pace and determine the activity. If the student seems to have difficulty in making the transition from private exploration to conversation with the counselor, the counselor might attempt to become involved in the student's exploration. One particularly effective method is to play a game (checkers, dominoes, cards, etc.) and talk to the student as the game is played.

Step 3: Students Are Encouraged to Give
More Personal Commentary

Embedded in the students' conversations are statements about themselves. The counselor can respond to these, encouraging students to talk about what they are doing in relation to themselves as persons. Expressions of likes, dislikes, and associations to other events should be noted in an effort to reinforce them. Once the students become used to talking about themselves, they will recall and relate more and more. Wishes and fears may begin to surface during the activity. Students may reveal their feelings about the counselor or the counseling situation. During this stage the counselor, being sensitive to these new elements, can encourage the students to give more of themselves—in both commentary and fantasy. Often at this point students become satisfied to talk without the activity gimmick or to talk after a quick game.

Step 4: Conversation Is Encouraged
Without Gross Motor Activity

As students begin conversing for longer stretches, they eventually mention or can be directed to mention their school experiences and problems. They express likes, dislikes, and annoyances. The counselor should respond to—and thus reward—the school-related discussions. Once the student converses comfortably the counselor has reached the presenting problem stage, which completes the transition from a nonverbal to a verbal relationship.

It is apparent that the four-step process is one of making finer and finer speech discriminations. At the start, only gross motor activity is possible (the nonverbal activity). This gross motor activity keeps the client in the office long enough to allow the low rate of fine motor activity (speech) to be increased. Once the rate is sufficiently high and stable, the content of the speech is shaped so as to become personal and then to focus on the problem area. Operant conditioning, then, merges with a client-centered approach and the use of play to facilitate a helping relationship.

A Case History

Three department heads referred Lloyd, an eighth grader, for counseling. He had been suspended numerous times for cutting classes and exhibiting disruptive behavior. He mimicked teachers, ran around the room, danced, and instigated similar acting-out behaviors in others.

The first sessions with Lloyd were conducted in almost total silence. Except to answer questions monosyllabically, Lloyd hung his head, stared at the floor, and took deep, heavy breaths. Because of his obvious discomfort and inability to verbalize, Lloyd was asked by the counselor if anything in the room interested him, and for the first time he raised his head to look around. Careful to avoid eye contact, which might prove too threatening, he surveyed the various "props" in the room. The counselor observed that Lloyd was eyeing felt-tip pens and a pad, so the counselor invited him to draw. Lloyd drew a primitive house with a dog and a person in the yard. At this time the counselor did not discuss the picture. Lloyd was reassured and scheduled for another session.

Lloyd approached this second session by announcing that he had something he wanted to draw. In this second picture he drew a prize fighter in a ring surrounded by spectators. As he drew he said nothing. He seemed to gain satisfaction from what was apparently a working out of his current feelings through the drawing. (The counselor learned later that Lloyd had been in conflict with his science teacher prior to his appointment.)

A third session was marked by Lloyd's discovery of the checkers. As he became more comfortable and trusting, he was able to move beyond drawing to a further exploration of the room. His selection of a game requiring two players was an invitation for interaction. For the next twelve to fifteen visits, student and counselor played checkers. Lloyd kept a careful tally of his win/loss record. (His power struggle—the fighter—was now transferred to the checkerboard.) From grunts, grimaces, and a few infrequent words, he progressed to talking about other things during the games, especially his dislike for the teachers and the effects of his negative interactions with them. The importance of the games and his winning them slowly diminished. Lloyd was now comfortable enough to discuss his difficulties in the context of a verbal, helping relationship with the counselor.

Of course, counseling with Lloyd also involved contact with the administrators, teachers, and family. School testing records indicated that in sixth grade Lloyd had functioned just below the tenth percentile, although up until the fourth grade he had tested at the low average level. Something at that point must have impeded Lloyd's development of verbal skills. The counseling, then, was a series of learning experiences designed to develop the verbal function where it had left off in the fourth grade. When Lloyd's problems were explained to administrators who were concerned with his lack of adjustment, they became more understanding and placed him in a self-contained classroom with remedial reading equipment. Thus, as Lloyd became more comfortable in expressing his anger and frustrations through counseling, he became less of an acting-out student, less of a discipline problem.

Discussion

The methodology presented here for successful counseling with the nonverbal secondary student is certainly broad enough to accommodate a number of different approaches, or counselor styles. For instance, the case history illustrates the use of play primarily as "bait" in the transition from nonverbal to verbal interaction; the fact that feelings were expressed through the play was deemed secondary in importance. Other counselors might want to concentrate on the content of the play or use the play projectively to determine underlying problems and feelings of the student. Counselors of a behavioral bent might use the play as a reward for verbal interchange. It is important, however, not to stop the sequence of steps with the play. The student needs to be brought to the final step of verbalization, as it is verbalization that is recognized and rewarded as a necessary skill by the school and the community at large.

Students vary in their procession through the four steps. Some are quite verbally developed, as can be witnessed by their peer interaction. They become reticent only when confronted by school personnel or by uncomfortable settings—such as counseling. These students move through the outlined steps quite rapidly. Those who are less verbally developed take considerably longer. The counselor needs to be sensitive to the student's progress and needs to tailor reactions accordingly. The length of the sessions can vary according to the amount of time each individual can comfortably tolerate. Experience here is a good guide, as is carefully watching each student. Sessions can vary in length from a few minutes to an entire period and in frequency from one a week to one every other day.

Our experience with this method has been with adolescent students in inner-city junior high school and senior high school settings.

It may also be applicable to children at the elementary level. The characteristics of the given counselee dictate the method more than does age.

Conclusion

Gross motor activities used to bring about increased speech can be a useful device, one that is very suitable for the school counselor. It is especially helpful with students who are verbally underdeveloped, depressed, withdrawn, and anxious. Our experience has indicated that the psychotic, the hard-core characterologically disturbed, and the mature or older student do not respond well to this method. One must then keep in mind that this is only one technique of many that can be employed to facilitate counseling. Counselors must develop their skills generally and then use activity techniques to extend their effectiveness.

SECTION IX

Eclectic Counseling

The most compelling indication for adopting the eclectic approach to behavioral study and psychotherapy is the complexity of the psychological states and life situations involved in even the simplest clinical problems. Behavior normally is in constant flux and change. Behavior occurs phenomenally in a sequence of psychological states of Being, each reactive to a constantly changing existential situation. Integrative dynamics not only are tremendously complex but also are determined by almost infinite permutations and combinations of organizing factors. Only the eclectic approach is capable of dealing with such complexity and change.

— *Frederick C. Thorne*

To be an eclectic counselor means to develop a combination of theoretical approaches that effectively deals with human behavior. The eclectic counselor is not satisfied with one theorist's explanation of behavior and therapeutic change agents. He or she feels this is too restrictive, confining, and ineffective. To be effective, the counselor must utilize the experience of many divergent theorists in his or her own practice. In order to do this the counselor must borrow from a spectrum of theoretical approaches, those that are felt most relevant for the clientele.

Frederick Thorne is one of the leading proponents of the eclectic position in psychotherapy and counseling. He strongly advocates that all therapists examine a number of different theoretical models in order to find the best personal combination of theory and technique. However, consistency throughout the theoretical framework is essential. All of the varying elements must form an interdependent, interrelated system. Every counselor must eventually settle on one philosophy and theory of personality that explains human behavior. The specific techniques of counseling are chosen from those that have been proven effective in therapeutic settings. The best features of each approach are then selected for inclusion in the personal framework. When the counselor adds new techniques in order to increase his or her effectiveness, they must be consistent and congruent with the already existing framework.

The readings in this section are intended to help encourage the reader to consider the eclectic position. In the first article, Lazarus presents a thoughtful plea for therapists to continually seek additional techniques that will broaden their practical expertise. However, he emphasizes the need for a system or framework of therapy, and he believes that new techniques must be incorporated into the total system.

The two remaining articles describe different combinations of theoretical positions that are examples of eclectic frameworks. Ponzo focuses on blending five different epistomologies into one coherent and applicable system. Gronert combines reality therapy, Adlerian psychology, and behavior modification. He concludes by applying the model to specific cases involving youth.

In summary, eclecticism may be characterized by both diversity and consistency. Diverse theoretical positions are synthesized into a consistent framework that is personally satisfying and professionally effective.

29

In Support of Technical Eclecticism

Arnold A. Lazarus

The plethora of psychological theories is exceeded only by the dearth of testable deductions emanating therefrom. Harper (1959), for instance, described thirty-six separate systems of psychotherapy which he regarded as "the main types of psychological treatment." There are, in fact, many other clearly identifiable "systems" which can be added to Harper's list. These would include: Transactional Analysis, Psychosynthesis, Reality Therapy, Reparative Psychotherapy, Integrity Therapy, Implosive Psychotherapy, and Morita Therapy, to mention a few.

Faced with this complex, contradictory, and often confusing array of psychological theories and systems, most practitioners seek refuge in those notions which best satisfy their own subjective needs. Yet one may legitimately inquire whether the consequence of adhering to a particular school of thought is to exclude from one's armamentarium a significant range of effective procedures. Who, even in a lifetime of endeavor, can hope to encompass such a diverse and multifarious range of thought and theory? Indeed, an attempt to imbibe and digest this overwhelming mass of information (and misinformation) may be no more rewarding than gluttony at any other level. Is there a way out of this morass?

Reprinted with permission of author and publisher from: *Psychological Reports*, 1967, *21*, 415-416.

To luxuriate in a metaphor, we might conceivably wield Occam's razor the way Alexander the Great used his sword, to cut *through* the Gordian knot instead of becoming involved in its intricacies. Occam taught that explanatory principles should not be needlessly multiplied. In keeping with this, the general principle of scientific thinking is that given two equally tenable hypotheses the simpler of the two is to be preferred. Add to this London's (1964) profound observation that: "However interesting, plausible, and appealing a theory may be, it is techniques, not theories, that are actually used on people. Study of the effects of psychotherapy, therefore, is always the study of the effectiveness of techniques."

Can a practicing psychotherapist afford to ignore any effective technique, regardless of its theoretical origins? Obviously, a technique derived from a source or system which is at variance with one's own theoretical beliefs may nevertheless possess healing properties—not necessarily for reasons which attach to the theories of its originator. Consider the case of a highly anxious patient who received relaxation therapy (Jacobson, 1964) to diminish his overall tensions, while receiving systematic desensitization (Wolpe, 1961; Wolpe & Lazarus, 1966) to various subjectively threatening situations and also being trained to be "excitatory" (Salter, 1949) by assertively standing up for his rights and by giving vent to his feelings. This was extended to embrace self-disclosure (rather than a life of concealment and camouflage) as a means of achieving social harmony (Jourard, 1964). The patient's irrational ideas were handled along lines advocated by Ellis (1962).

Now, the theoretical notions espoused by Jacobson, Wolpe, Salter, Jourard, and Ellis are very much at odds with one another. The eclectic theorist who borrows bits and pieces from divergent theories in the hope of building a composite system must inevitably embrace contradictory notions and thus is likely to find himself in a state of confusion worse confounded. But it is not necessary to accept or reconcile divergent theoretical systems in order to utilize their techniques.

And so it is with Harper's (1959) three-dozen systems and the dozens of others we could add to his original list. To attempt a theoretical *rapprochement* is as futile as seriously trying to picture the edge of the universe. But to read through the vast mass of literature on psychotherapy, *in search of techniques*, can be clinically enriching and therapeutically rewarding.

However, this should not presuppose a random melange of techniques taken eclectically out of the air. While the basic point of this paper is a plea for psychotherapists to try several effective techniques (even those not necessarily prompted by the logic of their own theories), it is nevertheless assumed that any selected maneuver will at least have the benefit of empirical support. Complete unity between a systematic theory of personality and an effective method of treatment derived therefrom remains a cherished ideal. Meanwhile it is well for the practicing psychotherapist to be content in the role of a technician rather than that of a scientist and to observe that those who impugn technical proficiency are often able to explain everything but to accomplish almost nothing.

References

Ellis, A. *Reason and emotion in psychotherapy.* New York: Lyle Stuart, 1964.

Harper, R. A. *Psychoanalysis and psychotherapy: 36 systems.* Englewood Cliffs, N.J.: Prentice-Hall, 1959.

Jacobson, E. *Anxiety and tension control.* Philadelphia: Lippincott, 1964.

Jourard, S. M. *The transparent self.* New York: Van Nostrand, 1964.

London, P. *The modes and morals of psychotherapy.* New York: Holt, Rinehart and Winston, 1964.

Salter, A. *Conditioned reflex therapy.* New York: Creative Age Press, 1949.

Wolpe, J. The systematic desensitization treatment of neuroses. *Journal of Nervous Mental Diseases,* 1961, *132*, 189-203.

Wolpe, J., & Lazarus, A.A. *Behavior therapy techniques.* Oxford: Pergamon Press, 1966.

30

Integrating Techniques from Five Counseling Theories

Zander Ponzo

An eclectic approach can provide the best of all possible counseling worlds; the strengths of one system often balance the weaknesses of another.

When she was annoyed with me, my mother would say, "Zander, there is a time and place for everything." I did not appreciate the depth of her wisdom then but saw the statement only as a precursor to more physical means if I did not stop inappropriate "time-and-place" behavior. However, maturity has enabled me to appreciate and utilize the wisdom of my mother's words in many areas of life.

I have lived through an era of proliferating therapies, each of which asserts that there is a time and place for its system—and it is always. It was a time in which the various systems vigorously competed for their place in the sun, a time when dogmatic "true believers" deified the leaders of their therapy cults and verbally annihilated the teachings and followers of other gurus. Fortunately, I sensed that dogmatism and deification contradicted Mother's wisdom, and I resisted the demands. Instead I worked to become a wise, time-and-place-for-everything counselor/therapist, a person who sought to integrate the wisdoms of the gurus into a system in which the different teachings worked together rather than against each other. I would like to share with you how I have done this.

Three Phases of Counseling

I conceptualize my counseling as being organized into three interrelated phases. Each stresses the achievement of different basic goals, and each differently uses the philosophy and techniques from five counseling systems. Client-centered counseling, Gestalt counseling, transactional analysis, rational-emotive therapy, and behavioral counseling are the systems I use the most in my "time-and-place" orientation.

Phase 1: Awareness. People enter counseling because they, or someone with power over them, believe that there is a discrepancy between their current and their preferred feeling, thinking, and behaving. The task of the counselor is to operate in a way that increases both the client's and the counselor's awareness of the situation and communicates a caring, an honest, and a competent atmosphere. Within this phase of counseling, attempts are made to increase awareness and to establish a good relationship. If these attempts are effective, clients may begin to develop new ways of thinking about themselves and life, and their behavior may change in significant ways.

I draw on Gestalt and client-centered counseling most heavily during this phase. Both systems view the individual as being capable of self-direction toward satisfying and rewarding goals. However, individuals slowly sacrifice their own well-being when they attempt to live by other people's rules instead of following their own feelings. Client-centered and Gestalt methods are geared toward helping people become more aware of their feelings.

From a client-centered perspective, clients are provided with a nourishing environment of acceptance, empathy, warmth, openness, and genuineness. The prime conveyers are reflecting responses and a counselor who models health. A basic belief is that under these conditions clients will be freed from their need to please, become more trusting of themselves and the counselor, become more aware of their feelings, and increasingly act in health-producing ways. Client-centered methods are very useful in building a trusting relationship, training the counselor to be an understanding listener, and increasing awareness. A criticism of client-centered counseling is that it might be too slow and superficial, that the awareness-building process would be quickened and deepened if the client-centered methods were supplemented with more direct and powerful ones; Gestalt counseling does just that.

Gestalt methods are geared toward helping clients become more aware of what they are feeling in their here and now. Most people have learned to use words to hide from themselves and others. The counselor focuses on voice quality and nonverbal behavior. Clients are asked to become aware of how they sound and what they are doing. Role-playing situations are established in which clients are asked to give words to their tears or voice quality, play both sides of a conversation between different parts of their body (e.g., a clenched fist and an open hand), and play all of the roles in a conversation among significant others. The novelty of Gestalt methods enhances their strength. Clients are thrown off guard, and their typical ways of defending themselves are reduced. In these moments clients can learn a great deal about themselves. The danger is that Gestalt techniques often move too quickly for clients and raise their anxiety level. In reaction, they leave counseling or become more defensive.

A criticism of both systems is that they pay too much attention to feelings and not enough to thought patterns and behavior change. Counseling can provide a place where clients indulge themselves in their feelings but make scant efforts to constructively control injurious feelings and change harmful behavior. This limitation can be avoided if counselors resist becoming dogmatic client-centered or Gestalt counselors.

Phase II: Cognitive Reorganization. Building on the accomplishments of Phase I, I question and challenge my clients' assumptions about life and teach them to do the same. Clients are taught to think in rational ways that lead to greater satisfaction of needs and wants, healthier emotions, and improved self-concepts. During this phase, counselors must guard against getting too rational, cold, and ambitious and losing touch with the gentler sensitivities displayed in Phase I.

I draw heavily on transactional analysis (TA) and rational-emotive therapy (RET). Basically, both systems view individual disturbance as the result of following conscious or subconscious learned programs that are irrational. The counseling tasks are to make clients aware of irrational thought programs, demonstrate how they are harmful, offer healthful alternatives, and insure that rational programs gain power over irrational ones. RET and TA are very similar, and they are both used to accomplish these tasks. The main difference between them is in their strategies.

A basic TA concept that facilates the evaluation and debugging of irrational programs is the Parent (P), Adult (A), and Child (C), conceptualization. Parent programs tell us what we and others should do; they tend to generate self- and other-directed hate and anger. Child programs make us fearful and insecure; they tend to limit the risks we are willing to take, because the programs magnify the consequences of failure and rejection. Adult programs are rational and keep us in touch with what is; they encourage constructive behavior that is based on calm and thoughtful decision making. The PAC model is taught to clients, who are encouraged to apply it to their own lives. In most cases the road to improved health is through having more of the client's thinking come out of the rational Adult.

In RET the road to rationality is lined with lectures, written materials, and the ABCD model. Lectures and written materials are used to transmit knowledge that could help clients live more effectively. The ABCD model is a technique that enhances people's ability to determine the thought programs that are linked with their emotions. (This tool is explained in a later section.)

In contrast to the feeling emphasis of Gestalt and client-centered counseling, TA and RET emphasize thoughts. Both have developed powerful methods for diagnosing and changing irrational thought programs. This is their strength—but also their weakness. When people are so tuned in to thoughts, their feelings can be neglected, and counseling can turn into a cold and inefficient tutorial. Combining the feeling orientation of client-centered and Gestalt counseling with the thought orientation of TA and RET should increase the power of counseling to help a person make desired changes. Incorporating behavior modification methods will also increase counseling potency.

Phase III: Behavior Change. Awareness of feelings and knowledge of rational and irrational thought programs are important ingredients in effective counseling. Improvement through counseling is further facilitated if the client is involved in a behavior change program that builds on the awareness and cognitive reorganizations of earlier phases. During this phase, counselors need to be supportive but demanding, as clients work to implement behavior change programs that were designed with and for them.

Behavioral counseling is founded primarily on the notion that behavior is learned and that systematic training programs can free people from limiting behavior and help them develop more desired behavior patterns. Behavioral counselors do not deny the importance of feelings and thoughts but believe that changed behavior will result in changed feelings and thoughts. Desensitization, counterconditioning, positive reinforcement, assertiveness training, implosive therapy, contracting, relaxation methods, and role modeling are among the many techniques behavioral counselors use.

The major strength of behavioral counseling is the recognition that in most cases lasting change is bought only at the expense of spending time and energy in systematic practice. A prime criticism of behavioral counseling is that it tends to overemphasize the behavior to the neglect of affective and intellectual components. As with the other four counseling systems I use, the strength of behavioral counseling is also the seed of its weakness.

The Process of Integration

Within these systems are found ingredients needed for effective counseling. Like the nutritionist, the wise counselor realizes that no one ingredient is sufficient unto itself. Nourishing counseling is composed of a combination of many factors. The five systems mentioned all have nourishing ingredients. Effective counselors draw from each in accordance with their skills and the needs of their clients.

Following is a case example showing how one eclectic approach was used effectively with a client.

Awareness

On the recommendation of her friend, Jo, a college student in her early twenties, called and arranged for a counseling appointment. When we met, I was struck by her smile, her excess weight, and her eyes, which rarely focused on me (Gestalt). Initially I functioned mostly as an understanding listener, getting a clearer picture of her concerns and helping both of us feel more comfortable with each other (client-centered). Interspersed among moments of crying and nervous laughing, Jo talked about her difficulties in handling a broken love relationship, her weight problem, and her anxiety about speaking out in class.

In addition to functioning as a Rogerian listener, I negotiated our counseling contract (regarding time, place, purpose, and methods), encouraged her to read *A Guide to Rational Living* (Ellis & Harper, 1973) and *Born to Win* (James & Jongeward, 1971) (TA, RET), and examined my feelings about working with her (Gestalt). I have a prejudice in favor of thinness; I wanted to insure that this, or any other bias, would not detract from our relationship.

In either the third or fourth session, we agreed to focus on Jo's difficulty with expressing herself in class. By this time I was aware that she was more comfortable with me and with the counseling situation. I learned this by asking her about it and by observing that she not only looked at me more but smiled more appropriately (Gestalt). Therefore, I was encouraged to be more confrontive with Gestalt methods.

We were discussing her fear of speaking out in class when I noticed that she was rubbing one hand against the other. I asked her to focus on this behavior and to continue doing it, but in an exaggerated fashion. While she was doing this, I asked her to decide who her right and left hands were and what they were doing. She said that one hand was her strong and confident side, and the side that wanted to speak; the other was her weak and scared side, the side that wanted to melt into the chair (Gestalt).

Jo then became involved in Gestalt role playing. She played both sides of her personality, an empty chair being used to represent the side she was talking to. The role playing helped her become much more aware of her conflict. During the Gestalt work, I supported and guided her with empathic listening and questioning (client-centered).

Then I asked Jo to link her role-playing work with the material in the two books she had been reading. With some help from me, she was able to see that her strong side was her more rational being, or her Adult being, and that her weak side was her Child, which was composed of many irrational thoughts (TA, RET). Her strongest irrational thoughts were that she should be liked and approved by everyone and that in order to be loved and worthy she had to behave perfectly (RET). Jo began to see how these thoughts limited her ability to function in class and in most of her relationships. With these awarenesses, we were able to begin the transition into Phase II.

Discussion. At this stage the counseling environment should be relatively nonthreatening. A step in this direction comes from reducing the ambiguity of the situation, by reaching agreement on issues of confidentiality, time, place, length, purpose, and anything else that might detract from the ability to focus on problems. The depth and length of these contract negotiations are a function of the client's counseling sophistication and the degree to which counseling was entered into with determination to work, vis-à-vis reluctance and apathy.

Throughout counseling I use the powerful data-gathering and relationship-building tools of client-centered counseling, including paraphrasing, clarification, and reflection of feeling. As the relationship develops, I use them less frequently but with a more powerful and penetrating slant (Means, 1973). For instance, instead of saying, "You feel bad when John laughs at you," I might say, "When you suspect others are laughing at you, you readily get in touch with your self-hatred."

A Gestalt orientation encourages me to focus on the client's and my own nonverbal behavior and to be aware of how I am feeling about working with the client. I particularly concern myself with noting the client's posture changes and any correlation with the subject matter. Based on these and other observations, I develop hunches and hypotheses. I store these data for future use when the client is ready to act on them.

When my clinical judgment tells me that the client is comfortable with the counseling process, I encourage the client to engage in Gestalt exercises that sharpen awareness. Some clients will find the novelty and power of these exercises threatening, and I therefore explain the process and purpose of the suggested exercise. This sharing of information makes it easier for clients to become involved in, to enjoy, and to benefit from exercises. In general, clients respond more favorably to different counseling methods when they have an understanding and appreciation of the methods. This can be accomplished through assigned readings or counselor instruction. I tell clients why they are being encouraged to do the reading and to discuss it with me. *Born to Win* and *A Guide to Rational Living* are helpful in preparing clients for the heavy doses of TA and RET during Phase II. These books also increase their self-awareness and their store of functional wisdom.

Returning to Gestalt, the exercises I primarily use are behavior exaggeration and empty-chair role playing. In the former, I ask clients to become aware of what certain body parts are doing and then exaggerate these movements. I ask them to share their thoughts and feelings while doing this. I sometimes guide them by asking whom they are hitting or petting, what they are keeping down, whom they would like to do that to, or what parts of themselves are interacting. Given a little thought and honesty, these and similar questions enable a person to become aware of some very important data. Other similar Gestalt exercises can be found in a number of publications (Fagan & Shepherd, 1971; Perls, Hefferline, & Goodman, 1951; Polster & Polster, 1973).

A behavior orientation encourages me not only to negotiate a counseling contract but also to reinforce any client behavior that facilitates the counseling process. For instance, I might verbally or nonverbally reinforce any behavior indicating that the client was working to be more open and honest and simply not respond if the conversation shifted to the weather or something similar.

The counseling enters Phase II when clients have a high degree of awareness of their problems and are comfortable with the counseling process.

Cognitive Reorganization

Jo wanted to improve her ability to speak out in her classes. We selected for analysis a class in which she was having a moderate amount of difficulty. The purpose of the analysis was to help her change thought patterns that inhibited her ability to speak out. The main work was a combination of RET and TA, but Gestalt work was still used to keep Jo in touch with her feelings.

Jo quickly recognized that she was operating from her Child when she thought of speaking in class. She saw herself as small and ineffectual, a person who desperately needed the support and approval of others. Teacher and students became parent figures to whom she gave overwhelming power to determine her self-worth. PAC diagrams and discussion helped her conceptualize her thinking about the class (TA).

Jo also did Gestalt role playing in which she played both herself as a young child and her parents. She learned that she believed her parents would love and respect her only if she were highly competent and achieving. These role-playing sessions were very emotionally trying, for they brought up her strong feelings of hurt and resentment (Gestalt). The sessions opened an avenue for discussion of her parents and also gave Jo important clarity on the genesis of her Parent–Child method of relating in class and in other situations. It was at this time that Jo became more aware of the fact that her Parent–Child way of relating dominated not only her class behavior but also most of her relationships with people. This did not frighten her; instead it gave her a sense of power, for she had gained a handle for understanding and controlling her reactions in a wider array of situations. The Child and Adult labels made a neat and easily recalled package that Jo frequently used to enable her to understand situations and prepare herself for various encounters (TA).

Interweaving them in the TA and Gestalt work, I employed RET methods and ideas to help Jo see the irrationality of her thinking and change it. RET helped her develop a more potent and rational Adult and helped her free her Child of many irrational thoughts. Over time, the proportion of RET to TA and Gestalt increased, but elements of all were generally woven together. Table 1 explains how this was done in my work with Jo.

With time and repetition, Jo could, given any situation, identify her irrational thoughts at the Parent and Child levels and replace these with more rational thoughts. She increasingly believed it was her thoughts and not the situation that were bothering her and that she could change her thoughts (RET). However, she was still not sure if she could put this and other knowledge into action. It was at this point that we began to develop and implement strategies that would convert rational thoughts into satisfying action (behavioral counseling).

Discussion. Table 1 and the previous paragraphs are representative of my work during this phase. I fully analyze a situation a client is having difficulty with. I employ Gestalt role playing to bring the situation into the here and now and to give clients a clearer picture of their thoughts and feelings in the situation. These thoughts and feelings are classified in terms of whether they are Parent, Adult, or Child and whether they are rational or irrational. Clients generally do not cherish realizing that they are handling life in Child patterns, and

Table 1. Putting Together RETs, ABCDs, TAs, PACs, and Gestalt Role Playing

(A) *Situation: Jo is sitting in class, thinking about speaking out*

Irrational Level

Gestalt Role Playing	(B) Thoughts	(C) Emotions	(D) Behavior
Jo, playing herself, the teacher, and selected students	*Parent*: You should do well. You're worthwhile when you do well. *Child*: This is too much for me. I can't do it. They will laugh at me. I'm a failure. I'm no good.	Anxiety, anger, fear	Trembles, sits quietly, leaves class

Rational Level

Jo, playing herself, the teacher, and selected students	*Parent*: It is nice to do well. It often helps you see what you want, and it feels good. *Adult*: I will try. If I do not do as well as I would like, tough. I am not a failure, but a person who has failed at something. I'll correct my mistakes and do better next time. *Child*: This should be fun. Let me give it a go and see what happens.	Interest, excitement, joy	Speaks out

this stimulates them toward Adult modes. Also, realizing that parts of their Parent are destructively irrational and usually based on their parents' parenting encourages clients toward constructing a healthier Parent and a stronger Adult.

Some clients are capable of easily changing their thinking to constructive modes once they realize the destructiveness of their present Parent and Child. Some find it difficult to change their thinking even with their new insight, and others find it difficult to recognize the destructiveness of their thinking patterns at all. I involve all three types of clients in RET.

Clients are taught the ABCD method of RET until they can accurately construct a table for themselves. It is also important that they fully accept the fact that they are responsible for their feelings and can change and control them. The accomplishment of both objectives is facilitated by the fact that they have read *A Guide to Rational Living* and that we have established a trusting and caring relationship.

I find that analogies are very useful in my work. A favorite is the tightrope one. Clients are shown that by agonizing over how catastrophic it would be if things do not go the way they want (failure, rejection) they are putting themselves on a hundred-foot tightrope with neither a net nor any experience. It is easy for most clients to see that they would walk it with such fear and tension that they would fall off. I then suggest that they consider how it would be to walk on a tightrope that is only three feet off the ground. Most see themselves doing this with little fear, because they know that if they fell off they would still be alive and healthy. We then work to change their thinking about failure or being rejected so that they can lower their personal tightrope from a hundred feet to a much more manageable level. Jo saw that she was putting herself a hundred feet up when she made her self-esteem contingent on the approval of others. She got down to the three- to five-foot level when she realized that she would be bruised, not crushed, if people did not approve. Most clients find this analogy useful; I often build other analogies that are based on my client's own interests.

The tightrope analogy frequently leads into a more behavioral approach. I point out that the tightrope walker still has to practice in order to improve, whether at five or a hundred feet. We now begin to focus more on developing and implementing practice programs that will convert wise and rational thinking into constructive, effective, and satisfying action.

During the practice-action work, if a client becomes frustrated and discouraged because wisdom and rational thinking are not resulting in immediate and dramatic change, I empathically listen, support, encourage, and understand. It is important to make sure that clients are thinking rationally and to convince them that real and lasting change takes time and effort. Even with a well-developed Adult and an accurate awareness of how to perform a skill or a combination of skills (speaking in class, calling someone for a date, being assertive, skiing down a slope), it will take time and practice before the new patterns are firm enough to allow for smooth, efficient, and spontaneous performance.

Behavior Change

This phase has taken the longest. It is ongoing. It has been the hardest for both Jo and me. Despite her increased awareness and rationality, Jo became very agitated when she thought about speaking in class. Her more recent programming put her on a three- to five-foot tightrope, but her stronger and older programs rapidly elevated her to previous heights. Jo became very discouraged. She thought she had made real progress, but had she? She needed assurance that she had, but more work was necessary. We would have to go step by step, making her new programs stronger than the older ones (behavioral counseling).

Together we worked out a schedule that moved her step by step from simple fantasy work about speaking in class to actually speaking in class. After fully relaxing herself, she was to take herself on a fantasy walk to class and then speak. At any point in the journey when she felt herself getting tense, she was to stop and focus on the feeling and the irrational Child thoughts that were producing it. She was then to replace these thoughts with more rational Adult ones and move on in the journey with reduced negative affect (TA, RET, behavioral counseling). In addition to engaging in this fantasy work, she progressively got to a point where she was asked to observe students who seemed to have no difficulty speaking out in class. She was to use them as role models (behavioral counseling).

In time, Jo's confidence increased and she decided she was ready to speak in class. She also decided, with much coaxing, that it would be helpful if she shared her fears with the teacher of the class—which she did. She was afraid that this parent figure would severely disapprove of her for being so afraid. To her surprise and benefit, the teacher was understanding and supportive. Encouraged, she confessed her fear to her friends. To her delight, she found acceptance and fellowship in the fact that even friends she had assumed were totally confident shared her fear (behavioral counseling). The ball was rolling, and, in good old they-lived-happily-ever-after fashion, Jo was soon (with a little nervousness) asking and responding to questions in all of her other classes.

Going from fantasy to reality took a couple of months. I served mainly to support and encourage Jo (client-centered). We role-played situations she was preparing for and used TA and RET to help her keep thinking more in the rational Adult.

Discussion. I think life is simple. By that, I mean life's tasks are relatively simple to understand, although they are complex to do. Exposed to readings, discussions, and demonstrations, a person with reasonable intelligence can readily understand how most skills of living are accomplished. The complex part is molding the understanding into a deeper, more pervading mind–body integration that allows the person to perform with skill, grace, and ease. In most cases this takes a great deal of work.

For counseling to be effective, both counselor and client have to be prepared for hard work, and they usually are not. Both get enthusiastic about the progress made in awareness and the reprogramming of thinking but quickly get discouraged when this does not directly translate into skillful action. Counselor and client must persist. One way to insure mutual persistence is by accepting the need for it, recognizing that new ideas are not that difficult to grasp (although they are hard to live by), and knowing that progress comes from being willing to do the hard and grimy work of changing one's habit-laden behavior patterns. It is also vital to build a creative program that takes into consideration the human need for success. People have, ultimate goals. Most will reach those goals only if along the way they have smaller successes that tell them they are getting there. I see myself, at this stage in counseling, as a coach who is involved in building a training program that, through successive approximation, will get the person to the desired goal.

With Jo, the kind of thinking just described reinforced both of us. Some of the specific techniques were desensitization, fantasy work, role playing, role modeling, relaxation, and on-site practice. Fuller discussion of these and other methods can be found in many books (Krumboltz & Thoresen, 1969; Mink, 1970; Osipow & Walsh, 1970). Using these methods wisely is very important. Equally important is the full recognition that behavior change is not a mysterious process but one that mainly requires a great amount of persistence and hard work. Counselors and clients have to fully recognize and appreciate this fact. The more they do, the more beneficial the process will be.

Epilogue

At this time Jo still has problems, but she is happier and much more of an adult. She is involved in a relatively healthy love relationship, eating better, and speaking out in class with minimal anxiety. And, just as Jo must continually work to improve herself, I am working to insure that my counseling is also changing for the better. I want my counseling to match the needs of my current—not previous— clients and to take into consideration the impinging forces of the larger society we live in. I hope my orientation encourages you to develop your own eclectic approach. For, as my mother said, "There is a time and place for everything."

References

Ellis, A., & Harper, R. A. *A guide to rational living*. North Hollywood, Calif.: Wilshire Book Co., 1973.

Fagan, J., & Shepherd, I. L. (Eds.) *Gestalt therapy now*. New York: Harper and Row, 1971.

James, M., & Jongeward, D. *Born to win: Transactional analysis with gestalt experiments*. Reading, Mass.: Addison-Wesley, 1971.

Krumboltz, J. K., & Thoresen, C. E. *Behavioral counseling*. New York: Holt, Rinehart and Winston, 1969.

Means, B. L. Levels of empathic response. *Personnel and Guidance Journal*, 1973, *52*, 23–28.

Mink, O. G. *The behavior change process*. New York: Harper and Row, 1970.

Osipow, S. H., & Walsh, W. B. *Behavior Change in counseling: Readings and cases*. New York: Appleton-Century-Crofts, 1970.

Perls, F., Hefferline, R. F., & Goodman, P. *Gestalt therapy*. New York: Dell, 1951.

Polster, I., & Polster, M. *Gestalt therapy integrated: Contours of theory and practice*. New York: Brunner/Mazel, 1973.

31

Combining a Behavioral Approach with Reality Therapy

Richard R. Gronert

This study is an attempt to demonstrate how behavioral counseling and a Reality Therapy approach in elementary education can work together in the child's total development. Data for these two cases come from my work as an elementary school counselor in Janesville, Wisconsin.

Inasmuch as this paper deals with combining counseling approaches, it is necessary to examine the relationships of Reality Therapy, Adlerian Psychology, and Behavioral Modification.

Glasser's Reality Therapy (Glasser, 1965) is an excellent tool for identifying situations and problems; it serves well in helping a troubled client to internalize the fact that he is acting irresponsibly. When the counselor involves himself with the client's situation, then alternative client behaviors can be explored effectively. The client also is made to realize that he alone is responsible for his successes and failures, and if he is going to extend an accusing finger toward someone, he should point it at himself. Reality Therapy employs both positive and negative reinforcements for the purpose of "administering" life's consequences, that is, reality. Examples of this are

Reprinted from *Elementary School Guidance and Counseling*, 1970, 5(2), 104-112. Copyright 1970 American Association for Counseling and Development. Reprinted with permission.

scattered generously through chapter three of Glasser's work cited above, which discusses the Ventura School for girls. He defines reality as that which has long-range benefits for the client as opposed to more immediate reinforcement of short-term pleasures.

Reality Therapy sets the stage and arranges the counseling relationship for the introduction of the Adlerian Psychology of Dreikurs (Dreikurs & Stolz, 1964) because it has determined that the total responsibility of the client's actions are directly on his own shoulders. Therefore, logical and natural consequences of the client's behavior are consistent and appropriate (Dreikurs & Stolz, p. 76). One of the tenets of this paper is that Adlerian Psychology aids in situation identification because the counselor begins to focus on the determinants of a situation when he considers the natural and/or logical consequences of the client's behavior. Even though Dreikurs does not endorse punishment, his view of Adlerian Psychology nevertheless serves as a bridge to Behavioral Modification in that his discussion points out the necessity for the parent or teacher to determine to what behaviors they will attend. Behavioral Modification goes a bit farther than Dreikurs because it endorses positive and negative reinforcement (Glasser, 1965; Krumboltz & Thoresen, 1969; Patterson & Gullion, 1968).

In combining a method of using natural and/or logical consequences with behavioral positive and negative reinforcement, we may think of the teacher or parent as analogous to a hot stove. A hot stove cooks meals (positive reinforcement). The logical consequence of using a hot stove properly is to eat hot meals; but, if one misuses the stove by bumping into it, he will be burned (negative reinforcement/natural consequence). Touching a hot stove repetitively would be similar to frequent disruption of a teacher's class by inappropriate behavior. The decision regarding how to use the hot stove is up to the individual, and he experiences in his behavior the natural consequences (good and bad). From such coping experiences with life's consequences the client should developmentally learn to sidestep problems.

After a situation is identified with the resulting realities of natural and logical consequences, then Behavioral Modification can be very useful. Reality Therapy combined with Adlerian Psychology can be thought of as setting the stage for Behavioral Modification.

The relationship between Adlerian Psychology and Behavioral Modification is strong because both methods indicate that the administrators of the child (parent, teacher, counselor, psychologist) need to sort out their own behaviors in a specific situation and quietly determine which behaviors in the children they will attend. (The act of responding is reinforcement—social reinforcements are smiles, praise; material reinforcements are M&M's, playtime, etc.) They must also determine which inappropriate behavior they will attempt to ignore and hope for considerable reduction in behavior. Any positive reinforcement is an encouragement that acts as a cement in strengthening the desired behavior. As the appropriate behavior sets, it usually carried its own reward (i.e., accomplishment, social acceptance, etc.) for the individual, as the behavior becomes assimilated, the material reinforcement gradually diminishes.

Jane's Case

Jane, eleven and a half, had had two years of ineffective psychological counseling concerning her grossly inappropriate, hyperactive classroom behavior with little or no results. Her behavior was so gross that the school psychologist said that any method that would cure this problem would be a rare accomplishment in psychological case studies.

Jane's five teachers approached me at the point of complete exasperation and stated their feeling that she should be sent away—perhaps to Mendota State Hospital. With reservations, however, they agreed to work with me in a behavioral approach. So, the challenge for elementary counseling was on.

First, a staffing was held with Jane's teachers to identify one of her most disturbing behaviors, namely, her vociferous outbursts. Second, it was explained that only one major behavior change should be dealt with at a time; teachers should ignore the behaviors that did not disrupt too much, thus not reinforcing other inappropriate attention-getting mechanisms. They also agreed to reinforce Jane's appropriate behaviors that they wanted her to repeat, thus encouraging desirable behavior. One teacher was asked to chart the frequency of Jane's vociferous outbursts. Finally, we agreed on the most important part of the method—the administration of a psychologically sterile Time-Out. When her behavior became so gross that it could not be ignored, the teachers had to act. In Jane's case we used a Time-Out in order not to reinforce her inappropriate means of getting attention (Briskin & Gardner, 1968).

A Time-Out is a physical area relatively void of visual or auditory stimulation though not frightening for the youngster. It is rigid, but in Jane's case it probably serves as one of the most loving acts in her behalf because it caused her to taste the realities of a balance between her inappropriate/appropriate behavior. The choice of appropriate versus inappropriate behavior is hers alone. The teachers are to reinforce her selected behavior if it is appropriate, attempt to ignore her mild inappropriate behavior, and, when the behaviors are gross, arrange the logical consequence for handling an inappropriate attention-getting mechanism. Then Jane goes to a Time-Out.

With no visible emotion, the teachers were to send Jane to the Time-Out area for each vociferous outburst no matter how many times a day it occurred. The Time-Out area is a blind, semidark, narrow hallway far removed from other people but close enough to my office for both visual and auditory observation. This device not only helped Jane but it also immediately took the pressure off the teachers and the classroom when it was most urgent. A Time-Out might possibly become a damaging experience for one's psychological makeup; therefore, it should be administered in school only with the advice of a psychologist or a counselor. If improperly administered, a Time-Out could perhaps teach a child to withdraw, so it would become a reality-avoidance mechanism. What is meant by proper administration of a Time-Out is the significance of such a procedure with each individual. A child is evaluated by the counselor and/or psychologist to determine whether he has withdrawal tendencies. If so, he is not placed in a Time-Out.

Jane's teachers watched for her next vociferous outburst which came soon, followed by her first Time-Out experience. Jane had already experienced a trusting counseling relationship; therefore, it was explained to her that her own behavior had put her in this situation and when she decided to behave appropriately again according to classroom standards she would be welcomed back in class. Her first Time-Out lasted thirty-five minutes; she did not enjoy it because she had nothing to do. Her purse, pencils, books, and so on, were all removed, leaving her with nothing to do but sit in boredom.

Purpose of the Time-Out

The purpose of the Time-Out is to produce a larger conflict for Jane than her present conflict of appropriate classroom behavior. Because her major goal has been getting attention inappropriately, we were convinced that by removing Jane's audience we would thwart her attention-getting fulfillment. The removal to the Time-Out area then became a negative reinforcer stimulating less maladaptive behavior and raising in Jane a conflict that needed resolution. When she chose appropriate alternative behavior, it was positively reinforced, thus achieving a welcome balance in the consequences of her behavior. An inference from Piaget's conflict resolution through alternative exploration would be that we choose the lesser of two conflicts by resolving the greater conflict by means of choosing alternative action or by avoidance (Piaget & Inhelder, 1958).

The victory in behavioral changes came from the staff's consistent actions and emotions. There was no reason to attach a label to Jane in an attempt to "pigeon-hole" her psychological behavior. Her name was the only label used in describing her. Jane was handled behaviorally with positive and negative reinforcements combined with Reality Therapy in which she had to admit that her behavior had been inappropriate at times and that she alone must pay for her irresponsibility (Glasser, 1969).

Table 1 shows what I consider the cycle of a person's behavior.

Table 1. Cycle of a Person's Behavior

According to:	Leads to:	Leads to:	Leads to:
G: Responsibility	Irresponsibility	Consequence	Responsibility
P: Conflict	Avoidance	Larger conflict	Lesser conflict
D: Classroom be-havior	Misuse of class	Painful consequence	Appreciation of class
J: Jane's behavior	Vociferous out-burst	Time-Out	Responsible be-havior

Note—Glasser (G); Piaget (P); Dreikurs (D); Jane's case (J).

Within three days of this consistent, nonemotional teacher reaction, Jane was very much improved. It took two days of the teachers' appropriate behavior in ignoring Jane's mild misbehaviors, their reinforcements of her slightest attempt to behave appropriately, and their consistently sending her to a Time-Out room for gross behavior (two times in two days). The Time-Out served as a strong reminder for Jane to think twice before she misbehaved in class. By the end of the week the teachers were delighted with the modification of Jane's behavior and they began to realize that she had something to offer. More importantly Jane realized this herself, so her self-concept began to improve. Her peers began to accept her and teasing diminished. Jane began to effectively cope in life and her job became that of a student with little time for excuses or crutches.

One day a teacher even left Jane alone in charge of the class and she was pleasantly overwhelmed by such attention. She had found that appropriate behavior was much less a conflict than inappropriate behavior because she had tasted the reality of consequences. The quality of the psychologically sterile Time-Out is what delivered that reality to her and she experienced a necessary comparison between the consequences of her appropriate and inappropriate behavior. (Since this episode a new Time-Out area has been devised, which is a multisided opaque screen that can be used in an open-pod area.) The positive reinforcement/encouragement effort effected a significant balance in Jane's experience of the pleasure of appropriate behavior and the painful consequence of inappropriate behavior. After the first week with these behavioral methods, Jane went for one month without a Time-Out and her teachers praised her instead of registering complaints. One day Jane said to me, "How come the teachers are being so nice to me?" In reply I asked her if it might be because she was being nice to her teachers.

Jane is fully aware that she alone is responsible for her behavior and about every four weeks her behavior (described as hyperactive) sends her to a Time-Out. She is no longer dreaded by teachers, however. Frequently, while she is behaving appropriately she comes to me for general attention, counseling, window-washing therapy, and folk guitar sessions. Jane certainly has earned these privileges and they are timed to encourage only the behaviors we want repeated.

Jane was helped because of an effective combination of behavioral counseling, Reality Therapy, Adlerian Psychology, and teacher cooperation, which is an important element—because without their support, elementary counseling effectiveness is severely diminished. Perhaps two words synthesize the combined approach—encouragement and involvement.

The major limitation in this approach is that the frequency charts of Jane's inappropriate behavior were not carefully maintained by the teacher. However, everyone felt the impact of Jane's swift behavior modification, and they were convinced the system was operating efficiently and saw little need for charts as proof. I kept my "druthers" to myself on this less significant point because teachers are very busy people with many things to chart.

The only danger now is that the teachers will rest on their oars in consistently dealing with Jane because she is no longer a threat; and they have been consulted on this point. If they let up in consistency of balancing positive and negative reinforcement, she may experience more reversals than necessary.

Mark's Case

Mark's case is more baffling and also more difficult than Jane's. However, the above methods were used to return Mark to appropriate behavior in the classroom and at home.

Since age two Mark had constantly wet his pants as many as five times or more a day. Mark was still wetting when he was referred to us. He was, and is, in second grade. He wet so often that his clothes were thoroughly saturated both at the end of the morning session and again at the end of the afternoon session, which had been preceded by a fresh change of clothing.

In despair, his teacher brought him to me. Mark was saturated and stank. His teacher was nauseated and desperate. Mark visited three teachers every day and the situation was urgent because he had been thoroughly wet every day of the first month of school. He remained soaked at school because he refused to cooperate with his teachers or mother in this elimination process. This was not a healthy condition mentally or physically and Mark was shunned by his peers. The next morning, after studying sphincter control and the like and receiving no useful information, Mark and I went into the following Reality Therapy session. I explained to him that no longer would he sit in the pod (multiclass area) with wet pants because it was not sanitary or fair to the others around him or to himself. Besides, wet pants really smell bad (the realization of how he smelled was a direct thrust of Reality Therapy). His mother had mentioned that he had brain damage, but we determined that brain-damaged or not, Mark had to keep living in the world. Mark (and his mother) had had several years of psychological, neurological, psychiatric, and occupational therapy sessions with no progress.

Mark's mother had mentioned that he did not take enough time to go to the bathroom. Therefore, this morning he was told that he was going to have as much time as he needed for elimination. In fact, he was instructed to stay in the extremely small toilet area of the nurse's office until he did eliminate and I would stay outside the door to hear the water tinkle.

Before Mark went into the toilet area, we chose three pieces of candy that were placed on the desk outside the toilet area. He was told that if he eliminated he would get the three pieces of candy; if he did not eliminate then I was going to eat them.

Within ten seconds after Mark entered the toilet area, I heard the water tinkle. Mark was pleased and I was jubilant. Not only did he get the candy but also he was made to feel as if he had won an election by the principal, his teachers, and me. Mark came in to the nurse's toilet four times that day, and four times that day Mark was 100 percent successful. He went home with a pocket bulging with eight pieces of candy in a pair of dry trousers. He was so proud he did not even eat the candy; he wanted to save them to show his mother.

For one month, Mark had no reversals in school. We set him on an hour and a half schedule to visit the nurse's toilet and coordinated this as best we could with his home routine. The schedule was set up this way in case Mark could not feel bladder distentions; also, we needed a string of victories to reinforce our efforts. Later, the candy reinforcements became intermittent but we always used social reinforcements. We tried extending the schedule to an hour and forty-five minutes, but the teachers had more difficulty keeping track of Mark's schedule, so we returned to the original schedule. Mark did become somewhat dependent on seeing me for his eliminations, and we tried to get him to take the initiative. He is now much more successful in initiating the elimination response independently.

Just before Thanksgiving Mark had three days of reversals after a month of successes. His mother said this was because of an upsetting weekend with her divorced husband disrupting the home atmosphere and Mark was reacting violently. The therapist and psychiatric social worker thought that Mark was purposely not cooperating because he felt hostile toward his mother because of the divorce situation. When asked to see the data supporting this idea they avoided responding four times and eventually admitted they had nothing to substantiate this claim. (What is this need for labels—brain damage, revenge, etc.? Do therapists really believe that a label aids treatment?)

When Mark was wet he did not go back to the class at any time. He spent two long sessions in a sanitary Time-Out situation, which he did not like. He wanted to be back in class and felt most uncomfortable. He knew his wetting behavior put him in the Time-Out, but he persisted. In fact, he missed the Thanksgiving party because the last day before vacation Mark spent considerable time in the Time-Out. It was Mark's fault that he was wet; and he could not sit in the pod area because of sanitation and damage to his increasing peer acceptance. Some may feel Mark was being punished, but, if so, he punished himself.

After Thanksgiving vacation, Mark was right back on a no-wetting schedule and is still functioning well. He had suffered the logical consequences of a lonesome Time-Out because he was wet. While consulting with his mother, we determined that she needed fresh legal advice concerning her divorce status for Mark's sake and for the whole family.

If Mark cannot feel bladder distention, then later when he can tell time, he can have a wrist alarm watch to remind him to visit the toilet. The diabetic needs to remind himself to take insulin, and there is no reason Mark cannot go through life as a normal person.

Instead of labeling irresponsible behavior and then using the label as a crutch to continue on irresponsibly, we could instead start without a label and realize that the troubled person, no matter what he is called, has to make it through life. Because of the urgency of some of our client's cases, we had better begin employing usable alternative behaviors that will adequately substitute for irresponsibility. This means, however, that we must get involved.

It seems that the younger the client, the more effective a behavioral reinforcement technique is. This presents a strong case for the great need for elementary school counselors who are capable of coordinating behavioral approaches with other approaches, such as Adlerian, developmental, Reality, self-concept, and play therapy.

References

Briskin, A., & Gardner, W. Social reinforcement in reducing inappropriate behavior. *Young Children*, December 1968, *24*(2), 84-89.

Dreikurs, R., & Stolz, V. *Children: The challenge.* New York: Meredith Press, 1964. Pp. 76, 276-277

Glasser, W. *Reality therapy.* New York: Harper and Row, 1965. Pp. 67-106.

Glasser, W. *Schools without failure.* New York: Harper and Row, 1969. Pp. 21, 131.

Krumboltz, J., & Thoresen, C. *Behavioral counseling*. New York: Holt, Rinehart and Winston, 1969. Pp. 89-114.

Patterson, G., & Gullion, M.E. *Living with children*. Champaign, III.: Research Press, 1968.

Piaget, J., & Inhelder, B. *The growth of logical thinking from childhood to adolescence*. New York: Basic Books, 1958. Pp. 339-340.

SECTION X

Recommended Additional Reading

This final section is a brief bibliography of books on the theory and practice of counseling or therapy. It is intended as an additional source for the serious reader who wishes to expand his or her understanding of and expertise with one or more of the different models. The bibliography is therefore organized by theoretical model, and each theory covered in the preceding nine sections is represented by several texts. In order to help the reader select additional reading, most of the texts are annotated. One note of caution for the reader: this bibliography is not intended to be exhaustive or divinely inspired; it is merely this editor's choice for additional in-depth exploration in the field of counseling and therapy.

Rational-Emotive Therapy

Ellis, A. *Reason and Emotion in Psychotherapy*. New York: Lyle Stuart, 1962.

This text represents the original treatise on rational-emotive therapy. All of the basic RET concepts and procedures are contained herein. Should be on every counselor's basic reading list.

Ellis, A., Wolfe, J.L., & Moseley, S. *How to Prevent Your Child From Becoming a Neurotic Adult*. New York: Crown Publishers, 1966.

This volume is oriented toward the nonprofessional. It applies RET principles to common and not-so-common problem areas of children. The authors emphasize rational ways for parents to treat their children and how parents can teach their children to adopt a rational philosophy of life. Stimulating reading for the professional as well as a good source book.

Ellis. A. *Growth Through Reason*. Palo Alto, Calif.: Science and Behavior Books, 1971.

This book is written for the nonprofessional who is interested in developing new strategies for coping with problem situations. It presents Ellis' RET model in a nontechnical, pragmatic manner. It is interesting supplemental reading for the professional, but it could also be used as bibliotherapy by the serious rational-emotive counselor.

Further Reading:

Beck, A.T. *Cognitive Therapy and the Emotional Disorders*. New York: International Universities Press, 1976.

Ellis, A., & Greiger, R. *Handbook of Rational-Emotive Therapy*. New York: Springer, 1977.

Ellis, A., & Harper, R.A. *A New Guide to Rational Living*. Hollywood, Calif.: Wilshire Books, 1975.

Ellis, A., & Whiteley, J. *Theoretical and Empirical Foundations of Rational- Emotive Therapy*. Monterey, Calif.: Brooks/Cole, 1979.

Hauck, P. *Rational Management of Children*: New York: Libra, 1972.

Reality Therapy

Glasser, W. *Reality Therapy*. New York: Harper and Row, 1965.

This text is the original publication by Glasser, which presents the postulates of reality therapy. All of his later work is based on this material. Serious students of counseling and therapy should add this book to their reading lists.

Glasser, W. *Schools without Failure*. New York: Harper and Row, 1969.

In this book, Glasser applies the principles of reality therapy to the classroom setting. He suggests that teachers adopt reality concepts in their total conduct in the classroom. In effect, the teacher creates a counseling or therapeutic learning environment. The focus is on positive feedback and instilling a success orientation in the children. It is written for both elementary and secondary school situations. It could be a good consultative tool for counselors to use with school personnel.

Glasser, W. *The Identity Society*. New York: Harper and Row, 1972.

Represents an extension of the author's earlier publications. The major portion of the text is devoted to Glasser's views of educational and societal problems and their solutions. Included are loneliness, failure, drug abuse, sexual behavior, crime, and welfare. However, chapter six, entitled "Reality Therapy," is devoted to a discussion of his counseling model. This chapter succinctly describes the major principles of reality therapy, with examples of their application. It provides interesting and informative reading for professional or non-professional.

Further Reading

Glasser, W. *Positive Addiction*. New York: Harper and Row, 1976.

Glasser, W. *Stations of the Mind*. New York: Harper and Row, 1981.

Behavioral Counseling

Bandura, A. *Principles of Behavior Modification*. New York: Holt, Rinehart and Winston, 1969.

As the title suggests, this volume investigates the underlying principles of behavior modification procedures. The development and control of a behavioral program are adequately covered. The main strength of this text is its comprehensive coverage of behavioral techniques, including social modeling, desensitization, inhibition, positive and aversive control, extinction, and counterconditioning. Beginning counselors and experienced therapists could benefit from Bandura's comprehensive treatment of the topic.

Buckley, N., & Walker, H.M. *Modifying Classroom Behavior*. Champaign, Ill.: Research Press, 1970.
A small manual that deals concretely with behavioral procedures. Organized as a programmed learning text, the questions presented realistically reinforce the material that the reader has just completed. Because of its diminuitive size and readable format, it can easily be perused in several hours. It is an excellent resource to use in conjunction with a more comprehensive text like Bandura's.

Ferinden, W.E. *Classroom Management Through the Application of Behavior Modification Techniques*. Linden, N.J.: Remediation Associates, 1970.
A small, inexpensive reference manual for counselors, therapists, or other professionals working in a school setting. It surveys a wide range of modification techniques that professionals could use directly with clients or in consultation with teachers and parents. Ferinden discusses approaches to classroom management as well as methods of dealing with problem children and problem situations in groups or individually.

Krumboltz, J.D., & Thoresen, L.E. *Behavioral Counseling: Cases and Techniques*. New York: Holt, Rinehart and Winston, 1969.
Presents a collection of techniques for behaviorally oriented counselors. The emphasis is on the "how" of practicing behavioral counseling. The book is very readable, with the focus on technique rather than theory. Impressive array of techniques for treating a multitude of child and adolescent problems. A very close approximation of "everything you always wanted to know about behavioral counseling," without being overly prescriptive or cookbookish.

Krumboltz, J.D., & Krumboltz, H.B. *Changing Children's Behavior*. Englewood Cliffs, N.J.: Prentice-Hall, 1972.
A good supplement to Krumboltz's previous work on behavioral counseling. Relates specific reinforcement techniques to normal and abnormal behavior situations. School oriented at both the elementary and secondary levels.

Ullman, L.P. & Krasner, L. *Case Studies in Behavior Modification*. New York: Holt, Rinehart and Winston, 1965.

An excellent presentation of specific case examples. A wide variety of dysfunctional behaviors are treated using behaviorally oriented counseling procedures.

Further Reading

Kanfer, F.H., & Goldstein, A.P. *Helping People Change*. New York: Pergamon Press, 1980.

Krumboltz, J.D., & Thoresen, C.E. *Counseling Methods*. New York: Holt, Rinehart and Winston, 1976.

Adlerian Counseling

Ansbacker, H.L., & Ansbacker, R.R. *The Individual Psychology of Alfred Adler*. New York: Harper Torchbooks, 1964.
A scholarly and systematic presentation of Adler's psychology. Comprehensively treats the philosophy, the theory, and the technique of individual psychology. A must reading for any counselor or therapist seriously considering Adlerian or Dreikursian counseling methods.

Dreikurs, R., & Soltz, V. *Children: The Challenge*. New York: Hawthorne, 1964.
A thorough presentation of the family counseling model of Rudolf Dreikurs. Grounded in the theoretical aspects of Adlerian psychology, it discusses all of the major aspects of family counseling. It provides a good introduction for counselors, teachers, or parents.

Dinkmeyer, D., & Dreikurs, R. *Encouraging Children to Learn*. Englewood Cliffs, N.J.: Prentice-Hall, 1963.
This is a manual for teachers, parents, and counselors to assist children in overcoming their emotional difficulties. The focus is on the educational system, and the authors attempt to integrate psychological principles with educational practices. The use of encouragement is the major process emphasized.

Mairet, R. *Problems of Neurosis*. New York: Harper Torchbooks, 1964.

A thorough presentation of Adlerian concepts and techniques. Presents thirty-seven case histories, which reveal how personality disturbances develop and are treated, through the eyes of an Adlerian therapist.

Further Reading

Adler, A. *The Problem Child.* New York: Capricorn Books, 1963

Dreikurs, R. *Fundamentals of Adlerian Psychology.* New York: Greenberg, 1950.

Dreikurs, R. *Psychology in the Classroom.* New York: Harper and Row, 1968.

Gestalt Counseling

Fagan, J., & Shepherd, I. *Gestalt Therapy Now.* New York: Harper Colophan, 1970.

Perls, F. *Gestalt Therapy Verbatim.* Moab, Utah: Real People Press, 1969.

Perls, F. *In and Out of the Garbage Pail.* Moab, Utah: Real People Press, 1969.

Passons, W. *Gestalt Approaches in Counseling.* New York: Holt, Rinehart and Winston, 1975.

Polster, E., & Polster, M. *Gestalt Therapy Integrated.* New York: Brunner/ Mazel, 1973.

Client-Centered Counseling

Hart, J.T., & Tomlinson, T.M. *New Directions in Client-Centered Therapy.* Boston: Houghton Mifflin Co., 1970.
A collection of readings gathered with the professional counselor in mind. Comprehensively presents the Rogerian model in both theory

and practice. The main theme is a survey of new developments in this approach. Part one, "An Introduction to Client-Centered Therapy," and part four, "New Directions in Therapy," are the most appealing for the practitioner.

Rogers, C. R. *Counseling and Psychotherapy*. Boston: Houghton Mifflin Co., 1942.

The initial work by Carl Rogers that inspired the development of the entire client-centered school of counseling and therapy. It details Rogers' concepts of counseling goals, stages in the counseling process, and common therapeutic problems encountered by the client-centered counselor. This text is the basis for all subsequent research and practice in the Rogerian model.

Rogers, C.R. Client-Centered Therapy. Boston: Houghton Mifflin Co., 1951.

A further exposition of Rogerian concepts as they relate to the counseling process. It expands the initial work of Rogers as detailed in his first book. It reflects the considerable amount of research and practice that ensued after Rogers' first book was widely distributed. Play therapy and group therapy from the client-centered perspective are covered as well as the influential individual counseling model of Rogers.

Rogers, C.R. *On Becoming a Person*. Boston: Houghton Mifflin Co., 1961.

This is the final book in what might be considered the Rogerian trilogy, which, when taken together, present all of the central concepts of client-centered therapy. This book is a collection of speeches presented by Carl Rogers. The focus is on the basic counseling relationship and its importance in the progress of therapy.

Further Reading

Rogers, C.R. *Freedom to Learn*. Columbus, Ohio: Charles E. Merrill, 1969.

Rogers, C. *A Way of Being*. Palo Alto, Calif.: Houghton Mifflin Co., 1980.

Existential Counseling

Frankl, V. *Man's Search for Meaning*. Boston: Beacon Press, 1963.

A basic presentation of logotherapy, which is Frankl's interpretation of existential therapy. The central concept is each individual's search for meaning in life. Dr. Frankl movingly describes his concentration camp experiences during World War II, which led to his development of this approach. He briefly outlines the concepts and therapeutic methods that he advocates. A short, readable book.

Moustakas, C.E. *Existential Child Therapy*. New York: Basic Books, 1966.

A collection of articles, each dealing with the problem situation of a child client. All of the contributors are existential therapists, and they provide a unique and enlightening glimpse into their conception of the helping relationship and the therapeutic change process. A very readable book for either the established professional or the beginning counselor-in-training.

Further Reading

Frankl, V. *Psychotherapy and Existentialism: Selected Papers on Logotherapy*. New York: Simon and Schuster, 1967.

May, R. *Existential Psychology*. New York: Random House, 1961.

Play Therapy

Axline, V.M. *Play Therapy*. Boston: Houghton Mifflin Co., 1964.

This text is primarily school oriented but beneficial for any professional interested in doing therapy with children. It is a comprehensive exposition of the nondirective play therapy model. It can be used as a basic primer by the neophyte or as a source of stimulation and reference for the established practitioner. A basic text for anyone contemplating or currently conducting play therapy.

Axline, V.M. *Dibs: In Search of Self*. Boston: Houghton Mifflin Co., 1964.

A case history of the psychological development of a small boy. He moves, with the expert guidance of a professional therapist, from a severely disturbed condition to one of security, happiness, and effectiveness. In the process of telling the story, Dr. Axline presents the major techniques of nondirective play therapy. An interesting and professionally enlightening book. Recommended for all practicing child counselors as well as interested parents and teachers.

Moustakas, C.E. *Children in Play Therapy*. New York: McGraw-Hill, 1953.

Play therapy is comprehensively covered in this well-written and organized text, which deals with a plethora of presenting problems, from normal to disturbed. There is liberal use of case studies and dialogue transcripts to illustrate the author's work with children. A must book for the serious play therapists.

Further Reading

Millar, Susanna. *The Psychology of Play*. Baltimore: Penguin Books, 1968.

Eclectic Counseling

Thorne, F.C. *Tutorial Counseling*. Brandon, Vt.: Clinical Psychology Publishing Co., 1965.

A book that was written for the professional therapist but without a dependence on clinical terms and procedures. It describes the eclectic approach of Thorne with the focus on positive mental health for the general population.

Thorne, F.C. *Personality*. Brandon, Vt .: Clinical Psychology Publishing Co., 1961.

This book describes the phenomenal personality system developed by Thorne. The emphasis is on personality development of the "normal" person in society.